S̶S̶

754

RANK AND FILE

RANK AND FILE

Personal Histories by
Working-Class Organizers

Edited by
Alice and Staughton Lynd

Beacon Press   Boston

Beacon Press books are published under the auspices
of the Unitarian Universalist Association
Published simultaneously in Canada by Saunders of Toronto, Ltd.

9 8 7 6 5 4 3 2 1

Library of Congress Cataloging in Publication Data

Lynd, Alice.
  Rank and file.
  1. Labor and laboring classes—United States—
1914–   —Addresses, essays, lectures. 2. Trade-
unions—United States—Addresses, essays, lectures.
I. Lynd, Staughton, joint author. II. Title.
HD8072.L883 331.88′092′2 [B] 73–6247
ISBN 0–8070–0508–8

The editors gratefully acknowledge permission to
quote passages from *The Company and the Union*,
by William Serrin, © 1970, 1971, 1972 by William
Serrin, by permission of Alfred A. Knopf, Inc.

47.756

Table of Contents

Acknowledgments

We wish gratefully to acknowledge many kinds of help. Helen Michalowski spent many, many hours transcribing tapes in an effort to deepen her own understanding of history. Jim Wright and Fred Stern provided some of the first introductions. Betty Balanoff generously shared her own resources in oral history. Alfred Young, Ann Gordon, and the editors of *Radical America* and *Ramparts* took this work seriously and made it possible for us to publish fragments. Above all, we wish to thank the individuals in the accounts, their friends and families, who opened up their lives to us.

Alice and Staughton Lynd

Introduction

THE INDUSTRIAL UNION organizing drive of the 1930s was a movement for democracy. Talk to the mass production workers who took part in it, and they will tell you that what they wanted more than anything else was dignity. They wanted freedom from the petty harassment of a foreman who could send a man home at will and reward those who curried his favor with steady work, preferred jobs, and promotion. They wanted "unions of their own choosing" which could stand up to the power of corporate employers and bargain on equal terms. Like democratic movements in America before and since, they believed that the human right to a job should take precedence over the property right to manage an enterprise as the employer sees fit.

After World War II the labor movement fell silent, and the democratic impulse made itself felt in movements of blacks, students and women. These movements insisted that American society claims to be democratic but the reality is often the reverse. They asked, how can a society which calls itself democratic prevent blacks from voting? How can it treat students as IBM cards, and women as sex objects? How can it make war without consulting Congress, let alone the people? All these movements agreed that people should participate in the decisions which affect their lives.

Now American working people are stirring again. They are beginning to question foremen and corporation executives whom they did not elect, and union officials who have lost touch with their membership. The groups which took part in the cultural revolution of the 1960s are moving into the workplace. Blacks have become a majority in many automobile plants and steel mills, students have graduated and taken jobs in white-collar bureaucracies, veterans are returning from Vietnam, women have gone out to work in larger

numbers than at any time since World War II. A new restlessness
is evident in wildcat (unauthorized) strikes, in rank-and-file rejection
of contracts, in demands for humanizing work and for a pollution-
and hazard-free work situation.

Two events in 1972 symbolized the ferment. At the General
Motors assembly plant in Lordstown, Ohio, workers struck against
speed-up and arbitrary discipline. Their average age was under
twenty-five. Many were veterans. Long hair and New Left life styles
were common. In the Appalachian coal fields, the Miners For
Democracy ousted the incumbent leadership of the United Mine
Workers. Their movement grew in part from a campaign against
unnecessary mine disasters and the slow death of Black Lung from
breathing excessive coal dust.

It is by no means clear whether the lasting impact of the new
working-class consciousness will be progressive or reactionary.
Miners For Democracy is widely supported by working people but
so is George Wallace. Even supposing (as we do) that the thrust of
working-class revolt is essentially democratic, what will protect it
from betrayal by those whom it elects to office? Among rank-and-file
working people there is universal resentment about union reformers
who, once in office, kick the ladder away and forget to look back.
It is hard to know how to prevent this.

Thus difficult problems present themselves as workers sense their
power and make their feelings known. This book is by and for
people struggling with these problems.

II

In the following pages, a number of men and women tell of their
experience as organizers. About half were active mainly in the 1930s
and about half since World War II. About one third are currently
involved in rank-and-file movements. Most grew up and worked in
the Midwest and many in the steel industry, since this is the principal
industry in the Chicago area where we lived while making the book.

They were not selected at random. What unites these remarkable
individuals is that, in our judgment, they belong to a tradition of
working-class democracy. "Go see so-and-so," we would be told,
"if you want to meet someone who expressed the spirit of the rank

and file." Led in this way from one person to the next we put together *Rank and File*.

What do working people mean when they say "rank and file"
and what do we mean by using it for the title of this book? Rank
and file, in a general way, refers to workers on the job, not paid
union leadership. Rank-and-file activity usually means people on the
job taking whatever action they think is necessary, doing something
for themselves rather than waiting for someone else to do it for them.
It means people acting on their own, based on their own common
experience. In the words of Percy Llewellyn, who helped to unionize
Ford in Detroit,

> It wasn't the international [union]* doing it. We were doing it. This
> was on our own. We knew what the problems were in the plant,
> and we didn't have to go to some political officer to tell him we
> needed some help on this problem. We just went out and did it. And
> that was the big reason that Ford was organized. Ford was organized
> mainly because the workers in there did the job themselves.

Rank-and-file activity may be directed against an intolerable
employer or an unresponsive union bureaucracy. Neither the
individuals in this book, nor we ourselves, are anti-union. "Don't
get me wrong," says Clarence Stoecker, a retired farm equipment
worker from the McCormick Works in Chicago (site of the strike
which led to the Haymarket "Riot" of 1886). "I'll never say that
you're better off without a union, that you'd do better to save that
five bucks a month or whatever the dues is. You just can't do that."
The fact remains that too many industrial unions have become
bureaucratic closed corporations, like the craft unions of the old
AFL. At best they are concerned with material benefits for their own
members, not with the welfare of working people everywhere. At
worst they have become a new kind of company union, financially
independent of the rank and file because the company deducts union
dues from the worker's paycheck (dues check-off) and politically
all-powerful because the contract takes away from rank and filers the

*National unions (as opposed to local unions) in the United States refer to them-
selves as "internationals" when they include Canadian members.

right to strike (no-strike clause). This is the situation that makes some union men and women say that they have two enemies, the company and their union leadership.

How did this degeneration of the trade unions come about? The collective action of working people springs from the need for self-protection. Those who are in a position to decide what others will do, when, where, and how they will do it and how much they'll get paid, have tremendous power over the lives of the people who work under them. It is extremely difficult for any single individual or any single local union to deal with that power. When the industrial unions were being organized, they were up against the power of national corporations which could transfer operations from one plant to another, or could take a loss for a while in one place and make it up in another. So workers turned to the CIO and to national unions which could match the corporations in money, full-time staff, lawyers, and access to media, and which could shut down all the plants of a corporation at the same time.

But this power came at a price. Once unions gained recognition and union dues were automatically taken out of the workers' paychecks, unions took on a new character. The militancy, democracy, and local union autonomy which flourished in the organizing period faded away or were crushed. Taking leadership in the union, which once meant working for nothing and living with the risk of being beaten or killed, became a way of moving ahead personally. It was a way of getting out of the workplace and getting a higher income. A successful local union officer could then go on to a career on the staff of the international union or, having come to the attention of management as a person with supervisory ability, a better-paying job with the company.

The typical rank-and-file leader seeks to be neither a union staff man nor a foreman. Characteristically, he or she does not want to become separated from the people in the shop. Like Eugene Debs, the rank-and-file leader feels, "When I rise it will be with the ranks, not from the ranks."

The rank and filers in this book felt, in addition, that there had to be basic social changes. They were both militant, in demanding changes within their unions and workplaces, and radical, in the sense that they tried to democratize the larger society. They imagined both a union and a society which were more just, more humane, more of a community.

They came to feel that the union alone could not bring all this about and they turned to political parties or community organizations as well. Most were some kind of socialist. Many belonged at some point in their lives to an organized radical group. Some still do. Regardless of their political beliefs or associations, those who took a forthright stand in confronting either management or the union were commonly attacked as Communists, and in this way forced to deal with the question of radicalism.

Of those who joined or worked closely with an organized radical group, most of the organizers who were active in the 1930s were connected with the Communist Party, while those active after World War II worked with other groups. We did not set out to select those we interviewed with this pattern in mind. We think it reflects the extent to which working people felt the relevance or shortcomings of these organizations.

Among the organizers who tell their stories here, therefore, there are people who vigorously disagreed with one another's politics. We do not believe that any of the organized radical groups had a monopoly of wisdom in the 1930s, nor do we think any of them do today. As we see it, there is a rank-and-file experience shared by all the participants in this book (and of course by countless others) which is deeper than the words used by different individuals to talk about it. Even when two people use words which are contradictory, they may have in common the goal of building a movement of ordinary people for the general good.

III

When we came to interview people we would offer the following explanation. We believe that most of labor history is created neither by famous leaders nor by faceless masses in crisis situations. We believe that the labor movement draws its life from many thousands of committed persons who work, day in and day out for years, to bring unions into being, to resist their bureaucratization, and to better the lives of others, not just themselves.

We asked the people we interviewed about their childhood, how they became involved with the labor movement, what they did, how their ideas were shaped, and what they might like to say to young people today. Many famous events in labor history are recounted or alluded to in this book—the Pullman strike of 1894, the McKees Rocks strike of 1909, the steel and packinghouse strikes of 1919, the San Francisco general strike of 1934, the Memorial Day Massacre, the Taft-Hartley Act, for instance—but these events figure largely as background to the personal development of those who lived through them.

Although most of our material was edited from tape recordings, Christine Ellis and John Anderson both wrote personal histories of book length. We regret that we could only publish portions. Some accounts (Patterson, Reese, Sargent, Sims, and the three miners) were edited from speeches; others (Tucker, and in part Ellis and Nowicki) from presentations to a small group, the Labor History Workshop in Gary, Indiana. Mario Manzardo permitted us to incorporate in his account a moving memoir which he wrote about his father, and Nick Migas' account includes a leaflet which was passed out at the 1948 Steelworkers convention. John Barbero's account combines the transcript of a discussion with John and other members of the Rank And File Team (RAFT) with the transcript of an interview with John alone.

All accounts were trimmed to reduce repetition of the same material or themes. A few names and places have been changed, lest unsympathetic members of the family or employers become distressed. Every account was read and corrected by the person or persons concerned.

It may be said, "The individuals in this book were not typical." True, the individuals in our collection were organizers. They were leaders. They had radical ideas. But precisely because they did not start out as organizers or leaders or radicals, their accounts throw light on what has been experienced or may be experienced with variations by a much larger number of people.

Again, it is often said, "American workers do not develop radical ideas on the basis of their own experience, but only if influenced by middle-class intellectuals or foreigners." This book challenges that belief. A few of these organizers inherited their outlook on the world from their parents. Most did not. Moving through a variety of frustrating and demeaning jobs, finding themselves involved in struggles often not of their own making, rethinking what they had taken for granted, the contributors to this book developed their ideas on the basis of what they saw and did, felt and tried.

Even the details were sometimes similar. Christine Ellis and John Anderson rejected the church when it failed to respond to human need or to deal rationally with the world. The flag of the United States was a significant symbol to resist or uphold for Sylvia Woods, Stan Weir, and George Sullivan as children. Mario Manzardo and (after the period dealt with in their accounts) John Anderson and George Patterson were drafted almost immediately after they did things which stirred up the wrath of the international union. As members of the Armed Forces, George Sullivan and John Barbero were disgusted by the way Americans disregarded other cultures and gained respect for people on a worldwide scale. This experience had a profound effect on Sullivan and Barbero, foreshadowing the impact of Vietnam on other young working men in the 1960s and 1970s.

For all the organizers in this book, experience was the heart of the matter. But often a friend—Marko for Christine Ellis, Frank Cedervall for John Anderson, Herb and Jane March for Stella Nowicki, Mamie Harris for Sylvia Woods, a fellow seaman for Stan Weir, the United Labor Party for John Barbero—put into words a context for what they were feeling and offered a sense of direction for dealing with unresolved life situations.

We would be pleased if our book could play the part of such a friend in the experience of those who read it. Rank-and-file groups tend to be isolated from one another. Individuals trying to transform their work situations (among whom we include ourselves) are also isolated in a deeper sense. Family, church, school, army and workplace combine to make us distrust our own feelings and to be fearful that the dream of solidarity and human dignity is, after all, only a dream. This book stands at the side of anyone doing such dreaming. Here is a roomful of travelers who, after long journeying, still believe that all men and women *can* live as brothers and sisters, still affirm that democracy *must* be made to work in the plants and

offices where Americans work. We have found them encouraging
friends in seeking our own way from the movement of the 1960s
into the very different kind of movement which the 1970s require.
We hope readers will gain from this book encouragement to work
in their own lives for the release of the human spirit.

CHRISTINE ELLIS

CHRISTINE ELLIS recalls in detail the experience of immigrants coming to America and the support the foreign born gave each other in political as well as economic and cultural ways.

She joined the Communist Party, served as an organizer of the unemployed in the early 1930s, and was active in the Party for many years. Later she became disillusioned with the Communist Party as a possible instrument for creating a more just society.

After the period described in this account, Christine Ellis lived in Gary, Indiana and married a steelworker. She opposed the Korean War for reasons similar to those of the Vietnam War protesters. This led to efforts of the Justice Department to have her deported under the McCarran Act. She was jailed without bail for ten months in 1952–53.

While in jail she began to write the story of her life on the backs of Christmas and Easter cards sent her by supporters. After we met her she added to these recollections, writing about some incidents and telling others to us personally or to the Labor History Workshop in Gary during the summer of 1971. What appears here are several highly condensed fragments from a mass of vividly-remembered material.

CHRISTINE ELLIS

People Who Cannot Be Bought

I

ALTHOUGH I WAS ONLY FIVE when we left what is now Jugoslavia, I remember the compound where we lived and the tiny village where many of the poor peasants lived in thatch-covered huts.

Both my mother and father came from ancient communal families. We lived in huge compounds, two stories high, built of thick stone walls. There was a common kitchen and dining room where all the members of the family ate together.

In order for a commune to exist in the twentieth century, it had to have good management. At one time our family had owned a lot of land, with vineyards, many sheep, olive trees, etc. With the death of my great-grandfather our fortunes began to suffer.

My father was a good-hearted soul but he wasn't exactly a hard worker. He served his time in the army of Emperor Franz Joseph where he learned to be an excellent marksman. His marriage to my mother was pre-arranged. They hadn't even met.

My mother came from the village of Nadim, walking distance from our village of Tinj. Her mother was the head of the family in their compound. She was a widow most of her life. But she was a good manager and was the undisputed head of the household.

My mother bore twelve children but only six survived. The first four, all male, either died at birth or in early infancy. Then she had three girls.

The land-holdings of the family had dwindled to a very low point and we lived in poverty. My father, perhaps in disgust that he had lost four sons and now had three daughters, decided to go to America. He left in 1911.

His first job was digging with pick and shovel the foundation for the St. Louis, Missouri, City Hall. When that was done he joined some other Croatian immigrants in building railroad tracks in Minnesota. The extreme cold weather there did not appeal to them. Some of the men said there were coal mining towns in southern Iowa where a large number of Croatians lived, and that is how Papa came to Jerome, Iowa. Between these various jobs he managed to save up enough money to send us the fare to come to the United States via steerage on a German steamship plus train fare from New York City to Jerome, Iowa.

I can never forget the misery and suffering we endured on the ship. We traveled steerage which means down in the hold where there are no portholes for air. The place was jammed tight with double and triple bunk beds, very thin mattresses so that if a child slept in the bunk bed above you there was every chance of the urine dropping down on you. Passengers who were seasick simply vomited all over the place and the stench is impossible to describe. Early every morning everyone in the hold had to go out on deck. If a passenger was too ill to walk up, stewards came and dragged the person up the steps and threw them on the deck floor. Then buckets of sulphur were burned in the hold so that the fumes of the burning sulphur would kill the stench. The passengers had to stay out on the deck all day, regardless of the weather or their physical condition. If a passenger was seasick and lay vomiting where he or she was the stewards would come along and spill a pail of water over their heads. Sometimes they added a kick in the ribs as well.

I was the least seasick of our family. Mama suffered the most. She spent almost every day just lying on the deck floor, too ill to move or do anything. There were sinks on deck where you could wash your face or your clothes. I felt quite well and decided to wash my stockings. I foolishly hung them to dry on the ship's railing. Naturally they were gone when I went to look for them. The sad part of it is that I had only that one pair of stockings and had to do without stockings the rest of the trip.

We arrived in New York in late September so it was already getting chilly. Some enterprising immigrant showed my mother how to take any kind of paper but especially newspapers, wrap my feet in one section and then wrap another section around my legs and tie it so it stayed up. I imagine Mama must have had some string or she tore something into strips so that she could tie the newspaper securely to keep my legs warm—so I arrived in America without even a pair of stockings and my feet and legs wrapped in newspaper.

The story of our wait for three days on Ellis Island and what we had to go through because I was lame is a story in itself. Since we spoke no English we all had identification tags, our names and our destination, etc.—my mother, two sisters and myself. Mama was terribly frightened of America. She had been told in the old country that in America men rape women on the streets, openly. There was another strange thing we noticed—so many men without mustaches. Where we came from all men had mustaches, only the priest was clean-shaven. Mama was puzzled—so many priests and yet so many sinful men.

We were herded like cattle—first we were stripped naked (males in one room, females in another room) and then we were forced to walk through a huge pool of water that had Lysol in it. That was our bath. Then we went to a de-lousing room where they sprayed something on our hair to kill the headlice. After that, still naked, we each had to have a complete physical examination.

I had a congenital hip dislocation and had a limp. The doctor said I could not be admitted to the United States, that only completely healthy people could be admitted and that I would be returned to my grandmother in Europe by the first boat. Mama, though a timid and very frightened woman, totally illiterate, told the doctor very firmly that unless I was admitted she and my two sisters would also return to Europe—she would not tolerate the breaking up of the family. There was a long and very heated argument but Mama stood firm. The doctors had me walk back and forth, asked many questions. I was confused and frightened. The idea of being separated from Mama was beyond comprehension even though I loved my grandmother very much. Finally the doctors gave in and said I could stay.

The authorities [at Ellis Island] kept us in huge waiting rooms on wooden benches. There was a huge dining room where we ate at long tables. The food was so dreadful that even we who had known real hunger in Jugoslavia could hardly eat any of it. The rule was that the new immigrants had to wait till their name was called to board trains for their destination. When the immigrants arrived a telegram was sent to the person sponsoring the immigrants. Then when a return telegram of verification was received the immigrants' names would be called and they would be directed to the boat that took them to shore and to the proper railroad station. Usually it was only a matter of a few hours or a day at the most.

We sat on the benches on Ellis Island for three days. Mama was sure that either something had happened to Papa or he had changed his mind and we were stranded on Ellis Island. She wept a great deal in her helplessness. Mama was hard of hearing and that made matters even worse. An employee on the Island would go through the waiting rooms calling out the names of those whose telegrams of verification had arrived. Our name was simple enough, Stanich, but how the employee pronounced it I do not know. Fortunately for us a woman who sat near us, a Slavic woman, perhaps Polish, asked us our name and when we told her she informed us that our name was being called for the last two days. She helped us locate an Island employee and that sped up our departure from Ellis Island.

I remember very little about the long train ride from New York City to Jerome, Iowa. We had huge tickets pinned on like labels on packages and were herded on and off trains since there was no direct route from New York City to Jerome. I do remember that the seats in the trains were made of braided cane and were hard. There was no such thing as a reclining seat so we had to sit up straight on the hard seats all the way.

The "home" that awaited our arrival in Jerome was a miserable three-room frame company house, built on a dirt street along the railroad tracks and across the road from the coal mine. The year was 1913.

We lived in the company shack for several months. Across the road from us and right next to the coal mine were a number of black families. My sisters and I made friends with black children and spent most of our play time with them. I remember the delicious cookies one of the black mothers gave us. It wasn't too long before my parents were told by other Croatians that they must not allow us to play with black children. It was forbidden and we would get in trouble. So that was the end of our friendship and delicious cookies.

We moved from the company shack to other houses where we stayed only a short time. Later we moved to a long-neglected farm in Rathbun.

Rathbun was and still is basically a Croatian town. (Rathbun is the oldest Croatian settlement in Iowa and very proud of its history and tradition. Now almost a ghost town, its old-time residents hang on—their children, scattered everywhere, return for celebrations and religious festivals.) The majority of its residents were Croatian, with a few Italian families, one Czech family, and a small number of native American families.

Whereas in most places it is the foreign born who have an inferiority complex because of language problems, etc., with us in Iowa it was just the opposite.

The early settlers were of English descent. They lived off the land and income from services to those moving west. In contrast to the new immigrants, the Anglo-Saxons had a past in America, a past that had been exciting and ever-changing. Now things had settled down. Railroads criss-crossed the land, people settled in towns, industries flourished.

With the digging of coal mines, immigrants from Central Europe began to arrive. These new immigrants were peasants, long experienced in getting food from the soil. They were also ready and eager to enter industry. The new arrivals felt insecure in a foreign land. The need to have a piece of land on which to raise food, a house you could call your own for shelter in your old age was a driving force which enabled them to withstand all kinds of difficulties, to live frugally, to save for the lean years. They had no past in America, only the future and the future was unsure and unpredictable.

Perhaps in their longing for the old days the old settlers blamed the new immigrants for the change that was taking place. At any rate the old native American families around Rathbun never acclimated themselves to coal mining which became the chief source of earning a living in the hilly country thereabouts. Their farm holdings became smaller and smaller as they sold sections of land to the new immigrants who combined farming and coal mining.

Foreign-born people used to make disparaging remarks about the native American women sitting in the shade in the summer heat fanning themselves while the foreign-born women sweated in their kitchens putting up hundreds of jars of beans, tomatoes, preserves, jellies, pickles, beets, fruits of all kinds. Instead of putting up vegetables, meat, etc. for the winter, native Americans bought canned goods from the store. None of the foreign-born women would be caught dead with store bread on the table. Every bit of land was carefully cultivated and cared for.

When work was slack many of the native American families had to apply for county "charity" which was something none of the foreign-born families would even contemplate. In the old country there was no such thing as public relief. They didn't expect it or look for it in America. The foreign born all belonged to fraternal societies which provided sick benefits and insurance. In case of accident, sickness or death the foreign-born miners made provisions for the care of their dependents.

Native Americans had no fraternal organizations nor did they make provisions for their families in case of long illness or death. When misfortune came their way they had to get help from the county. The foreign born resented this. They felt that they were paying taxes to maintain people who were too lazy and thoughtless to care what happened to their women and children.

Religious prejudices entered into the picture also. All of the foreign born were Roman Catholics and they maintained a church. The native Americans were Protestants. They didn't have a church. They held their occasional religious services in one of the school rooms.

It was a matter of record that the foreign born were the most loyal and devoted union members. Some of the native Americans had to be forced to join the miners' union [United Mine Workers].

In other words, the foreign-born people had nothing but contempt for the native Americans. In our eyes they were worthless and shiftless. No self-respecting son or daughter of a foreign-born family would think of marrying into native American families.

Disturbing events deepened the prejudices and antagonisms and finally resulted in bitter hatred and distrust in the 1920s.

During World War I a large number of southern white families

migrated to the mining and industrial areas in Iowa. During the war
the mines worked every day. When the war was over, work in the
mines slackened. The mines worked during the winter months but
only a day or two a week during the summer.

The coal operators were quick to react. Wages were cut. Union
miners protested and went on strike [November 1, 1920].

I've already described how the native Americans lived. When hard
times came they were totally unprepared. Native Americans were
willing to work for any wages. Some of the smaller pits in predominantly native American towns remained open. Native Americans
became scabs.

The two mines in the town where I lived remained closed. No
one dared scab. The town where I lived was made up of perhaps
95% immigrants who were staunch union men.

Coal operators and politicians fanned the prejudices that had so
far remained only near the surface into open warfare. Epithets like
"hunkies," "flat-heads" were hurled at the foreign born. The
foreign born retorted with "johnny-bulls." Not even the children
escaped from the brewing storm. The school yard in Rathbun
became divided between "flat-heads" and "johnny-bulls" and
heaven help the "flat-head" that tried to be neutral.

The Ku Klux Klan took the offensive. The combination of resentment of the new by the old settlers and the influx of native stock
southerners who found kindred souls in the old native settlers during
World War I was what gave the KKK its mass base for a number
of years.

Night riders in white robes and hoods invaded Rathbun night after
night, shooting pistols and shotguns into the air. The fiery cross
appeared often in front of the Catholic Church and on the tip of
the slag pile of the slope mine. Dynamite was exploded night after
night. Crops were destroyed, barns and haystacks were burned
down. Livestock was slaughtered. The Klan had a newspaper, "The
Iowa Fiery Cross," which was sold publicly on the streets of Centerville (the county seat) by small boys.

Native Americans in Rathbun never dared admit they belonged
to the Klan although there were suspicions about some of them,
including the Scotts, our nearest neighbors.

The reign of terror lasted for about three years, although its peak was 1920–21. During that time my father always had a loaded rifle near his bed at night. We had quite a few boarders in this period. All of them had shotguns for hunting. My father let it be known that every man in our household had guns, ready for use, and if anyone dared come on our farm at night the men would shoot first and ask questions later. Nothing was touched on our place.

In order to keep the ignorant, prejudiced and poverty-stricken native Americans loyal to the Klan their leaders promised them that as soon as the ''foreigners'' were driven out the Klan leaders were going to give, I mean *give*, homes and farms to the native Americans. They went so far as to designate which house, which farm was to be given to whom. It was not unusual for a Rathbun resident to be approached on the street in Centerville by a Klan member and told, ''You damned foreigner, when we drive you out I'm getting your house, free.''

When the Klan began its open warfare against the foreign born throughout Appanoose County a delegation went to the county sheriff demanding protection for the foreign born and restraining action against the Klan. The sheriff laughed in their faces and told them he was a leader of the Klan. Every county official except the assessor was a member of the Klan. When our people discovered that the county officials were leaders of the Klan they appealed to the governor but the governor turned a deaf ear to their pleas. We were completely on our own.

The Klan was unable to carry out its threats. The foreign born were outnumbered in the county population as well as the state. It was impossible to launch any kind of counter-offensive but the foreign born were determined to sit tight and weather the storm. In time the Klan terror began to subside, especially when it became evident to the rank and file that the promises of houses and farms were nothing but empty boasts.

The way the strike was settled also helped to break the backbone of the KKK, at least in Appanoose County. The strike went on all winter, the following spring and on into the summer of 1921. The union miners were getting desperate. We were running out of food. The company stores would not give credit and the few independent

store owners were running out of money and could not get supplies
from wholesalers. The shelves in the small stores were almost bare.
The union (Lewis, etc.) deserted the striking miners. Not one penny
came to our aid. In desperation the local union leaders decided they
had to use force to get the scabs out of the mines.

In early September 1921, the union miners met in the town where
I lived. They were armed with shotguns and rifles. I remember my
mother weeping and begging my father not to go with the caravan.
She said, "Think of me and the children." My father said, "It's
because of you and the children that I go."

So the armed caravan in broken down jalopies left our town and
headed towards a nearby town where scabs worked the mine. When
they arrived at the mine they found the entrance to the mine guarded
by southern white women and teenagers armed with shotguns and
rifles.

Instead of shooting it out right there on the spot, the union leaders
wisely put their guns on the ground and approached the women and
youth with outstretched hands. A spokesman said, "We mean you
no harm. We don't want to shoot you. We know your men are working for low wages but in doing so they do harm to you and to us.
Our children are hungry. All we want is for your men to come out
with us. If we all stick together all of us will gain. Our children
won't go hungry and neither will yours. We want you in our union
so that together we can improve our wages."

The women and youths listened, put down their guns and allowed
a delegation of union miners to go into the mine and talk to the
men who were scabbing. The delegation succeeded in getting the
men to come out. Then the southerners who had been scabbing
joined the caravan and they went from one scab-operated mine to
another, only now it was white southerners who acted as spokesmen
and convinced the others to come out. In one day the companies
were defeated—no one scabbed and the strike was settled and the
enmity between southern whites and the immigrants gradually wore
itself out.

This was an important episode in my early years. These events
left a deep impression.

A number of people have influenced my life profoundly but

perhaps none so much as Marko. I was fifteen years of age. My oldest sister and her husband had been living in Cleveland. My brother-in-law was a steelworker. There were big layoffs [1922] and work was scarce. They wrote and asked Papa if they could come back and live with us. They also asked if they could bring a friend with them. This friend was a man whose health was bad and he needed a place to rest and recuperate. Marko had been in jail, one of the victims of the Palmer Raids.

I was fanatically religious. It was mainly the fault of radicals in the Iowa mining fields who made religion instead of capitalism the main issue. The more religion was attacked the more I defended it.

There was a reason why I clung to religion. One has to have a reason for living, a guiding philosophy, a purpose, a goal. While in school my teacher had encouraged me to study. She predicted a great future for me as a teacher or social worker. I had beautiful plans for high school and college. There were no limits to the things one could accomplish in America. But no one in my family shared my ambitions.

Instead of going to high school I went to work. My disappointment was crushing. I wanted to die, literally. I prayed for death. I had no interest in living. There was nothing to live for. I blamed my father entirely. I refused to accept the fact that it was financially impossible for my father to send me to school. All I could see was my world crashing about me. There was no future in a place like Rathbun. Nothing awaited me except housework. I was lame. No man would want to marry me. In my desperation I turned more and more to religion. There was nothing to live for except the reward I would get in heaven when I died. When my father and his friends attacked religion they attacked and tried to undermine the only thing left to me, my only purpose in living.

One hot summer day I was reading a history book in the shade of the grape arbor. I wore glasses, the same glasses I had worn since I was about nine years old. Marko came and sat across the table from me. He was interested in what I was reading and was very much surprised that it was a history book. He spoke words of encouragement about studying. This was the first bit of interest I had evoked in anyone about my dreams and hopes for an education. Here for the first time was someone who valued and respected books.

He told me he noticed that I needed new glasses. That opened the door to the resentment against my father which was hidden deep inside. I unburdened myself of all the bitterness I felt at being cheated of an education.

Then slowly, skillfully he picked up the pieces and put each in its proper light and perspective. First he took up the question of the glasses. He explained that he understood the glasses were important to me but had I talked to my father about my need for new glasses? No, I hadn't. He showed how it was that my father, a man who had never gone to school, a man harassed by economic worries, a long strike the previous year, could not be expected to know and understand what went on in my mind.

Then, most important of all, he took up the issue of higher education. Deftly, he asked one question after another. My answers to each of his questions cast a light on who was to blame for my broken dreams. Up to then my father was the culprit. It was he who stood in my way. It was he who had ruined my life.

Marko asked how many students had been in my graduating class. I told him. How many of them had gone to high school? Two. Who were they? Elizabeth Mills and Billy Robinson. Were their fathers coal miners? No. What did their families do for a living? Mr. Mills was manager of the company store. Billy was a nephew of the mine superintendent, his mother a clerk in the company store. Had any son or daughter of a coal miner in Rathbun ever gone to high school? No. Did I believe that all coal miners were cruel and deliberately prevented their children from getting an education? No. Are there any rich coal miners in Rathbun? No. How far is it to the nearest high school? Centerville, about eight miles. Is there free transportation to school? No. Does the student have to buy his own books? Yes. Is there a tuition? Yes.

I was ashamed of myself for thinking such terrible thoughts about my father. Marko talked some more. He didn't preach but in clear and simple terms explained why it was impossible for a coal miner to be rich, to give his children an education, to take care of their health properly. I saw things then as I had never seen them before.

Father Kaufman, the Catholic priest of the area, made the final contribution that swung the balance of power on Marko's side. The priest came to our house one cold winter day to ask for a donation of chickens for a banquet to be held in Centerville to raise funds for the Church. The priest was a large man, blustery, aggressive and overbearing. He was also under the influence of too much home-made wine by the time he got to our house.

Papa was home that day. There was no love between Papa and the priest. Instead of sitting on a chair the priest sat on the table. That was an insult that could not be overlooked.

When Marko walked in I left the room and hid behind the door of the bedroom where I could observe and hear everything that went on. Marko went to work on Father Kaufman—it was an opportunity he couldn't miss. Politely and calmly he began asking questions which challenged religious dogma, dogma that had been refuted by science. Blow by blow every pillar on which I had leaned toppled over. The priest could not prove anything. All he could say was that it was a matter of faith, that it was written in the Scriptures, that it was proclaimed by Pope so-and-so. On his side Marko had science, logic and man's own experience learned through centuries of investigation, trial and error. The priest couldn't take it any more. He became very angry. He bellowed, "Go to hell with your questions and science." He pointed an angry finger at Papa, "Mr. Stanich, Sunday from the altar I'm going to expose you and have you run out of town." With that he stalked out of the house.

Marko announced that he would attend Mass Sunday morning to hear what the priest had to say. He dared me to attend. I couldn't refuse.

The priest gave his sermon on the sinfulness of women. I could hardly believe [that he did not live up to his threat]. It was a great relief but at the same time a great disappointment. Why didn't Father Kaufman show the same courage as Marko and fight for his beliefs? Was it possible there was really nothing to defend and fight for? I would have admired and respected the priest if he had carried out his threat. Perhaps I would even have been won back to the fold. . . .

I began to earn my own living at the age of thirteen, and at the age of fifteen I left home to earn my living in industry, first in Cleveland and then Chicago.

I went to work for the American Can Company. I had to walk up five flights of stairs to go to work. They put me painting milk cans by hand.

Most of the fifth floor was the lithographing department. The piece of tin is painted and then it is dried through the kilns, through gas ovens. Men with leather gloves would take these pieces of hot tin and stack them up as they came out of the kiln. It was impossibly hot working up there.

The men who took the tin off the kilns had some grievance. Apparently they all agreed. They wanted higher wages. They went to the boss and the boss refused. So these men stopped working. Then what did the boss do? He called on the girls and other young men who were painting, like myself, and put us to work because there was a certain amount of tin already in the ovens that had to come through. They didn't even give us any gloves or anything. I worked only a few minutes handling this hot tin. I almost cut off three fingers. The tin cut to the bone through three fingers. So I went home, this hand all bandaged up.

And my brother-in-law said, "What happened?" So I told him. He said, "You dirty scab." He said, "Serves you right. You should have known." I knew about unions. My father was a union member. And I knew it was wrong. But you're frightened. You don't know what to do. The boss tells you, "Do this." And this is what you do.

There were many places in the old days where you had to sign what they called a yellow-dog contract. In order to get a job you had to sign a statement that you would not join a union as long as you were employed by that company.

In factories where I worked, with the American Can Company and with the Continental Can Company, if a man did something that wasn't right, that was deducted from his wages. Not only was that deducted from his wages but he would get bawled out. I have seen grown men stand there and take such horrible abuse that the tears ran down their faces and they just stood there. They had nothing to say because there was no seniority, nothing. You took all the abuse, whether you liked it or not, because any time the boss could fire you from your job, and he could bring somebody else there. This whole question of what unionism meant and why these people sacrificed so much was so that they could have some dignity, so they wouldn't have to stand the abuse.

I came from Cleveland to Chicago when I was about sixteen. In those days nobody worked a whole year at a time. You worked a few weeks and then you had layoffs for a month or two and then you got another job and you worked a few weeks. In my early youth, there was nobody that I knew who ever worked steady. There were layoffs constantly.

I finally got a job at Bauer and Black, makers of medical supplies and athletic supports. Bauer and Black was one of the nicest places I have ever worked for. I was quite happy there. The work had to be perfect. The stitches had to be small. Their machines were in good shape. It was clean. I made many friends there. The wages were only thirty cents an hour, but they had an extra Christmas bonus. You got $50.00, I think, for the first year. My last bonus was $200.00.

When the Depression came, when the big crash came in '29, they went bankrupt. They were bought up by the Kendall Corporation which still owns Bauer and Black. The Kendall Corporation decided to modernize the place. So they started bringing in different kinds of machinery. My sister worked for the American Can Company and she told about all the modern machinery that they were bringing, all the people they were laying off and the modern machinery that was taking the place of people. So I became very much concerned.

When I first started at Bauer and Black I worked in the corn plaster department. You put certain things on the corn plasters by hand. Well, shortly, they got machinery and the whole thing just went one-two-three. The machine put out by the thousands. I could see machinery taking the place of human beings and the people who didn't have an education would be without work.

Meanwhile, I had become [a member of the Communist Party]. When I came to Chicago, all kinds of cultural organizations were led by progressives. They had choruses; they had the various amateur acting groups in which we took part and which I liked very much. And I had become acquainted with a whole number of people who were Communists. The leading Communists among the Croatian people were cultured, educated, kind, devoted people. Among them were editors of a Croatian language newspaper. Most of the leaders were skilled workers, but in the group were factory workers and just plain laborers. The thing that impressed me the most was the stress on education, culture, respect for others, devotion to a movement that would by its example win the masses to the cause of communism.

So when I became very much concerned as to what was going to happen to the working class with the introduction of machinery, I went to a meeting. They were organizing a conference of working women. Well, I worked in a place with working women. So I talked to some of the girls in the department where I worked and told them that this would be a good thing and some of them promised to come. They thought the program was excellent, the idea of organizing women, but I was the only one who came to the conference.

When I came to the conference I saw a woman in disguise. She was the personnel director of Bauer and Black. So I thought, oh boy, there it goes, I'm going to be fired. When I got to work on Monday, instead of being fired I got promoted. I got promoted to assistant forelady (at the age of twenty) and they raised my wages to $20.00 a week salary, which was something! And so I decided that I would use my position to talk to the girls since I had to teach new people as they came to work.

When they changed the managers of the factory they called a meeting of all the foreladies, assistant foreladies and so on. The whole bonus system was done away with. All the paternalism was gone. The company picnics, everything was gone. They announced that they were going to make big layoffs, that they were going to keep only the most efficient employees. We had to increase the production so that the production would be the same with about fifty per cent of the employees. They had to be heartless. Regardless of how long these people had worked there, only the fastest workers were to be kept, and it was up to us, the foreladies and the assistant foreladies, to decide who was going to be laid off.

So they said, "Does anybody have anything to say?" Well, how can I sit there? I am so naive. So I raised my hand. I said, "I protest!" Everybody's flabbergasted. So I said, "What do you want these girls to do?" There were a number of elderly women who worked as inspectors and there were others who were slow workers. I said, "What do you expect some of these old women to do, go down to Indiana and 22nd to be prostitutes?" They were quite shocked. And [a man] said, "What do you recommend?" "Well," I said, "a beginner, at least, at least split the shift. Split it in half, that each of the girls work three days so they won't starve, they won't have to walk the streets." And he says, "I'll have you know that you are working for the *company* now. You are *company* representatives. We have to think of the company first," and so on.

Then I wrote an article for the *Daily Worker* in which I said that the company was going to lay people off regardless of how many years they had worked in the factory. They were going to keep only the most efficient and they would have to produce to make up for all those that were going to be laid off. Of course, I didn't sign my name to it. I ordered about six copies to be sent to me personally. I clipped this article out, I brought some thumbtacks, and as I was sent on errands through the different departments I stuck up this article that I had written in different parts of the factory.

I put it on the bulletin board in my own department. In the meantime, I had some messages to deliver to the main office. When I came back to my own department the whole place was a bedlam. The forelady was ready to tear her hair out. Nobody was working. Somebody was standing up on the work table, everybody was gathered around, and she was reading this article that somebody found on the bulletin board. It dealt with the workers at Bauer and Black, and they thought it was wonderful. Hooray! Somebody cares about us. Listen, it's in print. It's in a newspaper. Look at what they said, about us, about layoffs and all this. And the forelady and everybody else came running in and put everybody back to work. Nobody said a word to me.

It was my job at the end of the day, after all of the girls left, to make sure all the windows were closed, that the aisles were clear, the machinery was shut off. The forelady would leave right away at quitting time. But this particular day the forelady was still sitting at her desk. I finished, cleared the aisles, shut off the machinery, checked the fire escapes. Then she said, "Christine, you're wanted in the office."

I came down to the office and there was the woman in charge of personnel. She says, "Christine," in her highest Bryn Mawr or eastern college fashion, she says, "We don't think you're happy here. And we think it's best that we sever all connections. Here's your pay."

II

Our first test in organizing the unemployed was about May 1931. Another man and myself were assigned to organize the unemployed on the near west side [of Chicago] in an all-black neighborhood. We found a small storefront and we paid the rent on it. We cleaned it up, got some chairs, mimeographed a leaflet. We didn't know a soul—went from door to door to distribute the leaflets. In the evening a lot of people came. The little hall was full.

We spoke simply, explained the platform, the demands and activities of the unemployed council. And then we said, "Are there any questions?" There was a rather awkward silence. Everybody looked at each other to see who was going to speak up.

Finally, an elderly black man stood up and said, "What you folks figure on doing about that colored family that was thrown out of their house today? They got no place to go. They're still out there with their furniture on the sidewalk."

So the man who was with me said, "Very simple. We'll adjourn this meeting, go over there, and put the furniture back in the house. After that, anyone wishing to join the unemployed council and build an organization to fight evictions, return to this hall and we'll talk about it some more." That's what we did. We adjourned the meeting.

They didn't walk with us. They discreetly walked just a little behind us because they didn't trust us. They wanted to see what we were going to do.

The evicted family was just around the corner a block away, at 13th and Loomis. It was a little frame house. (All the houses were

small, frame, one-family shacks.) We walked up to the front door.
There was a big padlock on it. So the man who was with me said,
"Does anybody have any tools? We've got to break this lock." In
a matter of minutes men came with all kinds of tools. We broke
the lock on the door. Once he and I started taking in the chairs,
everybody else pitched in, began to haul in every last bit of furniture,
fix up the beds, set up the gas stove and break the seal that had
shut off the gas, and so on; and when that was all done, went back
to the hall. The hall was jammed! And we organized the best and
most effective unemployed council in the city of Chicago.

Later some of the landlords got together and they decided that,
come hell or high water, they and the police were going to put an
end to this business of people breaking the locks and putting the
furniture back in, turning on the gas and everything else.

Some family had been evicted early in the morning. People had
been coming there all day long trying to put the furniture back in.
Hundreds of people had been arrested.

We had a little meeting in the hall and I said, "Well, let's go.
We've got to get that furniture back. It's getting night. We have
to help this family." So we did.

Over on 13th Street, there was the woman and her children and
her furniture at this house. But there was not another soul on the
street anywhere, not even a dog. So we think, all right, we'll go.

A handful of us marched up to the house where this woman and
her children were. As soon as we got there—the police had been
hiding around different buildings—the police came and surrounded
us. They were ready to arrest us.

I tried to go up to the house. So one of the detectives jumped
up on the steps of the house with a sawed-off machine gun and he
says, "The first son-of-a-bitch that sets foot on these stairs is going
to have his head shot off."

Well, you can't let that go unchallenged! So I stepped forward,
and behind me comes a young white man, and behind him comes
a black man and his wife. And the four of us marched up, right
in the face of the sawed-off gun.

When we four went on the stairs the people came out of their
houses. They came swarming out and they surrounded the police.

And the detective didn't dare kill us. He just held his gun uselessly in his hand. The four of us stood triumphantly up at the top of the stairs and were kicking on the door.

And then the chief, or whoever was in charge, said, "Now look. We've arrested hundreds of people here today. The hell with it." He took off his hat. He said, "Take up a collection. Whatever we collect, that's going to be the rent." They took up a collection among all the policemen and everybody who was there.

The landlord was there and the policeman told him, "That's your rent." The landlord wasn't satisfied. And the policeman told him, "Now you take this money or you get nothing. We've had enough trouble with this one house. I don't want to hear another word out of you." He said, "These people are going to break down the door. Now you take this money and you go open that door." So the land-lord had to take the padlock off the door.

In July 1932, I [became an organizer for District 10]. District 10 comprised Texas, Oklahoma, Arkansas, Missouri, Nebraska, Kansas and Iowa. At first the district headquarters was in Kansas City, Missouri. We had isolated organizations in all of these states plus some devoted contacts in all kinds of small towns and rural communities.

In Kirksville, Missouri we had one lonely contact. He wrote to the office in Kansas City and said that he'd like to have me come out and speak. He had come to see us in Kansas City and he wanted me to come to Kirksville. He would organize a meeting in front of the court house on a certain Saturday morning.

I had been up in northern Iowa, so I hitch-hiked from northern Iowa down into Kirksville. They had been forbidden a permit to meet. They decided, to hell with this, permit or no permit we would meet. So somebody brought an empty barrel and first a man by the name of Mr. Martin, a local man, spoke on this barrel. The police came along and arrested him.

As soon as they arrested him I asked the fellows to hoist me up there on the barrel. Somebody had pointed out the mayor of Kirksville and the mayor of Kirksville was a real dandy! He must have had a Brooks Brothers suit on. Kirksville used to be a shoe manufacturing town and here the people were barefooted. So, being a very practical person, I pointed to the mayor. I said, "There's your mayor." I said, "I bet his suit and his shoes and his beautiful shirt and tie cost more than you spend for a month's groceries." And that won the people over.

Meantime, they had taken this man to jail. And I said, "What do you say we all march down to that jail and get Mr. Martin out? He has committed no crime." They said, "OK, let's go!" They took me off the barrel and all of us, hundreds and hundreds, marched down to the jail.

The mayor and the keeper of the jail said they wanted to talk with me. I said, "No sir! You're not talking to me. You talk to *all* of us." No, they wouldn't, they'd talk to me. I said, "I'll tell you what, we'll compromise. Let the people here elect a committee so that nobody can say I made a deal with you."

The people there elected a committee and we went inside. We made it plain to the jailer and to the mayor that these people were not leaving until Mr. Martin was released. Since all these angry people were out there, they had better let Mr. Martin go. But first the mayor told me, he said, "You don't know this guy Martin. He's a no good slob! He wouldn't work if he had a job. He's lazy, he's good-for-nothing, he's no good," he's this, he's that! And he just slammed the man down as if he was absolutely dirt and wasn't worth fighting for. But then finally he agreed to release Mr. Martin.

So one of the turnkeys brings Mr. Martin out. The mayor comes out on the porch, puts his arm around Mr. Martin and he says, "Fellow citizens! We are releasing Mr. Martin. And just to show you that my heart's in the right place," (Mrs. Martin was pregnant, they had a baby in a few days) "just to show all of you," he says, "that my heart's in the right place, I'm going to treat Mr. and Mrs. Martin to the best meal they've had in a long time."

Mr. and Mrs. Martin walked with the mayor to a little restaurant at the west side of the square, and all these hundreds of people following. They went into the restaurant and the mayor told Mr. and Mrs. Martin to order whatever they wanted.

Mr. and Mrs. Martin ordered a glass of water! And that's *all* they ordered. The mayor pleaded with them. He *pleaded* with them to order something else. They said, "No. This is all we want—a glass of water."

By the time we got to Martin's house there was a layette, there were blankets, there was coal, there was food, there were all kinds of things. And then we organized an unemployed council in Kirksville. I think I stayed there about three days to get the thing organized. We had sowbelly bacon—it's just nothing but fat, soft fat, and that's what these people got from the relief—sowbelly bacon and homemade biscuits and gravy and black coffee three times a day. But these people organized. And there are people like Mr. Martin everywhere who cannot be bought by the mayor or by anybody else.

And the women were more militant than the men. For instance, in Joplin, Missouri, a young housewife had a whole bunch of kids. She made a slab. She took a pole and she took a piece of board and she tacked it on. And then she took the sowbelly bacon that she got from the relief and tacked it onto this board. And she led the demonstration through town.

The women were usually the most outspoken because they had the children to feed and they had to provide the food for the family. You found women pounding their fists on the desks as well as the men.

I remember a big gathering once in Grand Island, Nebraska. Have you ever heard of Mother Bloor? She was an old-time radical and a marvelous speaker. She and her husband owned a farm in North Dakota and they brought a whole truckload of farmers from North Dakota.

There were thousands of farmers gathered and they had inexperienced leadership. People had gotten together but nobody knew what to do. Mother Bloor decided somebody ought to do something. She got up on top of the truck and she said (she had a voice that really carried, she should have been on the stage), "Would you like to hear greetings from the farmers in North Dakota?" "Yeah!"

So she told them about farming and the miseries of farming and then she said, "I hear that some of you men complain about modern equipment for the women. You think women are having life too easy. Well," she said, "let me tell you the women's side of the story."

She said, "Did you ever go to a cemetery and take a look at the gravestones? Here lies Joe Smith. Here lies Jane Smith, his first wife. Here lies Mary Smith, his second wife. Here lies so-and-so, his fourth wife." She said, "A man outlived four or five wives because the women had to work so hard. . . ."

I have to tell you about the Sears, Roebuck sales. Let's say, Farmer Smith's farm is up for sale and he has 200 or 300 acres of land. He has a tractor, he has a couple of horses, he has cows, he has a wagon, he has a buggy, maybe he has a car, he has furniture, all the different implements. Everything is brought out.

All the neighbors from miles around gather. The auctioneer gets up and he says, "What am I offered for this first-rate Jersey cow?" "Ten cents!" "Does anybody raise the price? Ten cents offered, ten cents, ten cents, ten cents." Nobody offers more than ten cents. "This first-class Jersey cow is sold for ten cents."

"What am I offered for this tractor?" "Fifteen cents."

"What am I offered for this stove?" "Five cents."

"What am I offered for this. . .?"

And then they would get the bills of sale from the auctioneer and everybody would turn back these bills of sale to the farmer and help him put back all his stuff.

The farmers, without anybody telling them how to organize, knew how to organize. And do you know where they met? They didn't meet in any small hall. They met in the school house! They were American citizens, they were native Americans, that school belonged to them. They paid the taxes.

Every meeting started with a song. In the middle of the meeting there was singing. At the end of the meeting there was singing. And then they served coffee and cake if they had it.

In the '30s an organizer did not have a car and there was no money for bus fare. Organizers had either to ride the rails or to hitch-hike. [But one time] our people in Sioux City thought it might be dangerous for me to hitch-hike back to Kansas City so they managed to get enough money together to buy me a bus ticket to Kansas City.

The bus wasn't a large one, not a Greyhound, but some smaller independent company that probably ran buses in the rural areas of the region. All the seats were filled. A young woman, she didn't look to be more than twenty to twenty-five years of age, had four small children with her. They looked as though they were scarcely more than a year apart. She was thin and poorly dressed, her hair straggly and poverty was clearly written all over her and the four children. They were all squeezed into one seat, the mother holding the youngest on her lap.

Not long after the bus got started we ran into a heavy summer storm. There was thunder and lightning and at times the rain was so heavy the bus driver could hardly see the road. The pace was agonizingly slow, the storm so violent it was impossible to sleep. The four children became fretful and restless, some of them were crying—probably a mixture of hunger, fear, and being so tightly squeezed in such a small space.

Now in ordinary times the other passengers would have cursed the woman and her crying children, disturbing all the passengers in the bus and making the trip even more miserable than it already was. But these were not ordinary times. The Depression was a thing known to all. Hard times, hunger, worry, fear of tomorrow, was like a dark cloud hanging over the country.

Instead of being angry with the poor young helpless woman and her restless and fretful children, one passenger after another, male and female, came to her and each passenger took one of her children to cuddle and soothe, holding the children in their arms and trying to get them to sleep. I had seen kindness and consideration for others before but nothing to match the wonder of human sympathy and help that I saw that night. The passengers took all four children so the mother could get some rest. Soon all the children went to sleep in the arms of total strangers, and in my heart I felt that this is the true America, this is the America where I belong and feel at home.

I am very happy that I was sent out of Chicago because then I really got to know American working people. I have such undying confidence in the American people, that once they understand what they are fighting for, nothing in hell can beat them. I saw it in Joplin. I saw it in Kirksville. I saw it in Des Moines. I saw it in all kinds of small towns in Nebraska. I saw it in small towns in Kansas. I saw it in Chicago.

Some day, I hope soon, the youth of America will build a new movement. I hope that they will take that which was pure and noble from the old and add new ideas and methods of leadership that will one day convince the American people that socialism is the answer, a socialism based on the history, best traditions and the courage and fighting ability of the American people.

JOHN W. ANDERSON

J OHN W. ANDERSON was a rank-and-file activist in the United
Automobile Workers from its beginnings until his retirement in
1966. These pages, which tell of his early life, are part of a
book-length manuscript he has written on his career in the UAW.*

After the Briggs strike in 1933 with which this selection closes,
John Anderson joined the Industrial Workers of the World. This was
the union at that time which most emphasized the need for industrial
rather than craft unions. For workers to build a strong enough force
to deal with massive corporations, it appeared to Anderson, it was
necessary to organize on an industry-wide basis. So for three years
preceding the launching of the CIO, Anderson was a volunteer
organizer for the IWW.

In November 1936, he was hired at the Fleetwood Fisher Body
plant in Detroit where he worked for the next thirty years. During
the General Motors sit-down strike of January–February 1937,
Anderson was chairman of the Fleetwood strike committee. As a
delegate to the conference which ratified the GM strike settlement
and the first GM contract, he argued that the union should insist on
a shop steward system. This was one of the first occasions on which
Anderson as a spokesman for the rank and file clashed with Walter

*This material is copyrighted by John W. Anderson. It may not be reproduced
in whole or in part without his written permission.

Reuther. In 1938, he left the Socialist Party and became a founding member of the Socialist Workers Party.

John Anderson served the UAW in many positions. In 1947, he was elected president of Local 15 and initiated a massive demonstration in Cadillac Square against the impending Taft-Hartley Act. As local union president, from 1947 to 1949, Anderson agitated for a cost-of-living clause in the GM contract. He was defeated for re-election in 1949 during a period of widespread and intense red-baiting throughout the American labor movement. When he left office, a sign reading "An Injury to One is an Injury to All" was taken down from the wall of the local union headquarters.

Many themes run through John Anderson's account of his early years and his gradual radicalization which also occur in the narratives of Christine Ellis, Stella Nowicki, and George Patterson: the desire for education; the irrelevance of religion as a solution to social and economic problems; the hunger and hardship of the Depression and their effect in destroying love and family life; the outgrowing of a narrow national loyalty and the ripening in its place of a sense of solidarity with working people everywhere.

JOHN W. ANDERSON

How I Became
Part of the Labor Movement

I WAS BORN on a farm in Lincoln County, Wisconsin, May 12,
1906. Merrill, the county seat, is located two hundred miles
northwest of Milwaukee. At the turn of the century and until the
early twenties Merrill was a sawmill and lumbering town.

Many of the farmers worked the land in summer and were
employed in the logging industry during the winter. The climate in
this part of Wisconsin is not good for some crops. I have known
it to freeze every month except July. There is much swamp land,
many lakes, steep hills. In some areas there are so many stones that
it is too expensive to clear the land of them. The farms have no
ready market for their product.

My Norwegian grandfather homesteaded a hundred and sixty acres
[nine miles north of Merrill]. To this wooded area he brought his
wife and five children from Norway about 1890. After a few years
he divorced his wife and returned to Norway. My father, Alex A.
Anderson, at the age of fifteen became the principal breadwinner
of the family. He had to quit school to work on the farm and in
the woods. As he grew older, in the spring of the year he followed
the log drives. These drives took place when the rivers were swollen
from melting snow. Men like my father were skilled at riding the
logs down to the sawmills. When a log was held up on some obstruc-
tion a log jam piled up. It was then the task of the drivers to find
the key log that was causing the jam. Finding this log was difficult
and dangerous work. When the jam was broken hundreds and some-

times thousands of logs shot forward down the river. Breaking a
log jam resulted in injury and death to many drivers.

Father knew all the skills of the lumberjack. In winter he helped
cut the trees down, cut them into logs and pile them up by the river
or at a landing where they were taken to the mills by sleighs or
by train. In summer he sometimes peeled the bark from hemlock
logs. The bark was used in the tanneries.

My mother was one of six children of Swiss immigrants who settled in Nakoosa, Wisconsin. Her mother died of childbirth when
my mother was only nine years old. She had to quit school after
the third grade and go to work as a domestic in the home of a well-
to-do family. Her wages were low and the hours long. She often
told us how hard she had to work and the indignities she suffered.
She married my father in 1902. From March 1903 to February 1913,
my mother gave birth to six children. My brother Carl was the oldest, my sister Julia came next, and then me.

My most vivid childhood experience is of a terrible forest fire
that swept over our farm and the surrounding area in early August
1910. There had been no rain for a period of forty days. Our nearest
neighbors were a mile away. The one to the west had been clearing
land. He let a brush fire get out of control.

My father, like the rest of these part-time farmers, had no knowledge of how to fight a forest fire. Hardly more than an hour before
this holocaust swept across the landscape burning our house, barn
and most of the livestock, my father put us on a wagon and took
us down to the lake located on the southern part of the farm. A
neighbor from the south of us joined my father in protecting us from
the fire. We children were made to lie on a bog on the edge of
the lake. We were covered with a blanket. My father and the
neighbor kept throwing buckets of water on us, on each other, and
on the wagon and horses standing at the edge of the lake.

My mother narrowly escaped death in the flames when she tried
to save some of the cattle by driving them into the lake. We found
several cows burned to death within a hundred yards of where we
lay. I remember seeing the flames shooting hundreds of feet in the
air over the lake. All that we saved was a team of horses with the

wagon, a few belongings and a cow. For hours after the fire there were burning embers everywhere. As far as the eye could see the landscape was black, not a green tree or bush in sight.

This fire was a harsh turning point in the life of our family. We went to stay with my grandparents who lived about seven miles from the farm. My grandmother had married again. After a week or so the rest of the family went back to the farm to build a log house and barn before winter set in. I lived with my grandparents for almost four years.

My grandmother was a domineering woman. Although her profane and derogatory remarks were in Norwegian, I soon learned what she meant. She sometimes pulled my ears if I didn't immediately do as I was told.

I started school at the French Ridge school. It was a one room school where the teacher had to teach more than thirty children in all eight grades. I got little attention and sat idle most of the time. I had no trouble in school but going to and from school I was harassed by some older boys.

I was very young when I began doing some chores. I brought in the wood for the night. I fed the goat, got the cows from the pasture and helped in other ways. A small creek ran through the farm. I enjoyed it because it gave me a place to go fishing and swimming.

Only once in my youth do I remember getting a gift for Christmas. The daughter of one of the neighbors was a school teacher. One Christmas she bought me a pail and a shovel. This kindness I never forgot.

In the summer of 1914 I returned home. I had seen little of my father or other members of the family during the years I lived with my grandparents.

My dad was a brutal man with a violent temper. We children and mother as well as the animals suffered from it. He said he wanted to make us boys tough to meet the hardships of life. To be kind and loving for him was to show a weakness. There was little love shown by either parent toward each other or toward us.

From eight years of age I cleaned the barn, drove the cattle to water, hauled water from the lake, and milked the cows. I picked rocks from the fields, planted, helped with the haying and the harvesting. In the fall I trapped muskrat and skunk for their skins. In winter I snared rabbits thus supplying most of the meat for the table. I often had to ride a horse when it pulled the cultivator or other farm machinery. As I grew older I broke the colts we raised so that anyone could ride them.

In the summer when it rained we went fishing. We were permitted to swim in the lake on hot summer days when there was little work to do. While we were rarely allowed to visit the neighbor children we did make friends at school.

My six years in the Heineman school were not happy ones. The teacher relied on the rod to punish those who failed to learn as well as those who broke the rules. I believe I got more whippings than any two children in the school. Yet even this school was better than staying home to work on the farm. We had a mile and a half to walk each way. Temperatures of thirty degrees below zero were not uncommon. Sometimes we had four feet of snow and there were no snowplows. Our school lunch, which was sometimes frozen solid, was most often bread and syrup or peanutbutter. We seldom had any meat, eggs or butter. These had to be sold to the store to buy clothing and the other necessities of life we couldn't raise on the farm.

I was baptized a Lutheran and sometimes attended church with my grandparents but from 1914 until 1925 I had no religious training. This didn't prevent me from developing strong personal ideas on conduct and life. My parents instilled in me an intense feeling against any alcoholic drink. My dad smoked but always spoke against it. We knew about sex only what we learned from the animals or from some older boys. With this strict discipline, together with a philosophy of work, I avoided most of the pitfalls of youth. We were forced to suppress our emotions. My dad would scold us if we laughed or if we cried.

Religious bigotry and nationalistic pride on the part of the adults were the principal cause of friction among the children at school. The farmers who sent their children to the Heineman school were of many nationalities. Father made derogatory remarks about people of other nationalities except American and Norwegian. From my parents we acquired a strong bias against Catholics and other religious minorities. The fights and arguments I had in school originated from this bias. It prevented close friendships and the happiness that might have been derived from them.

In 1916 our log house burned down. (I was to learn from my mother that Dad had set the house on fire to collect the insurance. He needed it to pay the taxes and the interest on the mortgage.) Following the fire we were forced to live in a small frame building that had been used as a chicken coop and granary. My brothers and I all had to sleep in the attic, not more than four feet from the floor to the ridge of the roof.

During World War I we were getting high prices for butter and eggs and other farm products. My dad was getting high wages in the lumber camps; my older brother, my sister and I were bringing home our wages. We, like most farmers, were prospering. My folks saw the need for a new home. They mortgaged the farm for twenty-five hundred dollars to build the house and buy necessary equipment for the farm.

After paying off the old mortgage and buying needed farm equipment there was not enough money to complete the house. The interior remained unfinished and there were no bricks on the outside. It was impossible to keep it warm during the cold winter months. A couple of years after the mortgage debt was incurred the price of farm products began to fall. It was not long before the income from the farm would not meet the expenses.

My older brother and sister and I were the only children graduating from the Heineman school who went to high school. Because of our poor preparation and home environment all of us had difficulties with our studies. Our parents wanted all of us to get an education. Their important contribution was in encouraging us, in permitting us to leave the farm and giving us what little financial help they could. I rode a bicycle to school during the spring and fall when weather permitted. I worked on the farm on weekends and during most of the summer vacations.

After school was out in May 1923 when I was only seventeen, I got a job in a logging camp. I drove a team of horses skidding

logs from the woods to a sawmill. It took all the strength I had
to throw the harness over their backs in the morning and take it
off at night. I slept in the bunkhouse with the other lumberjacks,
ate my meals with them and thus observed first hand the life of
these men. In later years when I heard ıww members refer to these
men as "timber beasts" I knew what they meant. There were no
facilities for taking a bath. Laundry facilities were non-existent or
poor. This lack of sanitation facilities resulted in a strong odor in
the bunkhouse. The food was good and we ate all we wanted. It
was high adventure for me to work and live with these lumberjacks
for six weeks. In this way I learned how my dad spent most of
his life.

The logs we brought to the mill were cut into lumber and timbers
for the construction of a dam at the Grandmother Falls a couple
of hundred yards down the river. When the logging job was com-
pleted I went to work for a construction company building Grandmother dam.

We were paid four dollars for an eight hour day. They deducted
a dollar a day for room and board. One day two men were hired
who began suggesting that we ask for more money. They were going
to ask for five dollars per day. They spoke about strikes that had
taken place in Lawrence, Massachusetts and Paterson, New Jersey.
Because of their references to those strikes in the textile industry
I concluded many years later these men had been members of the
ıww. They got little response from the workers for a strike demanding higher wages. I was prepared to support any demand for more
money.

When I returned to school in September 1923 I had almost a
hundred dollars, hardly enough to carry me through a year of school.
Some of my earnings I had to loan to my parents. I was always
trying to find work on Saturdays or after school. I joined the Wisconsin National Guard. For each drill period I would get one dollar.
Even this amount seemed a lot of money in those days.

During the fall I had another experience that was to have a long
term effect on my life. I fell in love. Not wanting to embarrass the
girl I decided not to date her or do more than speak to her when
we met. Being in love with her made me more determined than ever
not only to finish high school but to go to college. I felt that only

by this means could I escape poverty and the hard life of a worker. My love for her inspired me to work harder. From then on I seemed to be working for a cause thus making the bitterest toil more acceptable.

As soon as I graduated from high school I bought a train ticket for Milwaukee. With no previous experience and no one to advise me, I went from factory to factory asking for any job that was listed on bulletin boards at the employment offices. After two or three days of job hunting I was hired at A. O. Smith, a large employer making seamless tubing for the petroleum industry and car frames for General Motors cars. A. O. Smith was an anti-union company that checked the record of its new hires for union activity. My coming from a farm was assurance enough that I had no union ideas.

When I first went to work assembling frames by hand it took four or five men to assemble each frame. The parts for the frame were not only oily and dirty but they had sharp edges on which one could be seriously cut. The air was filled with smoke and dirt. At the end of a twelve hour day I would be completely exhausted.

By November of 1925, A. O. Smith had developed a machine that eliminated the difficult hand labor. It was controlled by one man on a raised platform. They could produce the same number of frames with two hundred men that they previously produced with twenty-five hundred. On this machine my wages were cut and I worked fewer hours.

When my roommate got a job metal finishing at Seaman Body I decided to follow him there in January 1926. It took me about a month to learn the metal finishing operation. We used a soldering iron, several heavy files, finishing hammers, and emery cloth. It required skill to use a soldering iron so that a minimum of finishing was needed; then one had to learn how to use a file to make the solder and metal perfectly smooth. The more skill one had the easier the work was. It was necessary to wear canvas gloves, not only to protect the hands but also to feel the smoothness of the metal. We wore out a pair of these gloves every day or so and we had to buy our own gloves.

It was a piecework job. When I began working on the job the company was paying seventy cents for finishing one door. It was estimated that the best finishers could earn up to a dollar and ten cents per hour. If too many of them began turning in more than that a cut in the piecework rate could be expected.

After I had been on the job about three months the piecework rate was cut. Now they were going to pay us only forty cents per door. When the men were notified of this most of them refused to work. They didn't walk out but just sat around talking about what ought to be done. There was no union or talk about a union. There was some hostility toward those men who turned in too many pieces and thus brought about the cut in piece rates. Some of us got tired of standing around. We went home at noon and returned the next morning. Most of the men had returned to work at the reduced piecework rate.

From June 1925 until September 1926 I held eight different jobs and saved over twelve hundred dollars. That was a lot of money for that time. My love for my high school sweetheart hadn't dimmed. All the hard work had been made easier just thinking of her. To gain her hand was one of the strongest motives for my going to college.

I wanted an education in order to escape from the drudgery of work that I had known ever since I was a child. I didn't know how to study. I am sure I read at a very low level. If fatigue is an enemy of the mind, as no doubt it is, then my entire educational experience had been handicapped by it. I had often been told that "knowledge is power." I decided to study economics because I thought it would give me a better understanding of the political and economic system under which I lived.

I registered at the University of Wisconsin in Madison, fearful that I wouldn't be able to do the work. By mid-term I was on probation and I continued on probation for the rest of the year. It took several months before I recovered from what turned out to be an unsuccessful love affair and a year and a half before my scholastic problems were cleared up. My studies took most of my time when I didn't have a job earning extra money for my expenses. My financial condition didn't permit me to devote much time to social activities.

When I went to the University I joined the Christian Science Society there. Later I joined the Mother Church in Boston. I looked to religion for answers to all my problems—economic, health and scholastic. Although a faithful adherent for eight years I found neither health nor freedom from poverty.

In the spring of 1928 I signed an agreement to sell a book about scientific agriculture in Marquette County, Wisconsin. I saw the book as a valuable help to the farmers. I was soon to learn that just as my folks were forced to abandon our farm in Lincoln County in 1925, many of these farmers were no better off than we had been. The depression had hit these farmers in 1921, soon after World War I. They were not too receptive to a book that would enable them to grow more crops on fewer acres. They wanted to know how to get higher prices for the crops they had to sell. When I began making deliveries I found that at least twenty per cent of the farmers who said they would buy the book either had changed their minds about its value or didn't have the money to pay for it.

I ate most of my meals with the farmers and often stayed with them overnight. I soon learned not to judge people by either their nationality or their religion. During that summer I went to a number of different churches with the farmers. There was ignorance and bigotry as well as intelligence and tolerance among these people regardless of nationality or religion. Some regarded institutions of higher learning as an evil forced onto the taxpayer. The majority believed in education and admired anyone who tried hard to get an education. I knew that some of those buying the book did so to help me, not because they were interested in the book. The summer was rich in experience but poor in financial returns.

Returning to school in September I found it necessary to find odd jobs to pay for my room and board. I knew students who didn't have enough money for food and clothing. Waiting on table for banquets, the difference in living standards between the rich student and those of us who had to work was impressed on my mind. This condition caused a number of us to organize a union of working students. We held a number of meetings but as far as I can remember we made no wage demands on our employers. I do remember making some pretty militant speeches.

It was too difficult for me to work and keep up my studies so I decided to take a year off and build up my finances. At the end

of the semester I quit school and bought a bus ticket for Detroit.
I heard that the auto industry was having a good year. Detroit had
a reputation for paying high wages. I felt certain I would be able
to find a job as a metal-finisher.

In a day or two I was hired at the Chrysler Kercheval plant. Metal-
finishing had changed considerably since I began finishing at Seaman
Body. Soldering had become a separate trade and a power tool, the
disc grinder, was used to do most of the work. There were two
of us doing the same operation, one man on each side of the body.
As we worked our disc grinders threw a stream of lead particles
in the face of our partner. It was impossible to avoid it. It was a
hard dirty job.

We were paid a piecework rate. I had only worked there about
five weeks before we got a cut in our piecework rate. I got in a
sharp argument with the foreman and I was soon escorted from the
plant. This was the first time I was fired from a job.

The 13th of March 1929 was cold and the wind was blowing about
forty miles an hour. I knew on such a day very few men would
be looking for jobs; my chances of getting hired would be good.
There were no workers in line that day when I went in to the employment office of the Briggs Mack Avenue plant. I was hired for the
second shift.

We were paid on a bonus plan which none of us could figure
out. We were earning about seventy-five cents per hour so we didn't
complain too much. The men were crowded together giving us little
room to work in. The floor was covered with dust and dirt. We
worked ten hours per day. It took me almost an hour on the street
car to get there.

I didn't work long at the Mack plant because one day I went to
Fisher Body plant No. 18 and was hired. I was able to walk to work
in about ten minutes. Working conditions were much better than at
Briggs. I was working on Buick bodies. Again this was a piecework
job and again I was to have the usual experience of having the
piecework rates cut when we made over a dollar per hour. The men
walked off the job, some leaving the plant while others sat around
outside.

A Communist union, the Auto Workers Union, put out a handbill advertising a meeting to be held in the evening in downtown Detroit. I went to the meeting which was attended by about sixty men. I didn't recognize any of them as my fellow workers at Fisher Body. The speaker, a leader of the CP in Detroit, didn't make a good impression on me. He did not appeal to the workers and there was no real representation of the people involved in the strike. There was no discussion. Workers were afraid to speak up because of spies being present and their general inability to speak, express themselves or have any program. They went to these meetings just to see what was being offered, more out of curiosity than anything else. After three or four days the men went back to work. I believe some concession was made to the workers.

At this time my two younger brothers came to Detroit looking for work. Chester and I got work together as metal-finishers at the Briggs Mack plant. He was put to work on a body line with me so that I could teach him the trade and help him out until he was able to take his turn on the line. In a week or ten days he was doing the work of a metal-finisher. We were receiving a dollar per hour and we were working ten hours a day six days per week. In the heat of the summer metal-finishing is an especially exhausting job but Chester knew he was quitting to go to the University in September 1929, and I would only be working until the end of January 1930. We were highly motivated because we thought by working hard for a few months we would eventually escape this bitter toil.

I was working at the Briggs Highland Park plant when the stock market crash came in October 1929. In a matter of days they started to lay off men. After the first layoff of ten per cent, the rest worked so much faster that it was necessary to lay off another twenty per cent to reduce production by ten per cent. The slowest man was always in danger of being laid off. The greater the number of unemployed the greater the effort on the part of those working. As the Depression deepened, the men tended to work close to the limit of their capacities. It was this speed-up which became unbearable and finally caused the workers to organize.

Most of the workers had no savings. There was no unemployment compensation or other relief available from local, state or the federal government. Workers sold everything they had, including their clothes, at bargain prices in order to buy food. Millions of unemployed workers went back to the farms they had come from. The future for many Americans looked gloomy. I was little affected by this gloom for I continued to work until I returned to the University.

I had been back in Madison about a month when one day a resentful thought about my father crossed my mind. I had a feeling of guilt at entertaining the idea. When I went back to my room there was a telgram there from Mother saying Dad had been critically injured. At fifty-three years of age he was doing a very dangerous job loading logs on flat cars. The job should have been given to a much younger man. I left for home at once but he had passed away before I got there.

The last time I had seen him was at Christmastime 1928. He made a weak apology for his treatment of the family during past years and he was not a person to readily admit his mistakes. He took great pride in the fact that he had two sons who were going to college. This was something that few workers could boast about in 1930.

My last three semesters at the University, from February 1930 to June 1931, were the most enjoyable and productive. I studied economics under Professors John R. Commons, Selig Perlman, and Don D. Lescohier. In the spring of 1931, I attended meetings in the state capitol where the legislature was debating and holding hearings on an unemployment compensation law. I heard the president of the Wisconsin Federation of Labor debate the issue with the head of the state Manufacturers Association. The AFL spokesman made a good case but it was 1936 before the law was passed and took effect.

While some of the professors and instructors did raise my interest in the labor movement they didn't influence me in a radical direction. They were satisfied with the craft unionism of the AFL. They couldn't envision anything like the CIO being formed. They didn't foresee the Depression lasting ten years or the coming of World War II. They spoke of the Depression ending in less than two years.

I dated a classmate who I would have proposed to if I had had prospects of a good job. Proposing marriage to her before I had a job was out of the question. When I kissed her goodbye in June 1931, I expected to be able to return to her in a year or so. We corresponded for a couple of years but as time passed our letters were farther and farther apart. The disruption of family life caused by unemployment and the breaking up of young people who wanted to get married was the cause of much unhappiness and suffering during the Depression.

When I received my B. A. degree in June 1931, I hoped to get a job in the personnel department of some large corporation. I had minored in personnel management in college. I wrote letters of application to General Motors and other companies but received no reply. It had long been the policy of General Motors and other large companies to use a labor spy system to deal with their hourly employees rather than employing personnel men to deal with the workers or a union. I was to learn years later that only ten per cent of the class of 1931 were able to get jobs in their field of study. The other ninety per cent had to make a living any way they could.

From June 1931 until December 1932, I tried to earn a living selling various commodities door to door. I signed an agreement with the Real Silk Hosiery Company to sell their products in Columbus, Ohio. To appeal to the anti-union elements, part of our sales pitch was that, "Real Silk is made by non-union labor." We salesmen soon learned that the Depression had eliminated hosiery and lingerie as necessities of life.

I was hired by the Chamberlin Weatherstripping Company. We told our customers the weatherstripping would pay for itself in smaller fuel bills but few people could afford it. I tried selling the Hoover Vacuum Cleaner in Lancaster, Ohio. In Cleveland, I went to work for the General Electric Company trying to sell refrigerators. Wherever I went I got the same story. Most people were having difficulty buying the necessities of life, food, clothing, and shelter. Workers were unemployed, working part-time, or were afraid of losing their jobs. What I had to sell, few could afford. I, like thousands of other salesmen, was unable to earn a living.

Near Lancaster I saw an apple orchard in December where the fruit hadn't been picked. The ground was covered with large red apples. In spite of this, workers and their children in the city of Lancaster were going hungry. I could see no reason for this hunger in the midst of plenty. It was my impression that the wealthy families in the community were doing little or nothing to help the poor.

One day I was walking near the heart of Cleveland when I felt dizzy. I was broke and hadn't eaten that day. I decided to go to the office of a Christian Science practitioner nearby. I had been seeing him for my problem. I told him I was from Wisconsin and was somewhat critical of our economic and political system which I thought was responsible for the problems of the unemployed. He saw nothing wrong with it. He said my problem was caused by my erroneous thinking. When I left he gave me fifty cents to buy food.

In the spring of 1932 I decided to return to Detroit to get work as a metal-finisher. Arriving in Detroit the latter part of April, I learned there was no hiring in the auto plants. They were laying off workers. I tried more door-to-door selling of a number of products.

During the summer and fall of 1932 I almost starved. I rented a room for two dollars a week and ate in the Penny Pantries. These were places where restaurants had been and they were remodeled to feed the unemployed. From fifty to a hundred people could stand at a counter or sit at small tables to drink coffee, milk or buttermilk, with stale rolls or donuts. Nothing cost more than a nickel. Two or three times that summer I pawned the expensive watch my father left me. The pawnshop would loan me five dollars on it. That was enough to keep me a week.

It seemed ironic that from the time I was eight years of age until I graduated from college I never had time for a vacation. During these days of Depression when I was in my most productive years I couldn't earn a living although I had the trade of a metal-finisher and a college degree. The only place I could afford to go was to the public library. I went there to read the help wanted ads and the latest reports on the state of the economy. That summer was the most depressing period of my life.

Detroit, like Cleveland and other cities, made no provision for the feeding and housing of single men. At one time thousands of them were sleeping on army cots in vacant factory buildings where in the boom days of the '20s they made bodies for cars. Promiscuity was common in the rooming houses where single men and women found shelter. Men didn't have to pay prostitutes because there were so many women looking for a meal or a place to sleep. There was little publicity given to these reports but quite often one learned of the bodies of men being found in box cars and other places where migrants hung out. They died of cold, malnutrition and lack of medical attention.

As the time approached for the auto makers to start hiring workers for the 1933 model cars, I began going to employment offices. Men and women would stand in line from four o'clock in the morning until the employment office closed in the afternoon. When there were reports of hiring, the lines in front of the employment offices would sometimes be two or three blocks long. Thousands of workers would assemble before the Ford Rouge employment offices and at times they were driven away by mounted police or with water hoses.

These employment offices were the most uncertain way of finding a job. Many workers bought their jobs through an employment agency. Others were related to a foreman or knew someone with influence at the employment office. Still others gave the foreman a gift such as whiskey or money to obtain a job.

The employers preferred young single men from out of town. These men were at the age when they have a maximum of physical stamina. This is what the employer wanted on the production line. Also they felt no responsibility to these men when they laid them off.

The unorganized worker during the Depression had no bargaining power at the employment office. He accepted the hours, wages and working conditions without question. If you didn't have a trade you bluffed your way into a job by claiming experience in any job you thought you were able to do. With hundreds of workers in line you didn't get much time to talk to the man at the window.

I was hired at the Dodge plant of the Chrysler Corporation on

December 2, 1932. I worked from twelve to fourteen hours a day seven days a week from the day I was hired until December 24, Christmas Eve. Not having done any hard physical labor for almost three years, the killing pace left me completely exhausted at the end of the day but being twenty-six years of age I was able to keep up with the other workers.

It was common knowledge that a worker in the auto plants was so tired at the end of a day that he had no energy left for his family. He came home, threw himself on a bed, lay there and rested; he got up, ate his supper and went to bed for the night. A man was just a machine that worked, brought home the paycheck and lived a bare existance. From this extreme he went to the other extreme of being unemployed. One of the grievances of the wives of the production workers was that many of their husbands could not play their sexual roles when employed in an auto plant.

The metal-finisher had other serious grievances besides that of becoming exhausted. He had to contend with the lead dust, iron filings, and the sand thrown into the air by the emery wheels and disc grinders. There was no attempt to ventilate the work areas or to take the pollutants out of the air. Lead poisoning was contracted by breathing the lead dust into the lungs, through eating with hands that had not been washed after working with lead which was used to solder the joints of the body. It was an accepted fact that thousands of metal finishers in the auto industry suffered from lead poisoning but at that time it was not recognized as an occupational disease. Those who received proper medical attention soon enough avoided permanent damage. Those who died, those who were crippled, suffered merely from neglect. (At the South Bend UAW Convention in 1936, I. Ruskin, M.D., reported 13,000 lead poisoning cases during the Depression years, 4,000 cases during 1934 and 1935.)

There were other grievances that weren't so well publicized. For example, the female not only had to do the bidding of the foreman on the job; to hold her job she was sometimes forced to go out with him and do his bidding off the job. It was common talk around the shop that some men, in order to hold their jobs, had to respond to the wishes of the foreman with their wife or daughter. The foreman would visit the home or take them out.

To call ourselves free men or free labor would have been a complete distortion of the truth. Men were forced to work under these conditions in order to feed themselves and their families. To complain of the working conditions might have meant the loss of your job.

On Christmas Eve 1932 at seven o'clock, my foreman came to me and said, "You are being laid off until further notice. We'll call you when we need you." During the twenty-three days I had worked almost three hundred hours and had earned about $150. The hourly rate of the metal-finisher was fifty-two cents. There was no premium pay for overtime, Saturdays or Sundays. Metal-finishers were among the highest paid workers in the auto industry at that time.

Knowing that the production season only lasted four or five months for most of the auto workers during those years, I didn't wait to be called back to Dodge's but went to find another job. Between Christmas and New Years I was hired at the Briggs Highland Park plant. This plant was making Ford bodies.

Because of the bad working conditions the Briggs plants were referred to as slaughter houses. In 1927 there was a fire and explosion in the paint department of the Briggs Harper plant that took the lives of over two hundred workers. Although Ford had other body and supplier plants, Briggs was by far the largest. It was said that the contracts Ford signed with his suppliers didn't allow for a large margin of profit except at the expense of the workers; the suppliers reduced the wages in order to increase their profits.

On being hired at Briggs I was given a job on the line finishing the roof rail, a strip of metal running from the front to the rear on the top of the body. There were about twenty men doing the operation. They worked as teams on opposite sides of the body. Every man was required to take every tenth body. The conveyor line could always be speeded up giving the men less and less time to do their operation. Whenever the foreman thought he could get more work out of the men he speeded up the line. To get behind in your work might mean a layoff or discharge.

Working conditions at Briggs were worse than at Dodge's. The air was full of dust particles. The floor was covered with dirt. There were no adequate facilities for washing your hands, none for taking a bath. There was no cloak room or dining area.

When we went to work in the morning we never knew how many hours we would work. The metal-finishers on repair were working as much as twenty hours per day. Workers in other departments doing work on sub-assemblies were often sent home without earning their carfare. This sometimes went on for weeks and months at a time. I was working near the limit of my capacity but it was only eight hours per day, sometimes less.

Briggs paid their employees on three different bases: some were paid at piecework rates, some on a bonus system, and others an hourly rate. When you worked on a bonus rate it was virtually impossible to figure how much money you had coming on payday.

I was hired at fifty-two cents per hour, the same rate I had been earning at Dodge's, but I was never paid that rate at Briggs. When I received my first check I discovered I had not been paid the rate on my hiring slip. I was paid forty-five cents per hour. I wanted to complain regarding the shortage but when I learned that everyone had been shortchanged I remained silent waiting for some of the older workers to speak up. None of them did. The following week everyone received a further cut in wages. Now we were getting forty cents per hour. There was a lot of grumbling among the men but there was no concerted move to raise the question of our rate of pay with the foreman.

The next week the men on the line began discussing their rate of pay among themselves. When Friday came and instead of getting forty cents per hour we only received thirty-five there was real anger and discontent among the metal-finishers. We were called in to work Saturday and Sunday. By Sunday noon the workers had become so stirred up by the shortages in our pay that most of us walked off the job and went home without notifying the foreman.

Monday morning several of the men refused to work. They wanted an explanation why they weren't being paid at the rate at which they were hired. The foreman's answer was, "If you don't like your job why don't you quit?" and "There are a lot of people waiting outside to take your jobs." For about two hours the men would work a while and then go to the foreman for some understanding as to what our wages were. Finally the foreman said, "Either go to work or quit." That statement provoked the strike. (Briggs spokesmen told the press the workers had been driven from their jobs by strangers armed with clubs.)

We decided we weren't going to walk out as individuals. We left the sixth floor in a body after changing into street clothes. The word "strike" was soon heard throughout the plant. From the sixth to the first floor the workers marched out. Soon there were hundreds of workers milling around in the street. They didn't know what to do. They had no organization, no one to speak for them. I had seen these situations before. The men stayed out a few hours or a day or two and then went back to work without having made any gains.

Now because of my experience and education, I felt an obligation to stand up and speak for these men. I got up on the fender of a car and put into words the ideas I thought were passing through the minds of these protesting workers. I spoke about our principal grievance, the shortage in our pay. I told them I thought we ought to meet with the company and demand that we be paid the fifty-two cents an hour called for on our hiring slips.

I spoke no more than five minutes and then suggested that a committee be selected to meet with Briggs management. There was general agreement. I volunteered to go if I could get two or three others to go with me. After some persuasion, two other workers volunteered to jeopardize their jobs by acting as spokesmen for the other workers. All of those on the committee were metal-finishers. Because of their large number and skill, the metal-finishers were the most militant of the workers. They had the most experience in work stoppages and strikes.

It took upwards of thirty minutes to arrange the meeting with Briggs management. After waiting this time we were taken to the sixth floor where the office of the plant manager was located. Mr. M. L. Briggs was the spokesman for the company. He asked us what the trouble was and we explained that in three weeks our hourly

wage rate had been reduced from the hiring rate of fifty-two cents
to thirty-five cents an hour.

Mr. Briggs agreed to restore our wage rates. I suggested that he
put it in writing. This he refused to do. I told him anything that
couldn't be put in writing was not worth telling the men. I thought
if we didn't have something in writing we would have nothing to
prove that Mr. Briggs had agreed to restore our wages.

We hadn't been in Mr. Briggs' office more than ten minutes when
he looked out the window and saw someone speaking to the workers.
He turned to us and said, "The Communists have now taken over
the strike." We continued to argue for a written statement from the
company assuring the men of the restoration of their pay scale. Mr.
Briggs finally said, "We will put nothing in writing. If you cannot
take our word for it you can leave." We left without making any
promise of getting the workers to return to work.

On the outside we found Phil Raymond, a well-known organizer
of the Communist Party and secretary of the Communist-controlled
Auto Workers Union and John Weissman, alias John Mack, speaking to the strikers. They asked them to go to Yemans Hall in Hamtramck where many Communist Party activities were carried on.
Most of the strikers, not wanting to take an active part in the strike,
dispersed and went home or to neighboring bars. Two or three
hundred went to Yemans Hall. A meeting was held to discuss the
issues of the strike. A strike committee was elected.

I didn't go to Yemans Hall because I didn't want to become identified as a leader of the strike. I still had hopes of getting a job
in personnel management. I didn't want to kill my chances of becoming a white collar worker. Instead of going to the meeting I went
to the Michigan Department of Labor and Industry to report that
the Briggs Company was violating the law by working women more
than fifty-four hours a week. I had seen the women working ten
hours a day six and seven days a week.

The man I spoke with was sympathetic to the strike. He belonged
to the AFL. He told me his office had neither the staff required to
inspect the factories nor the power to enforce the law. He said,
"Unless you have a union you can't enforce the law." He further
stated that the only way for the auto workers to improve their wages,
hours, and working conditions was to organize.

I went back to my room in Highland Park wondering what to do and what might happen. The next morning I went to see if the strike was still in progress. A block from the plant I met a worker who recognized me as the one who had acted as their spokesman the day before. Not knowing my name he said, "Shorty, you were elected to the strike committee." I knew nothing about being elected to the strike committee. He said, "We were told what you said to management yesterday, so they elected you to the strike committee." Reluctantly I accepted the responsibilities of that committee.

I began my activities by helping organize a picket line that marched on Manchester Avenue in front of the employment office and other entrances. It was a cold winter day to plunge into the charged air of a picket line. We had difficulty in getting the strikers out of the restaurants near the plant and onto the line. Before long we had upwards of a thousand marching in the line which sometimes stretched the three block length of the plant. This picket line was referred to as Anderson's and Murphy's army. Murphy was the name of another striker who led the picketing.

John Weissman, the CP member put in charge of the strike in Highland Park, was German-born and trained as a tool and die maker. He called a meeting of the strike committee for the purpose of electing a chairman and assigning duties to each member. I, among others, was nominated for chairman. A worker with a Polish name immediately raised a storm of protest. None of us were anxious to be chairman so the protester was elected chairman by a unanimous vote. He turned out to be a spy for Briggs management. I became chairman of the publicity committee.

Within a day or two after the Highland Park plant went on strike, three other Briggs plants were struck. There were nearly fifteen thousand workers on strike from the four plants. A strike of this size required an organization and men with experience to direct it. During the first crucial weeks of the strike the CP and its Auto Workers Union helped formulate the demands of the strikers; they provided the organizers, the meeting halls, the legal defense, and the money to pay most of the expenses. The strike was directed for the first weeks by Phil Raymond at the Mack Avenue plant, John (Weissman) Mack at Highland Park and [another] John Anderson, CP candidate for governor of Michigan in 1932, representing the

International Labor Defense. The ILD provided most of the money
during the first month of the strike. If it hadn't been for these three
men and the resources they had at their disposal the strike would
have been broken in a few days with no important gains made.

The membership of the Auto Workers Union was largely unemployed. The workers on strike didn't feel that their interests were
the same as those of the unemployed. Their language was not always
that of the worker but rather that of an agitator. Two of them were
foreign born. In spite of their important contribution to the strike,
Phil Raymond and the CP were largely discredited before the end
of the strike.

The mayor of the city of Detroit in 1933, Frank Murphy, was
a liberal but the two most important city officials dealing with the
strike were conservatives. Harry S. Toy, the police commissioner,
was a Republican. I met with him to get a permit for a parade
through the city. He refused to give us permission for such a parade.
We held it without his permission. There can be little doubt that
he gave the orders which finally broke up the picket line at the Mack
Avenue plant.

Joseph Ryan occupied the most important post in the city government during the strike. As commissioner of public welfare he determined the policy of not only denying the strikers any relief but order-
ing people on welfare to apply for jobs at Briggs; if they refused
to accept a job in the struck plants they would be removed from
the welfare rolls. Two suicides were reported to the strike committee. They were workers who couldn't bear to see their families go
hungry and cold. One left a note saying, as a widow his wife would
be able to get welfare.

When the strike was called, it was reported that the editors of
the three Detroit metropolitan newspapers had met and agreed that
there would be no publicity given to the strike. And there was no
publicity for the first three or four days. Following that there were
a few headlines branding the strike as Communist-inspired and led.
These headlines were of a nature that would antagonize public opinion. I, as chairman of the publicity committee, met with the city
editor of the *Detroit Times*. With me were two other members of
the committee. We had no experience at publicity work and had pre-

pared no statement for the press. We were not successful in getting any favorable publicity for the strike.

As a Christian Scientist, I went to see a practitioner who told me to go and see the Detroit representative of the *Christian Science Monitor*. He worked for the *Free Press*. When I told him that I represented the Briggs strike committee he backed away from me as if I were a carrier of the plague. He didn't want to hear anything about the strike. That is when I decided the church was on the side of the corporations rather than the workers, and I was going to break my affiliation.

Since our efforts at publicity brought no favorable results I and other members of the publicity committee devoted our efforts to other strike activities. There was no strike fund. It was necessary to set up a strike kitchen and serve food and coffee. To get money and food, women from the strike, Communist Party sympathizers and other left-wing groups, organized what were known as chiseling committees to solicit business places and others with money who were in support of the strike.

During the first few days of the strike we were able to keep a picket line of several hundred at the gates of the Highland Park plant. As the strikers ran out of money and the strike kitchen ran out of food the picket lines were harder to keep going. Sometimes there were less than twenty pickets. Then after much effort on the part of the strike committee we might get a hundred men in the line.

To break the strike at the Mack Avenue plant the company moved thousands of army cots into the plant where several thousand men and women were kept from Monday through Friday. They were fed by the company. Because of the economic pressure on the strikers the number of scabs sleeping in the plant and walking through the picket lines continued to grow. Since Briggs was the principal supplier of bodies to Ford, Ford was forced to lay off most of their force of a hundred thousand workers. Ford supplier plants in turn were forced to close.

Briggs officials never admitted there was anything wrong with wages and working conditions in their plants. Yet on January 27, 1933, without fanfare or publicity they corrected the worst evils.

Hours of work became more regular and there were improvements
in sanitation. Although the strike committee learned of these
developments we held out for union recognition, a dollar an hour
for metal-finishers and comparable wage increases for other classifications. We also demanded the return of all the strikers to their jobs
without discrimination, and the thirty hour week so as to employ
more of the unemployed. We had no hope of winning all these
demands. But we knew that without a union the gains that were
granted could be cancelled without notice.

Every few days there was a new attempt to break the strike. One
morning when I was leading the picket line in Highland Park, I saw
some twenty or thirty big burly men coming toward the picket line.
They were immediately recognized as Ford service men. (The service men were plant guards who were used to intimidate and sometimes physically attack the Ford workers.) Ford had three thousand
of these men at the Rouge plant. They had a reputation for brutality
against protesting or striking workers. They received much publicity
in March 1932 when five unemployed hunger marchers were shot
to death at the Ford Rouge plant. The pickets seeing these men were
afraid; they scattered. I followed several into the waiting room of
the Briggs employment office. Someone recognized me as a leader
of the strike and offered me a good job if I would get the men to
return to work. When I refused I was escorted from the building.

The Detroit police arrested many members of the strike committee
and rank-and-file members on strike. We would be held in one precinct station for twenty-four hours, which was supposed to be the
maximum length of time a person could be held, and then taken
to another precinct station and held for another twenty-four hours.
It was a legal way of kidnapping the strike leadership in order to
discourage the strike.

After about a month a number of organizations, rivals and sometimes enemies of the CP, became interested in the strike. The
Proletarian Party passed out two leaflets to workers in the area of
the strike giving them support. The Socialist Party began holding
public meetings in Detroit and New York City for the purpose of
raising money and gaining public support for the strike. As a result

of meetings sponsored by the Detroit branch of the Socialist Party I decided to join that party. But sp support of the strike was limited to holding meetings and collecting funds. The AFL had previously labeled the strike as a wildcat, which meant that picket lines need not be respected, but now Frank X. Martel, president of the Detroit AFL, came out in support of the strike.

The IWW rented an upstairs flat in Highland Park which they used as a soup kitchen and an office for the purpose of recruiting new members and giving support to the strike. John Oneka, George Lutzai and other IWW members went to the farms around Detroit and collected truckloads of potatoes, carrots, onions and cabbage to make soup for the strike kitchens. They went to the bakeries and got day-old bread, buns and rolls. They went to the dairies and got surplus milk and chocolate milk that otherwise would have been dumped into the sewers for lack of customers who could afford the milk. The IWW fed all who came to their hall.

A number of developments changed the leadership of the strike. The CP, wanting to exploit the strike for its own purposes, called a meeting of the strikers at a hall called Dance Land. Having had no previous experience with left-wing politics, a number of strikers and members of the strike committee attended the meeting. They got me to go on the platform to say a few words. When we realized that the purpose of the meeting was to recruit new members to the Communist Party, we knew we had been used by the CP. The reaction on the strike was immediate.

At about this time Phil Raymond was arrested by the Detroit police and held for several days. He wasn't charged with anything. They knew he was a member of the Communist Party and a leader in the strike. It took a writ of habeas corpus to get him out.

During Raymond's incarceration, Frank Cedervall of the IWW was invited to speak to the strikers in their hall on Mack Avenue. Cedervall was an unemployed plasterer who had never worked in an auto plant but he was a powerful speaker of great sincerity and ability who did much to build up the morale of the strikers. The strike committee, now hostile to the CP, voted to remove Phil Raymond as the speaker at our daily mass meetings and invited Frank Ceder-

vall to replace him. Phil Raymond and his group then announced
that they would no longer support the strike and they urged the
strikers to return to work.

Cedervall soon won the respect of not only the strike committee
but of most of the strikers. He was looked upon more as an
individual. While most of us knew the ɪww was a radical organization it did not have the foreign connotation of the ᴄᴘ. It was more
of an Americanized approach.

I spent most of my time at the Mack strike committee headquar-
ters. We had a joint strike committee, I being the representative from
Highland Park. Once when we were holding a mass meeting we re-
ceived a call from the Highland Park strike committee saying that the
Michigan State Police were about to break up the picket lines there.
We rushed all the strikers we could get to reinforce the Highland
Park picket lines. Our forces were too small to defy the State and
Highland Park police. Picketing came to an end there the latter part
of March.

Soon after the busting up of the picket lines, I was walking from
the ɪww hall and kitchen toward the plant. The Highland Park police
picked me up and took me to police headquarters. I was brought
before the chief of police, Dan Patch. He seemed a kindly man who
was sympathetic to the workers on strike. He said he had attended
some of the mass meetings and that I had a strong influence over
my audience. After hearing me speak he was of the opinion that
I was a potentially dangerous man. When he said the strike was
instigated by Communists I asked him, "Was the Boston police
strike of 1920 led by Communists?" He made no reply.

After the strike had been in progress for about six weeks Mayor
Frank Murphy appointed a committee to investigate the causes of
the strike. He wanted to bring Briggs and the strike committee
together in a meeting. The committee had no legal power and was
not able to get company representatives to testify or give them any
information. Several members of the strike committee, including
myself, testified before the committee and gave a detailed report on
hours, wages and working conditions in all the Briggs plants. The
committee, trying to remain neutral, got little notice in the press.

The mayor's Fact Finding Committee issued its report on April 24, 1933. None of the recommendations of the committee were carried out. Whatever improvements in wages and working conditions were brought about came as a result of the strike, not of the mayor's committee. The committee served the political interest of the mayor. It did nothing to improve the conditions of the workers on strike.

A week or so after the mayor's committee held their hearings, a meeting was arranged between Mr. Walter O. Briggs and four or five members of the strike committee. Mr. Briggs had been vacationing in Florida and was forced to cut short his vacation. I was selected by the Highland Park strike committee to represent them on the joint committee that was to meet with Mr. Briggs. George O. Cornell, Earl Bailey and two or three from the Mack committee were present. Cornell had been a Briggs foreman before the strike. After the strike he became a conservative Detroit politician.

We went to the main office of the company on Mack Avenue. We sat down across the table from Mr. W. O. Briggs, president, and other company officials. Mr. Briggs being the owner of the Detroit Tigers, it was natural to open the conversation with a few words about the Tigers and the coming baseball season. To my surprise this conversation continued for about fifteen minutes. When I became convinced that neither Mr. Cornell nor any other member of the committee was going to raise the issue of the strike I decided to do so. The response to my question was stunned silence. Mr. Briggs and Mr. Cornell looked at me as if to say, "You have broken the agreement." After a few moments the other members of the committee resumed the polite discussion of subjects that had nothing to do with the strike.

It didn't make sense to me going to see W. O. Briggs and not raising the issues of the strike and union recognition. Evidently other strike leaders had been told by Cornell that these issues were not to be raised. The purpose of the meeting, it seems, was to have it on record that the Briggs management had met with members of the strike committee. The failure of the committee to raise the issues of the strike gave some credence to the company's position that there were no serious grievances. To me it was disgraceful. Since we were no longer having mass meetings, few of the strikers learned of what took place at the meeting.

On March 4, 1933, Franklin D. Roosevelt took office as president of the United States. A few days later a banking crisis shook the nation. Most of the Detroit banks were closed for several weeks. Soon after the inauguration of Roosevelt, Hitler came to power in Germany. Following this event, FDR established diplomatic relations with the Soviet Union. All of these important events took the public interest away from the strike.

The number of pickets had declined to about two hundred at the Warren entrance of the Mack plant. One afternoon while the pickets were walking there, nuts, bolts and other metal objects were thrown from the upper floors on to the heads of the pickets. They picked up these objects and started throwing them back where they came from, breaking the windows.

As if they had been assembled for that purpose, several hundred Detroit policemen moved against the pickets and the spectators on the sidewalk. I was standing a half block from the plant. Soon I, like everyone in the area, was blinded and choking from tear gas. We hurled some of the tear gas bombs back at the police but the outnumbered pickets and their sympathizers were soon on the run. I saw shots being fired at the strikers as they fled from the scene although I don't believe any live ammunition was used at the time. Some strikers were injured by the policemen's clubs.

We were in no position to challenge the Detroit police. After this riot the picketing was discontinued. At the end of April members of the Highland Park and Mack strike committees met and voted to end the strike. We got no agreement of any kind from Briggs. While most of the workers went back to work in their various jobs, all the active leaders of the strike were blacklisted.

Little publicity was given to the gains made as a result of the strike. The gains were many and important. The wages of metal-finishers, which were thirty-five cents when the strike was called, went up to sixty-two cents an hour. That was a phenomenal raise for Depression times. Wage rates likewise went up for other classifications. Hours of work became more regular. Deductions for lost or broken tools were ended. Other arbitrary deductions were no longer made. There were improvements in sanitation. Women were no longer worked more than the fifty-four hours permitted by law.

Not only did the Briggs workers benefit but plants throughout the Detroit area raised wages and improved their working conditions to avoid strikes. General Motors and Chrysler feared that this strike might spread to their plants. Some other supplier plants did have short work stoppages.

Equally important as the economic gains was the educational development of the workers. Willing slaves became rebellious men and women. An understanding of the economic power of the workers was impressed on the minds of most of us who took an active part in the strike. Several leaders of the strike were to become organizers of the UAW-CIO.

I had no radical ideas when the Briggs strike began. But we learned that it was only the radical parties that were on our side. The left-wing groups, the Communists, Socialists, the IWW and other groups of the left, were the inspiration and the leaders of strikes. The Republican and Democratic Parties and their official representatives in state and local government were on the side of the company. My joining the Socialist Party put me in contact with young people my own age who wanted to do something about changing society. It was in the SP that I was to meet May Wolf, Roy, Victor and Walter Reuther as well as several other socially-minded workers. My experience in the strike made me aware of the political and philosophical differences dividing worker organizations. I saw enough of the CP and its leadership in action so that I never became identified with it. The strike also brought me in contact with Frank Cedervall and the IWW which I joined some months later.

Taking up a picket sign and walking the picket line was a difficult emotional experience for workers in 1933. Few of us had ever seen a picket line much less walked in one. The fear of physical injury or even death in those days were deterrents to workers joining a picket line or engaging in other strike activity.

One day I bought a copy of the *Detroit Times* and found a few lines on the front page telling of finding the body of a worker by the railroad track in southwest Detroit near the Ford Rouge plant. He had a bullet through the head. It stated he had been selling the *Daily Worker* in the area near the Rouge plant. The tone of the article was that the Communists should be shot and nothing should be done about it. Nothing was done. There was no further publicity of the murder. The *Times* treated the murder as if he were some gangster and good riddance. This worker, who had a wife and an eight-year-old daughter, had been murdered because he wanted to educate the workers. I felt that this might have happened to me or anyone else who was a leader in the strike.

I became immune to fear of physical danger when I was active in the struggle of the workers. I think this was true of many of the radicals who led strikes and carried on political activities for the left-wing parties.

Although I didn't want to become involved in the strike when it was first called, it was to become the turning point in my life.

STELLA NOWICKI

S TELLA NOWICKI was for ten years an organizer in the meatpacking industry on Chicago's southwest side, beginning in the early 1930s. This was the third major attempt to organize the packinghouse workers. Strikes had been crushed in 1904 and 1921, and it was not until World War II that the United Packinghouse Workers of America were recognized.

A major figure in the Packinghouse Workers Organizing Committee was Herb March. Through close association with him and his family, Stella Nowicki became involved not only in meatpacking but also in the political activities which were flowing through the Marches' home.

The Back of the Yards Youth Council organized by Stella Nowicki and several other young people preceded the community organization for which Saul Alinsky is best known, the Back of the Yards Council.

After World War II, Stella Nowicki married and had children. Three times in her lifetime she felt she was part of the ferment that was making history. Although her family responsibilities kept her from being as involved in the civil rights movement as other members of her family were, she belongs to a women's liberation group and again has the feeling that this movement will change events.

This account was compiled from two interviews. The first one, in October 1969, took place in Stella Nowicki's home with a group

of young people who wanted to do community organizing in the
area which had been known as Back of the Yards. The second was
a presentation to the Labor History Workshop, Gary, Indiana, in
the fall of 1971.

Back of the Yards

I RAN AWAY from home at age 17. I had to because there was not
enough money to feed the family in 1933 during the Depression.

I was brought up on a farm. We really roughed it. We had no
electricity. We had outdoor privies. We baked our own bread,
churned our own butter, raised and butchered our own hogs, made
our own sausage, did our own smoking of meat. All the things young
people are into today we did because it was a necessity. We worked
hard and long hours.

We used to fell our own oak trees, my older sister and I. We
would cut eight or nine foot logs with a cross cut saw and we'd
lift those logs up on the wagon and drive home, then pick them up
and run a buzz saw on them. We did all kinds of other heavy work.

My father was a coal miner at one time and he instilled pro-
unionism in us as youngsters. The coal miners, at least the foreign
born, were of socialist background. My father bought a few books
about Lenin and Gorky from socialists in the coal fields. I learned
Polish through these revolutionary books but only years later did
I make the connection.

I remember when Sacco and Vanzetti were executed. The foreign-
born people were in mourning for a week after that, and they were
not all pro-socialist. My mother was and still is a practicing
Catholic.

My father used to have this slogan, "No work, no eat." That's
a socialist slogan, he said. It was really carried out at home. If we
didn't work we really didn't eat.

I would challenge my father many times. Before I left home I had gone to a dance with a group of girls against my father's word. For two or three nights I slept in the barn and my mother would bring me food.

Agnes, a woman from Chicago, was on our farm for her health. She was going to have an experimental operation in which a bone would be transplanted from her leg to her back to help correct a curvature. She asked me to come back to Chicago with her. We hitch-hiked to Benton Harbor and then caught the boat. I then lived with Agnes and her family who were radicals.

One of the family was Herbert March. Herb March was a member of the Young Communist League. He was a young man. When he was just out of college at seventeen or eighteen years old, he felt that here was this country, very rich, yet all these people were out of work. Maybe college didn't mean much and maybe he should go into organizing people for socialism, maybe capitalism wasn't the answer.

I was not really introduced to socialism until I came to Chicago and the Marches began telling me about it. I lived with them at 59th and Ashland. They lived on the second floor and on the third floor they had bedrooms and an attic room. Anyone who didn't have some place to live could always find room there. It was near the streetcar intersection and when there were meetings blacks could come. (This was a real problem at that time.) The Marches would have meetings of the YCL in the attic and they'd ask me to sit in. The terminology was like a foreign language. I thought that I better join this outfit so that I would know what they were talking about.

They pointed out things to me that, in my very unsophisticated and farm-like way, I saw. There was so much food being dumped —the government bought it up—and people were hungry and didn't have enough to eat. (There were days when I didn't have anything to eat. That's when I picked up smoking. Somebody said, "Here, smoke. It'll kill your appetite." And it did.) I realized that there was this tremendous disparity. The people in our YCL group told me that the government was set up to keep it this way. They thought that instead of just thinking about ourselves we should be thinking about other people and try to get them together in a union and organize and then maybe we would have socialism where there would not be hunger, war, etc. They initiated me into a lot of political ideas and gave me material to read. We had classes and we would discuss industrial unionism, the craft unions and the history of the labor movement in this country. We talked about Debs, we talked about the eight hour day, many things.

I was doing housework for $4 a week and I hated it. I would cry and cry. I was horribly homesick because I hated the restraint of being in a house all the time. I was used to being out a lot on the farm. So Herb suggested that I get a job in the stockyards.

Herb was working at Armour's at the time. He bought me a steel, with which one sharpens a knife, and I took it with me. He took me down to the stock yards and (he tells this story) I said, ''Those beautiful cows! They can't kill those beautiful cows!'' At home we just had cows for milking. But here were all these cows and they were going to be killed and they were crying, mooing, as they were going to be killed. But one had to get a job!

One of the ways to get a job was to go down to the employment office. Every morning you got there by six or six-thirty. There were just so many benches and they would all be filled early. They would only need one, maybe two people. This woman, Mrs. McCann, women's hiring director, would look around for the biggest and brawniest person. At seventeen I weighed 157 pounds coming from the farm, rosy-cheeked and strong. ''Have you had experience?'' I said, ''Well not in the stock yards but we used to butcher our own hogs at home.'' I carried this big steel and that impressed her. Mrs. McCann hired me.

I was in the cook room. At that time the government bought up drought cattle and they were killed, canned, and given to people on relief to eat. The meat would be cut into big hunks and steamed. Then it would come on a rail and be dumped out on the table. The women would be all around the table and we would cut the meat up, remove the gristle and bad parts, and make hash out of it. The government inspector would come around to see that bad meat wasn't being thrown into the hash. But as soon as his back would be turned, the foreman would push this stuff right down the chute to go into the cans—all this stuff we had put aside to be thrown away he would push right down in, including gloves, cockroaches, anything. The company didn't give a damn.

The meat would be so hot and steamy your fingers almost blistered but you just stayed on. In 1933–34 we worked six hour shifts at 37½ cents an hour. We would have to work at a high rate of speed. It was summer. It would be so hot that women used to pass out. The ladies' room was on the floor below and I would help carry these women down almost vertical stairs into the washroom.

We started talking union. The thing that precipitated it is that on the floor below they used to make hotdogs and one of the women, in putting the meat into the chopper, got her fingers caught. There were no safety guards. Her fingers got into the hotdogs and they were chopped off. It was just horrible.

Three of us "colonizers" had a meeting during our break and decided this was the time to have a stoppage and we did. (Colonizers were people sent by the YCL or CP into points of industrial concentration that the CP had designated. These included mass basic industries: steel, mining, packing, and railroad. The colonizers were like red missionaries. They were expected to do everything possible to keep jobs and organize for many years.) All six floors went on strike. We said, "Sit, stop." And we had a sit-down. We just stopped working right inside the building, protesting the speed and the unsafe conditions. We thought that people's fingers shouldn't go into the machine, that it was an outrage. The women got interested in the union.

We got the company to put in safety devices. Soon after the work stoppage the supervisors were looking for the leaders because people were talking up the action. They found out who was involved and we were all fired. I was blacklisted.

I got a job doing housework again and it was just horrible. Here I was taking care of this family with a little spoiled brat and I had to pick up after them—only Thursday afternoon off and every other Sunday—and all for four dollars a week of which I sent two dollars home. I just couldn't stand it. I would rather go back and work in a factory, any day or night.

A friend of mine who had been laid off told me that she got called to go back to work. Meanwhile she had a job in an office and she didn't want to go back to the stockyards, so she asked me if I wanted to go in her place. She had used the name Helen Ellis. I went down to the stockyards and it was the same department, exactly the same job on the same floor where I had been fired. But it was the afternoon and Mrs. McCann wasn't there. Her assistant was there. Her assistant said, "Can you do this work?" I said, "Oh yes, I can. I've done it." She told me that I would start work the following afternoon.

I came home and talked with Herb and Jane. We decided that I would have to go to the beauty shop. I got my hair cut really short and hennaed (similar to tinting today). I thinned my eyebrows and penciled them, wore a lot of lipstick and painted my nails. Because I hadn't been working, I had a suntan. I wore sandals and I had my toenails painted, which I would never have done before. I came in looking sharp and not like a country girl, so I passed right through and I was hired as Helen Ellis on the same job, the same forelady!

After several days the forelady, Mary, who was also Polish, came around and said, "OK, Helen, I know you're Stella. I won't say anything but just keep quiet" if I wanted to keep the job. I answered her in Polish that I knew that the job wouldn't last long and I thanked her. She knew I was pro-union and I guess she was too, so I kept the job as Helen Ellis until I got laid off. (Later on I was blacklisted under the name Ellis.)

Out of the fifteen dollars, I'd have to try to save half of it almost, to carry me when I was out of work. I remember that at one time I had a three-room furnished apartment on East 47th Street and I was paying fifteen dollars a month rent. Sometimes there would be fourteen people living there besides myself. Those who worked supported those who didn't. Anybody who worked put the money in the one pot and we shared it.

At this time, Herb was in the AFL and was asking for an industrial form of organization. The American Federation of Labor was organized along a craft basis. In the stockyards there might have been some electricians or some steam fitters or mechanics who were organized in their own separate unions. The mass of workers who were working on the assembly lines and on the kills—the sheep kill, the beef kill, the hog kill—and in the canning rooms, the women, they were not organized. The wage scale was way down.

The AFL really wasn't interested in getting masses of people in because large numbers threatened their position. Being as they were in crafts they didn't want to see the expansion because they would lose control. They had nice-paying jobs. They were bought off in a sense.

There were many battles within the AFL. A group of people, including Herb March, would raise questions at union meetings whenever they could get the floor. Many times they couldn't get the floor to speak and were carried out of union meetings bodily because they insisted on speaking on questions that the workers were concerned with—conditions of employment, wages, and other things. Herb nearly lost his life a couple of times because AFL racketeers were tied up with the meat-packers. Then the left-wing group organized a Trade Union Unity League as sort of an answer to the craft organization.

The Trade Union Unity League used to meet on 47th and State. We would walk [a couple of miles] from 47th and Ashland to 47th and State for meetings—we didn't have car fare and were out of work much of the time—to get together and talk about how we were going to organize the stockyards. The meetings were with blacks and whites.

Even at that time we raised the question of more Negroes on skilled jobs. The proportion of Negroes when I started in 1933 was, I suppose, fifteen to twenty per cent at most. By the time I left in 1945 it was maybe sixty per cent.

William Z. Foster and Jack Johnstone used to come and talk with us. In the twenties William Foster and Jack Johnstone worked together in organizing not only steel but also the stockyards. So when the thirties came around and we started trying to organize the unorganized industrial workers, we had these meetings with them and they would tell us about what they did in the 1920s with steel. We took advantage of their experience in the 1919–1921 steel and packinghouse strikes as to how to try to organize this mass industry of unorganized packinghouse workers.

They talked about the kinds of tactics to use, step one, step two

and step three! One of the pamphlets that William Z. Foster wrote
was "What Means a Strike in Steel?" and this was our Bible. It
discussed how you did all sorts of things, how you contacted workers
—through the church, through their organizations, through your
nationality groups, including relatives. Just like in the steel industry,
the packinghouse workers were made up of different ethnic groups.
They were in the main Polish and Lithuanian, some Bohemian,
Croatian, some Mexican and there were the German, the Irish and
the Negroes (as we called them at that time).

When we met with Jack Johnstone and William Foster, we talked
with them about people that they knew. They were able to remember
names of people and they gave us these names. There was a small
shop called Roberts and Oake and there was this Polish guy, Stan,
that they talked about. Somebody said, "Does anybody know where
Stan is?" Sure enough, Stan was still working in Roberts and Oake
and he was contacted.

It was very underground because if you even talked union you
were fired. Jobs were at a premium. You didn't have the law which
guaranteed people the right to organize. So we actually had secret
meetings. Everybody had to vouch for anyone that they brought to
the meeting, that they were people that we could trust, because as
soon as the company found out that people were trying to organize,
they would try to send in stool pigeons. They paid people to come
in and try to get information.

What they didn't know was that the secretary to the vice-president
of one of the companies was the wife of one of the people who
was interested in organizing. We were able to take advantage of this.
We made copies of material and were able to use it to expose many
of the anti-union tactics of the company.

I remember one of the first big CP meetings when we had William
Foster come to talk. The hall wasn't big enough. Somebody had
gotten hold of a loudspeaker (they were very difficult to get in those
days) and we hooked that up so that people could hear down the
steps and into the street.

We had a YCL/CP unit. (There weren't enough people in either
the YCL or the CP to meet separately and so we met together, younger
and older people.) We would have meetings and marches and classes

on Marxism and Leninism. We would write articles on the history
of Marxism and Leninism which we would then discuss. These
would go into *The Yards' Worker*. We asked the old time friends
of Bill Foster from the different plants for news of what was going
on.

We contacted young people who were at the University of
Chicago and they helped in editing and getting funds. They would
help us in writing up material for leaflets and by distributing material at the stockyard gates. They would get up real early and be there
at 6:00 or 6:30 in the morning. (We would start work at 7:00.) They
did this because we could not do so, for if we were caught giving
out leaflets we would be fired. On the inside, we had to wear
uniforms all the time and any packages we carried in were examined.
The only way we carried in these leaflets about organizing was in
our underclothes, in our bras (the men too, in their pants). I would
come in real busty. Then I'd go into the washroom and leave the
papers around.

When I look back now, I really think we had a lot of guts. But
I didn't even stop to think about it at the time. It was something
that had to be done. We had a goal. That's what we felt had to
be done and we did it.

We got into sending people all over to different groups and into
different shops so that when union organization picked up we would
have people everywhere.

The broadest contacts of the left at that time were in the International Workers Order which was set up as an insurance organization
for people to have sickness benefits and insurance, and culturally
they were able to have their own social affairs. We had our songs,
folk dances, and picnics where we would have ethnic foods. Every
nationality had its own chapter which would meet monthly and
recruit whole families. The IWO was much larger than the CP and
the YCL. They were pro-labor because they had been coal miners
at one time and they were organized in a Miners Union and had
had experience. When we set up meetings with these groups we
would cue them in as to who were stool pigeons, learn from them
about stool pigeons whom they knew, and who doesn't have a big
mouth who we can trust.

We had what we called fractions, made up of CP members and sympathizers, many of them from the IWO, who would get together periodically to discuss major strategy within the organizing campaign. We would decide what things to take up, who would take up what and where and how, who would support whom, who would make the motion, who would second it and so forth. It was very important that people know how to do this; otherwise they would be overwhelmed by the politicians.

The predominant organization in the community was the Catholic Church. I was the only ex-Catholic in our YCL group. When I lived around 59th and Ashland I joined the Sodality (a Catholic young women's organization) and I became a member of the basketball team to have contact with other young people and to be around people who were out of the realm of the left.

I joined all the youth organizations that I could. We didn't work steady so we had a lot of time. I'd work for two or three months and then there would be a layoff.

Then it was decided that I should start to learn about casings —guts that you make hotdogs out of. You wore rubber boots and a rubber apron. It stinks like hell because it's shit work: you clean all the shit out. I went to work under the name Kramer at the Independent Casing Company and I worked there for six or seven weeks.

I had also joined the YWCA Industrial Division and was active in their sports program. I came in contact with other women in the Y. Women were not about to come into unions but they were in the Y. The Y was offering scholarships to young workers. In 1936 they had this School for Workers in Industry at the University of Wisconsin. They would select young people through the different industries and I was selected from the Back of the Yards Y to go with all of my expenses paid to Madison, Wisconsin for six weeks. There we learned about labor history, parliamentary procedure, public speaking, how you run meetings. It was Social-Democratic in outlook. We had a mock Farmer-Labor convention there and the three political positions were presented: the left, the center, and the right.

When I came back the YCL group decided after discussions with me that I should try to get a job at Swift's. We had people at

Armour's and we had some people in Wilson's but there was no-body at Swift and Company. They employed anywhere from two to five thousand workers and we wanted to get some of them into the CIO.

Swift's was in a different class than Armour's. Everyone who worked in Swift's was thought to be a higher class worker—they got more money. Swift's had a group bonus system called the Bedaux system. After you produced so much then each person in the gang got that much more money. It's diabolical. One worker slits the throat of another. They keep going so that the group production is great enough that they can all get a bonus.

Swift and Company had a strong entrenched company union with a paternalistic system to keep people sort of quiescent and controlled. The company actually selected the representatives from the different departments. They called it an "Independent Employees Organization." Anybody who spoke up about it was a troublemaker and they got rid of him.

I went to Swift's to get a job. The personnel director said they weren't hiring but what were my qualifications, where did I work last. I told her Independent Casing. "Well, why aren't you there now?" I told her that I got a scholarship to go to the University of Wisconsin through the Y that previous summer. And she said, "Well that's my Alma Mater!" So she hired me for the casing department.

Later I got sent to the sliced bacon department which is the elite department. It was the cleanest job and you made the most money. They had this visitors' ramp where people went by and would look down. We were freezing our asses off in this cooler of about forty degrees. I wore two pairs of wool socks and a couple of wool sweaters under my uniform and a cap. We'd have to go every two or three hours into the washroom to thaw out and spill out.

Swift and Company had a slogan that the premium bacon was "not touched by human hands." The sliced bacon came down on this conveyor belt and we women sat three on either side facing forward, sitting with a scale in front of us. One woman would just put the plastic see-through cover on the bacon. Then we would catch the bacon with our tongs, turn it over on the scale to make sure that each package was about eight ounces in weight—a quarter ounce less or more—then we would wrap them up, put them back on the belt and on they would go to the packer at the end of the line.

The women themselves had gotten together and they would turn out a hundred and forty-four packages an hour of bacon. We were making $15 a week at 37½ cents an hour, but if we each produced 144 packages an hour we got $7 more in our pay. We made 50 per cent more than anybody else but we produced 90 per cent more than the set group rate. A new girl would come in and the oldtimers would train her. They would help her out so that gradually by the end of a certain period of time she was doing the 144. But they would never let anyone go beyond that 144 packages. They maintained that limit and they did it without a union. One smart-aleck girl came in there once and she was going to show them and go beyond that number because she wanted to earn more money: all the bacon that she got from the girls further up the line was messed up and scrappy and she'd have to straighten it up to put it in the package. She couldn't make a hundred packages an hour. (We took a loss just to show her.)

The checker would come around with the stop watch. You learned to wrap a package of bacon using a lot of extra motions because it was a time study thing. When he wasn't there we eliminated all those motions and did it simply. This was done everywhere—sausage, wrap and tie, bacon, everywhere. (It's all done by machine now.) There is always a faster way to do something, a simpler way where you save energy and time. The older women, in terms of experience, would show the new women. It was a tremendous relationship of solidarity. But they weren't about to join the union. They weren't about to put out a buck a month in union dues.

At first the women were afraid. It took quite a bit of courage to join. They were concerned about their jobs. Many of them were sole breadwinners. Also the Catholic Church said that the CIO was red: you join the CIO and you are joining a red organization. To talk about the CIO then was like talking about socialism to some people today. Even to talk union, you talked about it in whispers. You had to trust the person and know the person very well because he could be a stool pigeon.

When I was at the University of Wisconsin, John Lewis made his speech that he was breaking away the coal miners union from the AFL and they were going to set up the CIO. We set up an organizing committee for the stockyards. There were seventeen of us that met, three women and fourteen men. One of them was an Irishman by the name of McCarthy who became the acting chairman of the Packinghouse Workers Organizing Committee. We met behind a tavern on Honore Street. The organizing of these seventeen people was on Communist Party initiative and we worked through contacts in the IWO, the International Workers Order. In this group of seventeen there were some Poles and some Slovaks who were indigenous to the community.

We didn't have money. We collected money in every way that we could. A delegation was sent to the Steelworkers Union to ask them for support—financial support, organizers, etc. We asked them to send some speakers and we would have a meeting. We had this first big CIO meeting at the hall behind the tavern where parties for weddings and all kinds of community social events would be held. The turnout was so overwhelming that there actually wasn't room for all the people who came.

Among the people who came was a delegation from the Paddy Brennon plant, which was in the AFL. The president was black and the vice-president was white. They had heard about our meeting and they came, ready to swing their whole local right into the CIO. They had women too and they brought in all the women. It was a tremendous thing. This little plant spurred us on.

We couldn't get the sliced bacon department at Swift's into the union because of the money they were earning. What could the union do that they weren't getting already, and they *were* organized! So I told them that it was the case that they had the money, but what about the conditions—it was colder than hell. What happens if you get sick? What happens if the foreman says that he doesn't like you and he wants somebody else to have your job? I said that the union could protect them on these real problems. But they wouldn't join. I think that I only got one or two out of that great big department.

They were all white, mostly Polish. There was one black woman who worked on scrap bacon way in the back so that no one would see her when visitors came through. The company could always say that they had one black woman in this fancy department. I raised this matter of discrimination but it didn't go over too well with white women.

One day the woman who worked in the coldest spot got sick. She didn't come to work. We found out that she had become paralyzed. The door from the cutting cooler opened as the men came back and forth. It was below freezing there and every time the door opened she would get this tremendous cold blast on her side. The whole right side of her body was paralyzed and she died. Within a week we organized that whole department. She was a young woman, probably around forty, and she died because of the freezing conditions in which we all had to work. It was easier on the company to have it this cold. There was less spoilage. But they didn't give a damn about the workers. We showed that we could handle bacon and that it didn't have to be that cold.

The National Labor Relations Act had been passed, giving workers the right to organize. But this was not easy because people were laid off. I was laid off, for instance, in the gut shanty and they tried to break my seniority. We had departmental seniority and I would be shifted all around. Besides casing and sliced bacon, I got to work in wrap and tie (hams), soap, glue, fresh sausage, pork trim, almost every department. By being shifted around I became acquainted with many more women. I kept the names and addresses of all the women because I knew that some day I would need them. When we started organizing I knew women all over the whole plant. I would call them and get information as to pro-labor union sentiment, problems and issues, and so forth. We would print it up in the CIO news—the *Swift Flashes* we called it.

The same women who had hired me at Swift's approached me and asked me if I'd like to work in personnel—they tried to buy me off. They offered me better-paying jobs.

They put me in the glue factory thinking that they could discourage me and I would quit. By that time I was down to 130 pounds. They put me to work with Essie. Essie weighed 325 and she chewed tobacco. She used to bring big pots of food to work and eat it all. She was my partner.

This is how they made the glue. (I won't lick a glue stamp for anything any more!) They had these vats where they put all the stinking stuff that they couldn't use, outside of the squeal. They put the bones and the hair, and then they'd add lime and it would deteriorate this stuff. They would cook it and melt it. They would pour it on something like a screen. It would come out of the vat looking something like liquid peanut brittle. The screens were put in something like a heating room to be dried. Then Essie and I would take the screens off the pulley, turn them over and with something like a rug beater we'd hit them a full swing to crack all that stuff which would go down the chute.

When I got through with that job the first day, I was wet with sweat from tip to toe. When I came home I couldn't move out of bed for twenty-four hours because of the hitting. I was so sore—my hands and joints were all swollen from the work on this hard job. And we'd smell from all that stinking crap. They had a public shower so we would go there and shower or we'd go to some friend's house that had a shower. But I got Essie into the union. When she saw that I really wasn't a slacker and that I would keep up my end I won her respect. You had to *earn* the respect of your fellow workers or you couldn't talk to them about new ideas or unions, etc. You always had to be a good worker.

Women often did much harder work than men. For instance, in wrap and tie department—where hams were handled, wrapped in paper and tied—it is heavy lifting a twenty-pound ham. Then you'd have to put those great big hams on a slip hook and hang them up so that they could be smoked in the smoke shed. In the sausage department women used to link sausages by hand; but the men would measure the meat and work with a pedal to shoot the sausage into the casings.

The women worked much harder and much faster but they got less pay. We were paid ten cents an hour less than men. There were jobs that men had done that women took over and they'd still get the lesser pay. I worked in a cooler cutting the fat from the lean with the guard on my thumb and the sharp knife. Work with a knife is a butcher's job, but they had a pay differential. (The union corrected this inequity later.) There was also a differential between the southern rates and the northern rates.

Women had an awfully tough time in the union because the men brought their prejudices there. The fellows couldn't believe that women in the union were there for the union's sake. They thought that they were there to get a guy or something else. Some thought that we were frivolous. I would be approached by men for dates and they would ask me why I was in the union, so I would tell them that I was for socialism and I thought that this was the only way of bringing it about.

Some of my brothers, who believed in equality and that women should have rights, didn't crank the mimeograph, didn't type. I did the shit work, until all hours, as did the few other women who didn't have family obligations. And then when the union came around giving out jobs with pay, the guys got them. I and the other women didn't. It was the men who got the organizing jobs. Men who worked in plants got paid for their time loss—women didn't. I never did. But we were a dedicated group. We worked in coolers and from there I would go to the union hall and get out leaflets, write material for shop papers, turn in dues, etc., get home and make supper, get back. These guys had wives to do this but there was nobody to do mine. Sometimes I'd be up until eleven, twelve, or one o'clock and then have to get up early and be punched in by quarter to seven and be working on the job by seven.

I became educational director of the Packinghouse District #1 because, after all, I was in college for six weeks! We had classes on public speaking and parliamentary procedure and labor history. I remember getting up on Sunday morning and going to churches to speak about our union. We got involved in activity against the southern poll taxes. We elected congressmen. We defeated people like Busby who was on the Dies Committee by 1500 votes. It was CIO people who helped to defeat him.

The union mushroomed; it spread. The union had a certain vitality about it that was just tremendous. We had many problems but they were all problems of growth. We tried to make sure that there were both Negroes and whites as officers, stewards, etc., in all the locals.

There were people vying for jobs—they wanted to be leaders of this union. It was a marvelous time.

For a long time I fought dishonesty within my local. There were some guys who would pocket the dues money. I would debate them on the union floor. Many times I was the only female there.

The women felt the union was a man's thing because once they got through the day's work they had another job. When they got home they had to take care of their one to fifteen children and the meals and the house and all the rest, and the men went to the tavern and to the meetings and to the racetrack and so forth. The fellows were competing for positions and the women didn't feel that that was their role. They were brainwashed into thinking that this union was for men.

The union didn't encourage women to come to meetings. They didn't actually want to take up the problems that the women had. I did what I could to get the women to come to the meetings but very few came—only when there was a strike. I tried to make the meetings more interesting than just a bunch of guys talking all evening.

We organized women's groups, young women's groups. They liked to dance and I loved to dance so we went dancing together and I talked to them about the union. The women were interested after a while when they saw that the union could actually win things for them, bread and butter things.

We talked about nurseries. In World War II we finally did get some because women were needed in greater quantities than ever before in the factories. But the unions had so many things they had to work for—the shorter work day, improved conditions—so many things that they couldn't worry about these things in relation to women.

Later on, during the war, there was one department where I got the women but couldn't get the guys in. They hung out in the tavern and so I went there and started talking with them. I didn't like beer, but I'd drink ginger ale and told them to show me how to play pool. I learned to play pool and I got the men into the union. I did what they did. I went into the taverns. I became a bowler and I joined the league. The only thing I didn't do is rejoin the Catholic Church.

I was on the grievance committee and I was on the Swift nationwide negotiating team. Before I left, there were a whole number
of job evaluations. It was one of the things we fought for on the
wage policy committees. I remember talking with Helstein (president
of UPWA) in the national office one day and saying that I thought
there should be a study made of jobs, especially for women, because
I didn't see that a job had a sex. He said that it was a very interesting
idea and that maybe I could do something about it. But I wasn't
equipped to go into research, nor did I have the time even if I were.
Later on they set up a Women's Department and did it.

There were only so many things that we could do and there were
so many big things, we couldn't handle everything. You'd have to
have socialism.

About socialism, you didn't talk about socialism per se. You
talked about issues and saw how people reacted. You talked about
how one could attain these things. The only time I ever heard anyone
from the union talk about socialism outside of the small meetings
was the head of another CIO local, a Scotsman. After negotiations
and they didn't get all they wanted, the guys were turning down
the contract. He said, "Look, you bunch of bastards, you're not
going to get all of this stuff, not until you have socialism." That's
the way he put it to them and I thought it was great. "This is a
limited contract under capitalism." I think the workers got the message. It all depends what your relationship is to the people you are
talking with.

If you are an honest leader, recognized and supported by the workers, you could raise and talk about issues. You couldn't talk about
socialism and what it meant in an abstract sense. You had to talk
about it in terms of what it would mean for that person. We learned
that you can't manipulate people but that you really had to be concerned with the interests and needs of the people. However, you
also had to have a platform—a projection of where you were going.

At certain times we felt that the union wasn't enough. We worked
in the stockyards with blacks but when we came home, we went
to lily-white neighborhoods and the blacks went to their ghetto. How
were we going to bridge that? There was unemployment and people
were being laid off. There were many young people who didn't get

jobs. There was no concern on the part of anyone, the city fathers, the church, the union and others, about the needs of young people and places to play. What are unemployed young people going to do? There were a bunch of young people—I was twenty-four or so—and we felt that our needs were not being met by the union.

The Yards YCL group got together and talked about getting more playgrounds for baseball, basketball and so forth. One of the things that we felt we should do was fight to get blacks into professional baseball. I remember being part of the delegation that went to see Fitzpatrick, who was chairman of the Central Labor Council, about labor exerting its influence to get blacks on organized professional baseball teams. It was one of the initial things our union did.

We tried to show the community that the union was concerned about the welfare of the young people. We raised the problems of youth; we raised the problems of women; we raised the problem of inequality. We tried through the National Youth Act to get some funds to set up facilities for young people in the community. We had to find ways to attract youth and women and keep all these people within the union.

We asked the union to back us up in calling a community conference to set up a council, a Back of the Yards Youth Council, which would be concerned about these kinds of things in the community. The union said OK. They gave us their blessings. We went ahead and we did it. Actually there were three of us young women who did it.

We had a successful conference. The place wasn't big enough, it was such a turn-out—young people from about 18 to about 25 from the neighborhood.

The man who really organized some massive youth activities was Bishop Shiel. I think he was the first major churchman to recognize the CIO. The first time this bishop of the Catholic Church accepted to come to a CIO meeting, it was historic.

Remember that the CIO didn't have bargaining rights in the different plants yet. This was 1938, '39, '40. We were in the organizational stage and there was tremendous ferment. There were strikes. There were beatings. There were people being fired and laid off and there were test cases in the NLRB. There was picketing going on.

The AFL was opposing it. During the early organizing meetings they sent goons with guns to threaten individuals to scare them so they would not organize. Twice they shot at Herb March.

But you had this sense that people were ready come hell or high water to get together, to protect each other, and come into the union. It did happen that people were fired but when people were fired the whole department just closed down. People refused to work until this person was put back. They had this feeling of solidarity, this sense, because they knew that if the company could get by with doing it to one they could do it to another, maybe me.

By the 1940s, we had meetings on every issue where we would call on the workers to come out. The union would come around with their sound truck and everybody would come to the CIO corners in the Yards. The butchers would all come out with their boots and their bloody white smocks. Thousands and thousands of people would show up for meetings right there in the middle of the stock-yards at noontime. Even people who were not in the union would come out.

There would be an issue a day, just about. The Armour Plant, Local 347, would have meetings on Wednesday. Friday was payday so it was sacrosanct and there were no meetings. Tuesday was our day. Wilson's on Thursday. Then for some overall issue we'd have everybody come out. There would be so many people coming that the companies would protest to the union—we had half hour lunch breaks and we would stay out for an hour. The companies never did a thing about it because the turnout was that tremendous and massive.

The union leadership would be negotiating within a particular plant on a grievance and the agreement was that if they hadn't received word that the matter was settled by a certain time, the department would walk out. The beef kill at Armour's stopped so many times! They were the best organized and most militant. (These were blacks, by the way.) And if this department went down, the whole plant went down. The kill floors were the key floors. This was true all over. The beef kill was the most important because more beef was killed; then the hog kill, then the sheep.

We participated in all sorts of things beyond just our own industry.

At that time there were no black bus drivers. Bus and streetcar driver jobs were considered very good-paying jobs and our union promoted the idea of having blacks work as streetcar and bus conductors.

The contract and recognition were the thing that everybody wanted. Armour's was the plant with the greatest concentration of people and the union came to be recognized there in 1941. Wilson went before our plant did. Swift's had to have two elections and it was the toughest. We won there during the war, I think in '42. We didn't have the militancy in the Swift plant that we did elsewhere. The Swift Company bought off many guys. Later on we found out that some of the white leaders were paid agents because they testified before the House Committee on Un-American Activities on a lot of us. They were stool pigeons.

I worked in the yards during the war because I thought that it was my patriotic duty. It was part of the thinking of everybody within unions that you just couldn't quit. We even tried to get people to produce more in our zeal to support the war effort. Besides, I had all this seniority and all this history. Then I got frozen on the job. There was a job freeze because white workers were leaving the industry to go to higher-paid jobs in defense plants.

No-strike was part of the deal. The men in the union felt that the company was making all kinds of money on the war and the workers weren't. During that time there were slow-ups and workers who didn't join the union were ostracized. Grievances were hung up without being settled or turned down because the company knew we couldn't do anything. We knew that the company took advantage of the war in a whole number of situations.

I left packing in 1945. With recognition and with the war ending, certain changes took place within the union itself and within the union officialdom. Soon after, a whole group of radical CIO unions were kicked out of the CIO and the McCarthy period set in. I think this ended that era. It was a privilege and a wonderful experience to participate in the excitement of those times.

GEORGE PATTERSON, JESSE REESE AND JOHN SARGENT

T HIS IS AN EDITED TRANSCRIPT of a community forum on "Labor History From The Viewpoint Of The Rank And File" held at Saint Joseph's College in East Chicago, Indiana on March 24 and March 31, 1970.

Patterson, Reese, and Sargent all worked in steel. George Patterson was picket captain at the Memorial Day Massacre in 1937 and first president of Local 65 of the United Steelworkers of America (United States Steel South Works, South Chicago, Illinois). Before the formation of the Steel Workers Organizing Committee in June 1936, Patterson built an independent union of 3,000 workers at the South Works mill. In September 1936 he was fired for union activity, and from then until he retired in 1969 he was employed as an organizer by SWOC and the Steelworkers Union.

Jesse Reese, a black man and an open member of the Communist Party, went to work at Youngstown Sheet and Tube in East Chicago, Indiana in 1929. Reese was a member of the Resolutions Committee at the first national convention of the Steel Workers Organizing Committee in December 1937.

John Sargent was first president of Local 1010, USA (Inland Steel, East Chicago, Indiana). Sargent was re-elected in 1943, 1944, 1946, and, despite vicious red-baiting, 1964. In 1958 and 1962 he took a strong stand against a dues increase at the Steelworkers conventions. In 1972 he was still working in the mill. Sargent is the "John Smith" whose experience and point of view are presented in the article "Guerrilla History In Gary" by Staughton Lynd, *Liberation*, October 1969.

Two major themes emerge from these accounts. First is the vigor of rank-and-file activity during the 1930s. Before the CIO was formed, George Patterson had organized the Associated Employees at South Works and Jesse Reese had organized a lodge of the Amalgamated Association of Iron, Steel, and Tin Workers (the old AFL union in steel) at Youngstown Sheet and Tube. John Sargent describes how in Little Steel, because there was no contract and no no-strike clause, wildcat strikes in particular departments continued for three or four years after the Memorial Day Massacre in 1937.

A second theme is the expulsion of radicals after the unions were organized, and the narrowing of goals which resulted. We wanted the union to be a watchdog for the working class, Reese concludes, but "Your dog don't bark no more."

These three accounts, together with talks at the same forum by Harvey O'Connor and John W. Anderson, were published as "Personal Histories Of The Early C.I.O.," ed. Staughton Lynd, in *Radical America*, May–June 1971, and reprinted as a pamphlet by the New England Free Press. The text as it there appears has been slightly re-edited to conform with the general style of this book.

GEORGE PATTERSON, JESSE REESE

AND JOHN SARGENT

Your Dog Don't Bark No More

I

GEORGE PATTERSON. I came here when I was sixteen years of age and went to work in South Chicago at the South Works. I became a roll turner's apprentice and went to night school at Englewood High. I worked ten hours a day in the mill and went four hours an evening to night school: I was self-educated. I graduated from high school and served my apprenticeship all at the same time, and it wasn't easy for a young fellow.

The first job I got was in a blacksmith's shop, and we got $5 a day. That was 50 cents an hour for ten hours. But I quickly got over trying to be a blacksmith. I wasn't built for it. So I went into the roll shop and became a roll turner, and I dropped down to 29 cents an hour. That was $2.90 for a ten-hour day. Of course every six months you got a raise.

We in the roll turner's trade began to form our own union, and I became the international vice-president of the United Roll Turners of America. This was my first experience with unions. I wasn't too interested in unions other than to get more dough; I was a typical steelworker. We had just come through the Depression. Those Depression years were terrible. I almost starved to death. The reason I got interested in the union was that I got married in the middle of that Depression, and then along came my son and I didn't have enough money to buy a bottle of milk.

The steel mill people came into the mill around 1933 and handed us a piece of paper. We looked at it, and it was called "An

Employee Representation Plan.'' Now the Employee Representation Plan was the company union plan. It was based on the fact that we had the right to bargain collectively. The company drew the whole thing up, and the workers in the various departments elected representatives of their own. I looked at this paper as a young lad and said, ''this thing could never work,'' because it said right at the outset that there would be five members from management to sit on a committee and five members from the union—the company union—to sit on the committee. I asked who settled the tie, and of course I found out management did. So you see how useless it would have been.

I talked to the fellows in the shop, and I talked faster than the others about unions. (I'd heard my dad talk about unions in the old country.) I said, ''I don't think this thing is any good.'' So they elected me to be their representative! And the first thing I did was to begin to destroy this company union idea. I believed in the legitimate form of union. I got in touch with the Amalgamated Association [of Iron, Steel and Tin Workers, the old AFL union in steel] through my craft union, the Roll Turners, and they wouldn't have anything to do with us. Leonard was the secretary. He wrote me nice letters, but never came to see me or invited me to come down and talk over joining with them. The Amalgamated Association was lying there and wouldn't do a thing for us.

So we formed an independent union. We tried to disband the company union, and we formed what we called the Associated Employees. This was just workers like myself attempting to do something by way of getting into a legitimate union.

Then, strange things began to happen. One night I came home —I'll always remember as long as I live, it was Lincoln's Birthday about the year 1936—and I walked into the house and there were two big fellows sitting there talking with my sister. They had a wonderful opportunity for a job for me. Now I was working in the mill as a roll turner, making pretty good money for that time. When I got to talking with these fellows, I found out that they wanted to hire me as a spy. So you see I became very quickly acquainted with labor espionage. We were trying to form a legitimate union, and these people invited some of us to come spy. Of course I turned this down and told them I had nothing much to offer them.

One day we read in the newspapers that they were trying to do the same thing [form an independent union] down in Pittsburgh. So I was elected to go down to Pittsburgh and talk matters over with the fellows who were attempting to do that. And I got to talking to a man named Johnny Mullin who asked me if I knew of a certain man named Hemingway. And I looked at him and said, "Yes. What do you know about him?" "Well," he said, "I work for him." I said, "You mean you're working for that spy?" He said, "Yeah." He had been approached by these same spies down in his plant in Pittsburgh, and he was taking the money. He was giving them the reports they wanted, and then he was turning them over to Clinton Golden of the National Labor Relations Board. We found out that Frick, vice-president of U. S. Steel, was the company man in charge of the spying. Mullin and I went down and testified before Senator LaFollette's committee, and there we revealed the beginnings of labor espionage in the steel mills and in other industrial plants.

I became president of the Associated Employees, and then we heard about a man named John Lewis who was very interested in trying to organize the unorganized. I wrote him a letter and said we had an independent union that would like to join up. He wrote back and told me if I held my shirt tail in he'd be down there in the near future and he'd send a man by the name of Philip Murray. So I got to meet Phil Murray and found he was a Scot, born about a mile from where I was born, and we got along pretty well. He was old enough to be my father. He was a United Mine Worker and could tell me more about unions in America than anybody else I knew, and I began to work very closely with him.

One day he said to me, "I'd like you to come down to Pittsburgh and do a little testifying against 'yellow dog' contracts." A company had quickly signed a "yellow dog" contract with a company union that still existed—the remnants of it. So we appeared before Madame Perkins and testified against "yellow dog" contracts, and these contracts were ruled illegal and the company unions were disbanded. But I was fired for doing this. I had twelve years in the steel mills. It was the only place I had worked. Just at that time the Steel Workers Organizing Committee began their drive. I was quickly picked up, thank goodness, by the Steel Workers Organizing Committee, and for the last thirty-three years of my life I've been working as an organizer for the United Steelworkers of America.

In June 1936 we started the drive to organize the steelworkers in this area. I had a lucrative place to go; I had all these company unions throughout the steel mills, and I knew nearly every one. I would go to these people and get them to start joining the Steelworkers Union. Of course, many of them were joining up at their own volition. I didn't do all this by myself. I was just an organizer.

By that time 1937 had rolled around, and we had already gotten a contract with U. S. Steel (Carnegie-Illinois at the time). When we tried to get a contract with Republic Steel on May 26, 1937, the workers went on strike because Tom Girdler [president of Republic Steel] said he would rather dig potatoes than ever sign a contract with any labor organization. So the strike was on.

I understand you want to hear just a little bit about the Memorial Day Massacre. I was there. I was there on the Wednesday night when the strike started. I watched the police march around in their military formation. They were very well oriented. And toward 11 p.m. they marched out all of a sudden and broke up our picket lines, and the next thing I knew I enjoyed being placed in jail for the first time. I was in jail many times after that, and I never found anything too wrong with jail except the bedbugs, which I didn't like. Otherwise I got along fine in jail. I always carried an extra $50 bill hidden away somewhere so I could get myself out. (You know, the Wobblies, they didn't have a $50 bill. But we young steelworkers were getting wise and saving our money a little bit by this time, because the Depression was beginning to get over with and we were working a little steadier.) So I ended up in jail on the first night of the strike with about eighteen other organizers. We got out immediately the next morning, charged with disorderly conduct.

Thursday I began to organize the picket line and we went down to picket, and they wouldn't let us picket. Mayor Da . . . Mayor Kelly—I've got to watch that, Daley and Kelly, there's no difference, you know—Mayor Kelly said at the time, "Yeah, you can picket all you want." But if we went down there the cops would beat the hell out of us. So we kept trying to picket and we got put back in jail.

On Friday night we got real angry. We marched, and we were determined that we were going to picket. We met the police again. This time they really took a swat at us, and they were beating the hell out of everybody in the front lines. If you were in the front you were pretty lucky if you could get away without being clubbed a little bit. Then they fired a few shots in the air, and that scattered us. There was no riot. We ran like hell. The cops were after us.

They always say we riot. We never riot. We wanted to picket. They won't let you picket, so they beat you up and then they say you rioted. This is the fact. The cops make you riot. They riot against us, always. I know it, I've been there too many times. I'm always well-behaved: I might talk to them, but that's about all. Anyhow, they chased us and they beat us again.

This got a lot of union people mad. They got mad over here at Inland Steel, they got mad at Youngstown Sheet and Tube, and they got mad down at Gary. So we decided to hold a big meeting the following Sunday, which was Memorial Day. We invited the public to come and hear us, and we were going to picket. We had been given the right; it was in the paper. Everybody said we could picket; now we were going to picket.

After the meeting was over we started to march, and I went down with the front group, right by the flag, and there we met about 650 cops lined up. It was getting to be kind of familiar. I was always ill at ease. I didn't like it. Don't ever think that anybody's that brave. But I was an organizer in charge of the picket line, so I walked along and saw my familiar old friends Mooney, the commander of the police, and Kilroy. They stood about six feet, six inches tall. They were big fellows, and I'm not very big. And I looked up and said, "Well, here we are. We'd like to go through. Would you escort us? We'd like to picket."

Well, he was standing there—Kilroy was the man—and he was reading a very official document asking us in the name of the people of Illinois to disperse. As soon as he said that, he put the paper down and all hell broke loose. They began to shoot us, club us, and gas us. Ten people died while sixty-eight were wounded and we don't know how many got hurt in all. It really was hell on that field. I ran back with the rest of them, and I got mad. I could see the cops there shooting away with their guns. At first I thought they were blanks—I really did. I could smell the gunpowder—I'll never forget it—and then I began to see people fall. I saw a boy run by, and his foot was bleeding. Then it dawned on me. They were shooting real bullets. This was for keeps. They didn't stop shooting and killing till an hour and a half later. They were chasing people and picking people up.

It was about a week later that I was picked up by the police, and this time I really got the treatment. I went in and was held incommunicado for four days and four nights. You know how they do it: every twenty-four hours they move you (they don't need to book you) and all the time you're being questioned. My wife didn't know where I was at. Nobody knew. I just disappeared. They picked me up on 95th Street at Torrence. I was going over to a meeting at the Burnside Steel Foundry, where I was organizing at the time. I never got there.

How did I get out of it? Well, after about the third night there was a boy in the cell next to me who had been picked up for drunken driving, and his mother came down from Joliet to get him out, and I asked this lovely lady, "Would you do me a favor?" She said, "Well, you look like a nice fellow." And I said, "Yes, I am. I've been in here for four days and four nights, and I'm trying to get word to my wife." And she said, "Give me your telephone number." And I told her. And she called my wife. When they got the information from my wife, my lawyers got a writ of habeas corpus and produced the body—which was me—and we were put out on $50,000 bond.

We were charged with exactly the same thing these seven fellows [the Chicago Seven] were charged with: conspiracy to commit an illegal act. They did it then, they'll do it next year, they'll do it any time. The police will react the same way, the mayors of Chicago will react the same way. Every time you put on a demonstration, always take for granted that this is what's going to happen. I haven't seen it change from the Haymarket days, to the Memorial Day, to the 1968 National Democratic Convention, when the police are faced with a plain group of citizens and are stirred up by the newspapers and foolish propaganda. I don't know what we can do to teach policemen that we're law-abiding citizens who are walking on the streets, we're demonstrating for something right. My heart bled the night of the Democratic Convention.

You know these things happen, and you'll have to be prepared to face them. We were ready to do these things. We stood up and we organized the steelworkers all over the country. Some people ask, "Was it worth it?" Of course it was worth it. We got a contract at Republic Steel.

II

JESSE REESE. You are looking now at living history: not reading from a book, but listening to a man who took part in the history of building a trade union in steel.

I went to work at Youngstown Sheet and Tube in 1929, and we had a skeleton union there called the Amalgamated Association. It had only three or four people in it. I worked down there for a few months, and I decided to join that union and see what I could do. The Party organizer of the American Communist Party came to my house and sat down and talked to me for two hours. He said, "I have an assignment for you." I said, "What is that?" And he said, "I want you to go into the old Amalgamated Association. I want you to build that union. You're going to meet many difficulties. You're going to meet Jim Crow; they're going to throw it in your face. You're going to meet racism; they're going to throw that in your face. But I want you to stand up and throw your ring around with the leadership. That's your assignment." I said, "Well, I have a few things on my mind." And he said, "What is that?" "Freedom, Tom Mooney, the Scottsboro Boys—nine young Negro kids framed for rape in Scottsboro, Alabama," I said. "If I can take a stand on that. . . ." And he said, "Well, you've got to go in there with the leadership, and report to me about every week or two how things are going."

I went in, and the first thing I met was old Jim Crow. They intended to run me out. So they said to me, "Well, we don't take colored people in here, we haven't been taking colored people. But since you're a steelworker and we need the trade union built, we'll give you a chance. But remember one thing. You'll have to organize to stay here." I told them, "That's my business coming here, to help organize the union." One of the secretaries said to me, "I love Negroes, but I like to see 'em in their place." I didn't say a thing, because the organizer had told me to take it cool ("Don't lose your cool, but stay there.") So when it came to my time, I took the floor. I said, "I met a brother here in this union, and he gave me something to think about and something to do. He told me he liked colored people, but he liked them to stay in their place." I said, "Brothers, I agree with him. The place of black people is in the labor movement and officiating in their place, and I'm going to see that everyone out here can be put in his place." I said, "Every working man should know his place. I don't know what place you belong to, but my place is in the labor movement. Is that the place you were telling me you wanted me to stay in?" So that went on.

A few days later, they said to me, "We heard the reds were coming in here, to take over the union. Stay away from the Communists. Stay away from them." I didn't say a word. I waited till my time had come, and I got on the floor. I said, "Mr. Chairman, fellow delegates to this union. I didn't come here to tell you how good communism is, I came here to help you build a union. I feel that if a man is in jail, and you have a piece of pie in your hand and tell him how good it is when he needs liberation, it is foolish, when you can't enjoy it under the present system that we live under." And they left me alone, and next time they said, "This brother, we're going to make him president of this local union. He's able to take care of stuff, and the rest of us don't." And they said, "We're making you president. How about it?" There were four of them. I said to them, "Well listen, you white fellows say you are free. Why do you want to put such a load on my shoulders?" They said, "Well, you're the man for it; you can do it; you can do a good job. You're president of the union—we're going to nominate you." So they elected me, and I took it.

I reported to the organizer and told him I'd done a good job, and he said, "Tell me what you did." I told him. I said, "They hit me in the face, they hit me everywhere, but I hit back. And they hit me with communism, but I told them I hadn't come there to tell them how good communism was, since they couldn't enjoy it anyway under the present society that we live under." And he grabbed me and kissed me. [It was the] first time I'd ever been kissed by a man in my life, but it was a true kiss. It wasn't a Jim Crow segregation kiss, but it was a kiss of an honest brother.

I went on there in the union. I wanted to know how I could get the people in the union. That was my next step—to get people to join the union—to get black people in there. So I kept talking to my brothers and working with them. Black folks had the key positions in the mill, the positions of the hardest jobs, like pickling. All the steel had to come through the pickles of the Youngstown Sheet and Tube tin mill. They fired our foreman, a nice fellow, and they brought over a slave driver from Gary. A white fellow told us he was an organizer for the Ku Klux Klan and said, "You all going to stand for that guy to come in here?" So I went down to the operators of the pickles and said, "Shut the pickles down." And they said, "We can't do that, man!" I said, "Shut the pickles down." And they shut them down. I went over to see Long, the foreman, and I said, "Long, you lost your job?" and he said, "Yes." And I said, "Well, give me five minutes and we'll make them tell you where your job's at." And he said, "You got all day."

I drove over to the hot strip where the white fellows were rolling hot steel, and I said, "Hey fellows, just stop a minute rolling that steel. We're shutting down over there. We're fighting for ten cents an hour and our foreman back on the job." (It would look foolish fighting for your foreman and not for yourself.) And they said, "Oh, you got it organized?" And I said, "Yes, we shut it down. Look over there. We're down, we're not moving. We want you to stop until our grievance is heard." So the white fellows said, "We'll follow you."

Before I could get to the superintendent's office every superintendent in the mill was there. When I walked in, this man by the name of Mr. Griffin said, "Hello. Come in, Mr. Reese. I heard you were coming." And I said, "Well, Mr. Griffin, you should have cooked a cake." And he said, "Well, if I had known it in time maybe

we could have had a cake. What's your story?'' I said, "Well, I'll
tell you. You fired our foreman, and we want him back on the job
if you want any steel rolled and any tin pickled." And he said,
"Well listen, you boys all made a mistake. We gave your foreman
a vacation with pay and a better job." Nobody had ever given anybody a vacation with pay before, not in the mill, not any place.
I said, "Did you give us ten cents an hour? Didn't you know that
we wanted ten cents an hour on our pay and an annual thirty-five
cents added onto that?" "Oh Reese," said Griffin, "that's too
much. Oo-oo, I can't do that. You'll have to go to Youngstown
Sheet and Tube." One of the superintendents said, "Give 'em three
cents." And Griffin said, "Well, I'll tell you, we decided about
a month ago to give you all three cents on the hour." So I said,
"You can't make it ten cents?" And one of the fellows came up
hunchin' me and said, "Take it. Take it and let it go." So I couldn't
go ahead of my army; you know, if I went too far ahead of my
army I would lose my gang. I looked around, and they said, "Take
the three cents and come on." And I said to them, "If we can get
two cents more, let's fight for it!" And I said to Mr. Griffin, "The
brothers say two cents more, Mr. Griffin, and we'll settle with you:
two cents." "Well, we'll think about it," said Griffin. "Boys, I
want to tell you this is your home, this mill is your home. Go along
back to the pickles and pickle the steel, and we'll see about your
raise."

We went back down there, and I said, "You asked for ten cents.
Why don't you . . . ?" And they said, "Yeah, we want ten cents.
But you know that's too much." And I said, "That's never too
much to ask from the man. Ask for the mill."

I went back to the hot strip and told the brothers, "Well, we got
three cents on the hour, and the foreman a better job with a vacation." And there was an iceman, whose name was Bill: Bill Anderson. He was a big, heavy, strong fellow. And he said, "Bring 'em
on up to the union, and we're going to initiate them, every man.
We're going to make a strong union." So I brought them into the
union and we made a talk [about the shutdown, and the three cent
raise] and how they got it. But the hot strip didn't get anything.
They just gave to the pickle. So everything was hot on the hot strip.

How were they going to get their increase? The hot strip boys were coming into the union. They were afraid of the union at first, everybody was scared to come in. But they were going to join the union.

I had a meeting in East Chicago, in Indiana Harbor. A candidate by the name of Mr. Fred Higgins was running for Lake County judge, if I remember right. And that was my smokescreen. I could bring forth my union, what my union was doing for the politician, so I could call for membership. I think I had about 2,000. Then I was called in on the carpet. Mr. Griffin called me in and said, "Hey, I thought you were satisfied. What are you doing now? I heard you got to be president of the Amalgamated Association, and you're calling mass meetings." And I said, "My viewpoint, Mr. Griffin, is politics." "Oh, that's all right," he said, "go ahead." But I didn't tell him what kind of politics I meant.

The years rolled on. We had a terrible Depression, 1932 and '33. Evictions were taking place. Black people were being thrown out from block to block and from street to street. And we were beginning to work one day a week—one day in the mill—and the rest of the days in the street putting furniture back in the houses. Lots of people had bought property on option lease. They thought that they had a contract until their real estate agents proved that they had only leased their houses: "We didn't sell it to them." (Something like what's going on in Chicago now.)

A Hunger March came through led by a man named Claude Lightfoot. So I got my gang ready, getting some of the people in Gary ready to meet the Hunger March, all those who could go to Washington getting aboard the train. The train was moving in for unemployment insurance, social security, and $6 a day with a five-day week. Those were the demands of the Communists in that day. Arnold Johnson, the Republican mayor of the city at that time, said, "No Hunger March is coming through Gary!" Well, Claude got an average number in his march (which looked about a mile long), and stopped about fifteen minutes and said, "Arnold, we are here! And we are on our way to Washington for unemployment insurance, social security paid by the government, and five days' work six hours a day." That was the way it was.

Sure enough, they passed social security (which you pay for). And

that's what you're getting today; that's how you got it. And if anybody here doesn't know how he's getting social security, that's the
way it was got: through a struggle. The old fellows here, I know
they know. Everything that we gained there came through struggle.
And it was a hard struggle. I came up some time in the union on the
strength of the slogan, "Five days' pay, social security. We must
organize our union and fight for those things."

We had a "rump" convention of the old Amalgamated Association in Pittsburgh, but we didn't have any money to send people
there. We had to have $100. One of the brothers there who red-
baited so bad told me, "I want you to go to Communist Party headquarters and borrow $100." And I said, "No, I won't. I'm the presi-
dent of this union. I'm going to let the delegation go, and you're
going to be on the committee." "Well Reese," he said to me, "I
thought you knew [the Party organizer]." I said, "You can get
acquainted with him!" So sure enough, they went on and borrowed
$100 to go to Pittsburgh. They never did pay it back. They couldn't
give social affairs to raise money because there was so much racism
in the outfit. They were scared of a black and white social affair,
but later on they began to see that there wasn't much difference,
and they had to do whatever they could to get money.

They went on to Pittsburgh. That was Mike Tighe's union, the
old Amalgamated. They called on Mike Tighe to come and help
build a union; they wanted his viewpoint. Mike Tighe came and
expelled all of us, calling us reds. I said, "Oh my goodness, this
bunch of Catholics. All of them are Catholics but me." I was the
only red in the bunch but he expelled all of them. I went back and
said, "Hey, I thought you were going to keep the reds out of the
union, you fellows turning red all the way around in one night. How
did that happen?" And they said, "We ain't going to have no red-
baiting in this union. We're going to be in this union, and Mike
Tighe is out to break it up."

In the year 1935 a resolution to organize steel was introduced at
the AFL convention. It was a knock-down, drag-out fight. John L.
Lewis and Bill Green [actually, Bill Hutcheson] got to fighting over
the resolution, and I understand that Lewis knocked Green down
and came out with a CIO industrial union council, ready to organize.

John L. Lewis told Philip Murray that he wanted our union built in steel and to go into Party headquarters and hire all the Communists. Philip Murray told him, "I don't want to have anything to do with the Communists!" He said, "Murray, if you were going to build a house you wouldn't go to the mines and get a dust blower, and you wouldn't get a plumber; you'd get a carpenter, wouldn't you? So I want you to go and get the know-how, go and get the Communists. We're going to build the union if we have to fight the Devil in Hell!" Well, he came out to Party headquarters, hiring everybody he could hire. So the Party organizer said, "Reese, you can get a job for $8 a day." I said, "A man can hire, a man can fire. I'm going to stay in the mill and build my union where I know I'll have security." I said, "John L. Lewis with his money . . . well, he can fire, but I have no security; but if I have mass security, I can have security in the mill."

Well brothers, we rolled on, building steel. I helped to organize Youngstown, and we had a strike in 1937. Republic Steel was scabbing. So we went to South Chicago with truckloads of people, working-class people. And we started our picket line like any union would be doing, and brother George Patterson was leading the strike. And while walking along I heard guns, and I thought, "Oh-oh, they're shooting blanks." I said, "Keep moving, folks. They ain't doing a thing but shooting blanks. File up; march!" But then I began to see people drop. There was a Mexican on my side, and he fell; and there was a black man on my side and he fell. Down I went. I crawled around in the grass and saw that people were getting beat. I'd never seen police beat women, not white women. I'd seen them beat black women, but this was the first time in my life I'd seen them beat white women—with sticks. There was this woman carrying a flag in her hand, and they took the flag away from her and began beating her with the flagpole. I thought, "I'm here with nothing. I should have brought my gun." But I didn't get hurt; I got out of there all right.

U. S. Steel signed a contract. And I think the steel plant where we were working signed some kind of state agreement [see page 107.] And later on we also got a contract.

I had always said that I wanted a union that would be a watchdog for the working class and guard its interests. So I always called our union the watchdog. If I ever had a chance I was going to turn my dog loose on the steel corporation. I always looked at Mississippi and Alabama. The lynching, Jim Crow, and segregation always stayed on my mind. How could we stop it? My aim was to do it.

The first [swoc] convention at Pittsburgh I begged to get on the Resolutions Committee, and I wouldn't tell anybody why. I wanted to draw up a resolution for Tom Mooney and the Scottsboro Boys, and I knew if I told them that they wouldn't put me on the Resolutions Committee. Well, I met a white fellow from Missouri, and I said, "How about nominating me for the Resolutions Committee?" And he did. I went in the resolution room (you had to bring the resolution from your committee onto the convention floor), and I had one of the biggest fights in that room with my own man—a black man. He was sent by the Alabama committee to keep me from bringing up our resolution in the resolution room. He didn't mean it, but he had to go back to Alabama; he had to make that fight against the resolution on the Scottsboro Boys. I said, "Listen, I'll tell you where I'm going to stand. You're from Alabama. I'm from Mississippi, but I happen to be here for a little while. I know how you feel going back, but I'm going to fight for this resolution on the floor of the convention." Well, I did. John L. Lewis called me on the floor. Yessirree, as the representative of East Chicago 1011, I had a right to speak on the resolution. I came forward and I spoke on Tom Mooney and the Scottsboro Boys, who had been framed. I said the union was the watchdog of the working class, and it must speak up on the misery of the working class of people. [Both resolutions were adopted.]

I want to say, friends, I have to give it to you like it is. The Communists built the union. After we got the union built, something happened to John L. Lewis, and Mr. Philip Murray carried out his aims: he fired every Communist organizer. He made an agreement with the steel trusts, it seems to me, that he would fire the Communists. And that's what happened, and the union's been going back, back, back ever since. It doesn't open its mouth.

Today we have in our unions a pet dog—what you might call a pet company dog—led by the caretakers; and the caretakers are the leaders of our union. And our dog is being fed red-baiting and his teeth have been pulled out (that's the no-strike clause) and your dog don't bark no more for you. So the only thing you can get to win now is a cat, and it's got to be a wildcat, organized as a blanket matter. You've got to use blanket cover to keep from being exposed.

Your so-called leaders are the leaders of the industrial pet dog. Your dog don't bark at no misery. Your dog don't bark no more. He can't hear. Makes no difference how many people they kill, your dog don't say nothing. He ain't the dog of 1937, when that dog turned loose nine boys—the Scottsboro Boys—and freed Tom Mooney. Your dog . . . what's the matter with your dog? I couldn't stay in that union, pay dues, and keep quiet. They'd have to do something about things. There's no justice, no justice! And we sit down with a big trade union, with intelligent people (people who are educated, they say), and you don't hear nothing, and you can't say nothing, and you can't see nothing. You can't see those people getting killed. They have declared war on color, and not just on one color, but on all color from the Kennedys to the Kings to the black ghettos to the Black Panthers to the mine workers. And they're now dancing on the doorsteps of Asia, and your dog don't bark. Because you don't have anything but the pet dog of the steel trusts.

You have no leaders. Your "leaders" don't say nothing: they're scared. Freedom is in the jail house. That's the way of freedom. It ain't worth being free if you're not willing to go to jail for it.

III

JOHN SARGENT. I got in the mills in 1936, and I [was] fortunate to be caught up in a great movement of the people in this country. And that doesn't happen very often in one's lifetime, but it's an experience that I think is important to anyone who has been able to participate in a movement of this kind. It's indeed a very important event in his or her life. Because a movement of the kind that we had in the Steelworkers Union and in the CIO was a movement that moved millions of people, literally, and changed not only the course of the working man in this country, but also the nature of the relationship between the working man and the government and between the working man and the boss, for all time in this country. There are some parallels in the movement today, especially among the young people and the black people, that I won't go into. . . .

I was hired at the Inland Steel Company in 1936. And I remember I was hired at 47 cent cents an hour, which was the going rate, and at a time when there were no such things as vacations, holidays, overtime, insurance, or any of the so-called fringe benefits everybody talks about today. But the worst thing—the thing that made you most disgusted—was the fact that if you came to work and the boss didn't like the way you looked, you went home; and if he did like the way you looked, you got a promotion. Anything and everything that happened to you was at the whim and will of the fellow who was your boss and your supervisor. Now fortunately Jesse [Reese] had a good boss. Ninety-nine per cent of the people did not have good bosses. As a matter of fact, in order to get a promotion—and sometimes even in order to work—you had to bring the boss a bottle of whiskey, or you had to mow the boss's lawn, or you had to do something to make yourself stand out from the other people he saw. This was the type of condition that existed as late as 1936 in the steel mills in this region.

When the CIO came in, the people were ready to accept a change. And because they were ready to accept a change, it was not a difficult task to organize the people in the steel mills. Thousands upon thousands of them, in a spontaneous movement, joined the steelworkers' organization at that time. And they did it because conditions in the mill were terrible, and because they had become disgusted with the political set-up in this country and the old tales told by the Republican Party about the free enterprise system in this country in which any man was his own boss, and there was no sense in having an organization, and organizations and unions were anti-American, and so on. All this fell off the backs of the people at that time. They realized that there was going to be a change—both a political and an economic change—in this country, and there was.

John L. Lewis had an agreement with the U. S. Steel Corporation, and they signed a contract. Little Steel—which was Youngstown Sheet and Tube, Republic Steel, Inland Steel, and other independent companies—had no contract with the Steelworkers Union. As a result in 1937 there was a strike called on Little Steel. And one of the things that happened during the strike was the massacre in South Chicago, the Chicago cops beating and shooting the people. The strike was not won. We did not win a contract. Neither Youngstown Sheet and Tube, nor Republic Steel, nor Inland Steel won a contract with the company. What we did get was an agreement through the governor's office that the company would recognize the Steelworkers Union and the company union and any other organization that wanted to represent the people in the steel industry. And we went back to work with this governor's agreement signed by various companies and union representatives in Indiana. At Inland Steel we had a company union; we had our own Steelworkers Union. When we got back to work we had company union representatives and Steelworkers Union representatives, and we had no contract with the company. But the enthusiasm of the people who were working in the mills made this settlement of the strike into a victory of great proportions.

Without a contract, without any agreement with the company, without any regulations concerning hours of work, conditions of work, or wages, a tremendous surge took place. We talk of a rank-and-file movement: the beginning of union organization was the best kind of rank-and-file movement you could think of. John L. Lewis sent in a few organizers, but there were no organizers at Inland Steel, and I'm sure there were no organizers at Youngstown Sheet and Tube. The union organizers were essentially workers in the mill who were so disgusted with their conditions and so ready for a change that they took the union into their own hands.

For example, what happened at Inland Steel I believe is perhaps representative of what happened throughout the steel industry. Without a contract we secured for ourselves agreements on working conditions and wages that we do not have today, and that were better by far than what we do have today in the mill. For example as a result of the enthusiasm of the people in the mill you had a series of strikes, wildcats, shut-downs, slow-downs, anything working people could think of to secure for themselves what they decided they had to have. If their wages were low there was no contract

to prohibit them from striking, and they struck for better wages. If
their conditions were bad, if they didn't like what was going on,
if they were being abused, the people in the mills themselves
—without a contract or any agreement with the company involved—
would shut down a department or even a group of departments to
secure for themselves the things they found necessary.

We made an agreement with Inland Steel way back in '38 or '39
that the company would not pay less than any of its competitors
throughout the country. We never had it so good, I assure you of
that. All you had to do as a union representative was come into
the company and say, "Look, we have a group of people working
in the pickle line, and at Youngstown, Ohio or Youngstown Sheet
and Tube in East Chicago people are getting more money than we're
getting for the same job." And if that was a fact, we were given
an increase in wages at Inland. In those departments where you had
a strong group of union members, where they were most active, we
had the highest rates in the country. We were never able to secure
conditions of this kind after we secured contracts.

What I'm trying to get at is the spontaneous action of people who
are swept up in a movement they know is right and correct and want
to do something about. Our union now has a grievance committee
of twenty-five people. In those days there were more than twenty
assistant grievers and hundreds of stewards. The grievance committee set-up could handle the affairs of the people on every shift and
every turn with every group. Where you did have contracts with
the companies (at U. S. Steel, for example) you had a limited grievance procedure. The U. S. Steel plant in Gary, the largest steel plant
of the largest steel company, had a grievance committee of only
eleven. Where union officials did not take over the union through
a contract with the company (as they did with U. S. Steel), you
had a broader, bigger, more effective, and more militant organization
that set an example for unions throughout the country. Where the
union and the company got together through union contracts (as at
U.S. Steel), you had a smaller, more restrictive, less militant union
that provided less representation for the people in the mill. U. S.
Steel has never had a strike (so far as I know) since the unions
organized, whereas unions like the Inland Steel union had a whole

series of strikes in order to protect their conditions and prevent the company from taking over or taking back the things they had earned.

What happens to a union? And what happened to the United Steel-workers of America? What makes me mad, and what makes thousands of other people in the mill mad, is that the companies became smart and understood that in order to accommodate themselves to a labor organization they could not oppose that labor organization. What they had to do was recognize that labor organization. And when they recognized a labor union they had to be sure they recognized the national and international leadership of that labor union and took the affairs of that labor union out of the hands of the ordinary elected officials on a local scale.

Now Little Steel was not smart. Little Steel had people like the president of Republic Steel, who said he would go out and pick apples before he would recognize the union. And our own dear Inland Steel Company said they would do nothing, they would rather shut their place down forever than recognize the Steelworkers Union. Now what happened to these companies that did not recognize the union, that forced the union to act against the company, was that the workers developed the most militant and the most inspiring type of rank-and-file organization that you can have. Now when the companies realized that this was what was happening, they quickly saw that they had gone off in the wrong direction, and they recognized the leadership of the union.

We used to bargain locally with the Inland Steel Company, and we had our own contract with the company. We let a representative of the international union sit in, but we bargained right in Indiana Harbor and settled our differences right there. But soon Inland began to realize that this was not the way, because they were up against a pretty rough bunch of people who had no ambitions to become political leaders and labor representatives on a national scale. They realized that the best way to handle the situation was to work with the international leadership of this union. And today, the company and the international union get along pretty well.

The union has become a watchdog for the company. The local union has become the police force for the contracts made by the international union. If a local union tries to reject a contract in the

Steelworkers Union, the contract is put into effect and the local union acts as the police to see that the men live up to the contract, even if it is rejected by the entire committee [of the local union] which negotiates the contract.

This is, I think, the normal growth which occurs when labor unions and most other organizations become legitimate and old and part of the general situation of the country. At the same time, I think it important to realize that the growth of the union in this country has changed the bond. We no longer have many of the sweatshops we had in the '20s and early '30s, or the terribly low wages we had before. The union taught the system—taught the industrialists of this country—that it is possible to pay decent wages and provide decent working conditions and still make a fortune. In fact the steel mills make more money now than they ever made before. They do it by paying people a fairly decent wage and by working people not nearly so hard as they were worked in the past. The union has taught the companies how to make money through recognizing the union organization. And the government and the employers have learned how to adopt, co-opt, and engulf the union and make it a part of the establishment. And in making it part of the establishment they took the guts, the militancy, and the fight out of the people who work for a living.

SYLVIA WOODS

S YLVIA WOODS' experience spans half a century of black struggle. As a child in New Orleans she took part in the movement of Marcus Garvey, which powerfully projected both the dream of a return to Africa and black pride. At the time that we interviewed her for this book Sylvia Woods was playing an active role in the national campaign to free Angela Davis.

Many black workers today believe that they must first organize as blacks, and only then (if at all) seek an alliance with white workers. Sylvia Woods, like Jesse Reese, came to a different conclusion: that only through the unity of black and white could black working people move forward. She describes in detail her gradual conversion to this point of view.

Sylvia Woods also had the good fortune of belonging to, and helping to create, a democratic local union. The UAW local in the airplane parts factory where she worked during World War II did not want the dues check-off, feeling that it would dampen voluntary participation by the membership. Local union officers worked in the shop. Like Nick Migas [see page 168]. Sylvia Woods always took the aggrieved individual with her in processing a grievance, rather than representing an individual who wasn't there. Departmental meetings at the end of the night shift made it possible for fellow-workers to form deep relationships. And education was a regular feature of the local union's meetings.

No wonder, then, that the day the plant closed down at the end of the war the members of this extraordinary local just stood around the gate, wondering, "What am I going to do without these people?"

SYLVIA WOODS

You Have to Fight for Freedom

I WAS BORN March 15, 1909. My father was a roofer. In those days they put slates on the roofs and he was a slater. It was a very skilled job. You had to nail the slate. They used to make a fancy diamond with different colors. Every time the white guys got ready to do this they sent him for the bucket of beer so that he wouldn't learn it. But when they got ready to send him for the beer, he would find something wrong. He didn't know where his hammer was or he had to get something before he went, and in the meantime he would be watching. He learned it and he could do it beautifully. He'd say, "I'm the best. I stole it from those bastards but I'm the best." He became so good he didn't have to work with contractors any more. He could go out on his own.

And he was a union man. There was a dual union—one for whites and one for blacks. He said we should have one big union but a white and a black is better than none. He was making big money—eight dollars a day. I used to brag that "My father makes eight dollars a day." But he taught me that "You got to belong to the union, even if it's a black union. If I wasn't in the union I wouldn't make eight dollars a day."

New Orleans is a trade union town. My father had seen the longshoremen organize and they made a lot of money. Unions were not new to this city. And I mean they had unions! When they came out on strike, there were no scabs. You know why there were no scabs? Because you carried your gun. The pickets had guns and they would blow your brains out.

My father got into the Garvey movement when the Garvey movement was being born. I was about maybe nine or ten at the beginning of the Garvey movement. We couldn't wait for Sundays to come because we went to the big meeting in Longshoremen's Hall. The band would be playing and we would march. Everybody had a title and everybody had a uniform. My husband used to say that any organization that puts a black in a uniform, that's all he needs. It makes him something special. If you have a uniform it gives you a little more dignity. The other thing was freedom. You want to leave this oppression and go back to the mother country and have some freedom. This was the beginning of my realizing that you have to fight for freedom.

I'll never forget, there was a little woman there and she used to speak every Sunday. When that woman got up to talk, my father would just sit thrilled and then he'd look at me: "Are you listening?" I'd say, "I'm listening." "I want you to hear every word she says because I want you to be able to speak like that woman. We have to have speakers in order to get free." And then when we got home he would say, "Now what did she say?" I could say it just like her, with her same voice, all of her movements and everything. This would please him no end.

He was a gentle man. He believed in women doing things. He never slapped my mother. If the housework didn't get done, he didn't see it. There were more important things to do.

He was a very kind man. He never raised his voice. He never wanted my mother to give us a licking and my mother was hard on us. She really would give it to us, but he would say "No" if he was home.

I had a grandmother who was very religious and my mother was kind of because that was her upbringing. After she married my father she sort of got away from it. But my grandmother made us go to church and she would frighten us: "You're going to die and go to Hell 'cause you're telling a lie and when I get through beating you, you're not going to tell any more lies." I was actually afraid I might go to Hell. My father would say, "That's a lot of crap. This is what the white folks tell you so that you will be scared. They go to church and come right out of church and lynch a nigger before

you can say scat. Now, are they scared that they're going to Hell?''
My grandmother used to get so angry with him. "Tom, you are
going to send those children's souls to Hell." He said, "The white
folks send them to hell every day. They were sent to hell when
they were born right here on earth, Ma." She would pray and we'd
all have to go and pray and he'd say, "Don't believe all that. Go
and kneel down but don't be saying all that crap."

My grandmother was born in slavery. It's a funny thing, we never
thought to talk to her about it. She never talked to us except to
say, "Scrub the kitchen," or do something or don't do something,
or "Come with me."

If she hadn't had a stroke I wouldn't have been married until I
was maybe forty because she took me everywhere. When I was
twelve years old she was still picking me up from school. "You
got to watch girls. You can't be too careful with girls."

When I was maybe ten years old, I changed schools. On the way
to school, I had to go through a park that was for white people
only. We could walk through the park but we couldn't stop at all,
just pass through it. There were swings in this park and, oh, I so
much wanted sometimes to just stop and swing a little while, but
we couldn't because we were black. I would walk through this park
to my school where there weren't any swings.

Every morning all the kids would line up according to classrooms
and we would have prayers and sing the Star Spangled Banner and
then we'd march to our respective groups after this business.

I decided I wasn't going to sing the Star Spangled Banner. I just
stood there every morning and I didn't sing it. One morning, one
of the teachers noticed that I wasn't doing it. So she very quietly
called me over and asked me why didn't I sing the Star Spangled
Banner. I said I just didn't feel like singing it. So she said, "Well
then you have to go in to the principal and explain that to him.
All of the children in the school take part and you've got to do
it too."

OK, I went in to the principal and he asked me why I wasn't
singing the Star Spangled Banner. He threatened me with a lot of
[stuff like] I'd have to bring my mother. I said, "I don't care. I'll
tell her to come but she won't come because she has to go to work."

I said my grandmother would come, not my mother. "Alright, then you'll have to bring your grandmother." I said, "She don't care if I don't sing the Star Spangled Banner." (I didn't know whether she would care or she wouldn't care.) He said, "You won't be able to come to school here." And I said, "So, OK, I won't come."

He says, "Why don't you want to sing it?" Finally I told him. "Because it says 'The land of the free and the home of the brave' and this is not the land of the free. I don't know who's brave but I'm not going to sing it any more." Then he said, "Why you've been singing it all the time haven't you? How come you want to stop now?" And I told him about coming through the park and if I could not swing in those swings in the park, and I couldn't sit in the park, and I could only walk in Shakespeare Park, then it couldn't be the land of the free. "Who's free?" He didn't say anything.

Then he said, "Well, you could pledge allegiance to your flag." I said, "It's not my flag. The flag is with freedom. If the land is free and the flag is mine, then how come I can't do like the white kids?" And then I told him that the next white kid I see, I'm beating him up. "I'm telling you right now, he's just going to get all beat up. I don't care." He says, "But you can't do that. You could go to Jones Home." So I said, "Well, I'll go to Jones Home. I don't care. But he'll get beat up. I know that!"

Anyway, he told me that I didn't have to sing the song and I didn't have to pledge allegiance but I had to stand in the back of the line. So who cares about standing in the back of the line? Sometimes the white administrators would come to the school and look the niggers over. (We called it that. "Well, there's the white folks looking the niggers over.") And he didn't want them to see me. But I didn't mind getting in the back of the line as long as I didn't have to sing that song. But I was so hurt and disillusioned, I would not have sung it no matter what. I'm sure that this man must have sympathized with me although he gave no indication that he did. He had said he was going to make me bring my parents but he never mentioned it again. I never sang it again from the time I was ten years old. I still don't pledge allegiance to the flag and I don't sing the Star Spangled Banner.

My mother had two children, my brother John and me, and then we had a brother Joseph. I'm eleven years older than him. She had to work and I had to take care of the two boys. Every morning when she got ready to go to work Joseph would cry, "Mama, please stay home!" She had to go off and leave him and I know how her heart must have been broken. In the evenings I would take him to meet her. We walked two blocks to the streetcar. The first street-car would come along and she wouldn't get off. He'd say, "Where is Mama?" I'd say, "She will be on the next one." So the next one would come and she wouldn't get off and he would cry, "When is she coming?" She left him crying; she found him crying. You know she felt sorry for me her little girl, her first born, taking this burden.

She went to work in "the white folks' yard," as the blacks would say. She did the washing—and then there wasn't any washing machine—she did it by hand. This man used to have fifteen white shirts a week. She took care of the child, the house, the washing, the ironing, everything but the cooking. I think she made two dollars a day.

My mother was very strict with me. The school used to have dances for the youngsters on Saturday. I could go if John went with me (that's my older brother). He would say, "Don't dance with him. I saw him carrying on in the corner. You dance with him and I'll be telling Mama." And then, "Come on. Let's go." "But John, just one more . . ." "Let's go! I'm ready to go." I'd say, "I'll bring in your wood for a week." "OK, bring in my wood for a week. You can dance another dance." Then I'd have to do all of his chores for a week in order to dance another dance.

They were really strict and tight, so I wouldn't get spoiled, so I wouldn't have a baby. (They didn't know that I wasn't going to have any babies.) Then my grandmother had this stroke and I had to take care of her. And I had to mind Joseph. I didn't mind minding him—we were happy.

Finally, I got tired of it. Then Henry came along and he was talking about we would get married and then we would go to Chicago. I had never been on a train in my life. I would have married just to get on that train and come to Chicago.

He lived two blocks away from us. We grew up together. But my mother didn't know his parents. The first time he came he asked my mother if he could come to see me and she said, "Have your mother come up here Sunday and we'll discuss it." I was fifteen. The next winter I got married. When he got serious my mother was sorry she had let him come. We got married and my mother just hated it. My father didn't want me to get married either. My father was a skilled laborer making eight dollars a day and here is this man who didn't even have a trade. Henry was working as a porter in a dress shop. "How do you intend to take care of her?" my father asked him. "She can't cook. She is lazy. You will not find anybody as lazy as that girl! I'm telling you what you are getting. She doesn't want to do a thing in the house and her mother has to get after her to wash the dishes. She slops them up. She don't dry them. You take down a plate to eat and water drops in your face. She is the laziest thing you have ever seen." Henry said, "Yes, sir. That's all right. We'll get married."

Henry came to Chicago. He got a job and he sent me a one-way ticket. I was so happy. It took him three months to send it to me because the train fare was $35. Thirty-five dollars was a lot of money. When I got the ticket I told my mother, "I got my ticket, Ma. I can go to Chicago!" She looked at it and it was a one-way ticket. She said, "Put that thing in that dresser over there and leave it there. When your father gets enough money, he'll buy you a two-way ticket and then you'll be able to go. You're not going away from here with a one-way ticket." I cried and cried. She said, "You take your round-trip ticket and if they say your eye is black you can tell them the devil with them and you'll come home." So I had to wait. It took almost a month before she got that ticket.

The minute I got off the train and I told Henry that I had the two-way ticket, he couldn't wait until the next morning to go down town and sell the other half of it so that he would have some money, because he had lost the job in the meantime. It was in the heart of the Depression. He's a little guy and in those days they just didn't hire little guys.

So I had to go to work. I had never had a job in my life. I came from a family that didn't allow the girls to work because they didn't know who you were going to work with and you couldn't mix and mingle with anybody and everybody. All you could do is go to school.

I got this job in a laundry. The first morning I went there, this guy asked me, "Did you ever work in a laundry before?" I said, "No." He said, "Well there's no point in your coming here because we only hire people who know how to work in a laundry." I said "OK" and I left. The next morning I went back because I didn't know any place else to go. "Weren't you here yesterday?" "Yes." He said, "Well, I told you that we don't hire people who don't know how to work in a laundry." I said, "Well, maybe you'll need somebody one day. I'll come back tomorrow." So the next day I came back. When I walked in the door he said, "Come with me." He took me upstairs and he said to the foreman, "Teach her how to shake out."

You had to shake these clothes out and put them on long poles. You know how things look when they come out of a wringer. You had to shake them out so that they could run them through the mangle. Two girls put the things through the mangle. One girl did the sheets and the other did the small things like towels and pillow slips. I worked really hard. I kept those poles full. The women would say, "You mean you never worked before?" I'd say, "I never had a job before."

When I went back the next day, my arms were aching. I just couldn't lift them up. The women were angry with me. They said, "You just don't want to work." There was this one big fat woman and she said, "That kid's tired. You know it's the first time she's ever worked. What in the hell do you expect of her? If anybody else says anything to her, they're going to have to reckon with me." She was pulling those great big bags and tying them up and pitching them just like they were nothing. Nobody wanted to reckon with her. I limbered up in the afternoon and I did a little better.

So then I wanted to start shaking sheets because there is an art to shaking sheets. You pick these sheets up and—wham—if you did it right they popped. You made the sheet pop and then you threw it over that pole. This fascinated me. "Come on over here. You can shake out the sheets." I was going so fast. There were four poles and if we kept those poles full, then I could monkey around.

I'd go over and watch the women feed the sheets into the mangle. One day I said to this white gal (only white feeders—black shakers and black folders, the hardest jobs—white table girls), I said, "Will you let me see if I can run this?" She said, "Sure." By the next week I knew how to feed.

So the next week I wanted to fold. I hurried up and filled the poles and they showed me how to fold. I wasn't there three weeks before I knew how to do everything.

I was working for ten dollars a week and I asked this white woman on the mangle, "How much do you make?" She said, "Fifteen dollars." I said, "You mean you're making fifteen and he's only paying me ten?" She said, "Yes, but I'm a feeder." I said, "Well that girl over there"—and she was a Negro woman—"she only makes ten and she was feeding. I'm going to ask him for a raise." She said, "Kiddo, don't do it because you'll be fired if you do." "He doesn't have to fire me. I'm going to quit. I'm not working for ten dollars a week."

The next morning I said to the owner, "Hey Charlie." "What do you want?" He never stopped walking. You had to walk behind him to talk to him so I walked right behind him. I said, "I'm not working for ten dollars any more." "What do you mean you're not working for ten dollars any more? I hired you, you didn't know how to do a goddamned thing, I did you a favor." I said, "I know how to feed and fold and stack." He said, "It's impossible. You've only been here three weeks. I don't believe it."

He came up and he watched me work. I stood at that mangle and fed those sheets in. He said, "Speed it up!" I put it up to its highest notch and ran it. He said, "All right, I want to see you fold." I snatched those sheets out of that mangle, me and this other girl. . . . He didn't say a word. He turned around and he walked out.

Everybody said, "He's going to fire you. He's going to get you." I said, "I don't give a damn if he fires me. I don't have to work here. I know how to feed and fold. I can go to King's Laundry down at the next block."

The next week he raised me to eighteen dollars. That was the top for the table girls. He said, "Now don't you tell anybody." The minute I got that check I went right back up and said, "Hey everybody, I got a raise!" "Aw, you're crazy." I said, "Look at my check! Eighteen dollars." So they called him up.and they asked, "How come she's getting eighteen dollars" instead of saying, "Give me eighteen dollars too!" He looked at me and said, "God damn you, I made a mistake when I hired you. I told you not to tell anybody."

Then they organized a night shift. There was so much work that they just couldn't get it all out. So they put all the black workers on nights. I used to work from five o'clock in the evening until three o'clock in the morning, every night. I was getting $18—top salary.

No whites. All blacks but the blacks were stealing them blind. They were wrapping sheets around them and wearing them home and taking everything. They said, "Well, hell, we are just getting the rest of our pay." The foreman would go downstairs and everybody would stop. They wouldn't do a thing.

One night a white woman was hired. "Who is this white woman?" Everybody was looking around. She was hired to watch us to see that we didn't do any stealing. The boss came up and said that this woman was going to be the forelady. I said, "I don't know what the rest of you think but I'll be goddamned if she's going to be forelady over me. We've been working nights for over a year. We've the most seniority. We're all black women here and if he has to have a forelady I don't know why he couldn't have one of us. She's got to go." So everybody got mad. They closed the mangles down.

And then the boss comes up. He walks right up to me and says, "What's going on here?" I said, "We're not working." He said, "Why not?" I said, "We're not going to have a white forelady over all black women. Until you get her out of here, we're not going to work. If you are going to have a forelady you have to get one of us. Either one of us or nobody." So he goes out and calls the cops.

The cops came in and said we had to get out if we weren't going to do any work. We really messed the place up. We mixed the bundles up until the cops didn't know what to do. They told them that I was the ringleader and they put me in the patrol wagon but the white policeman just took me home.

We went up to my house and held a meeting. It was all new to me and I didn't know how far to take it. We didn't fight any more. We just left. But they didn't put a white forelady over us!

My husband got fired that night—he was working there—and they fired my brother. I just went down the next block to another laundry and got a better job. I was making $20 a week as a table girl and all around girl.

From there I went to a laundry in Oak Park that paid 32 cents an hour, and that was a lot of money! This laundry was owned by a family and they would give us a turkey every year for Christmas and two weeks vacation with pay. This was unheard of. Other laundries were paying 18 and 20 cents an hour, their top rate was 25 cents an hour, but Brooks in Oak Park paid 32 cents.

When the union came to organize, I went to all the meetings and I was the spokesman for our laundry, for Brooks. The union said that they had negotiated with the laundry owners for 26 cents an hour. And I said, "You have got to be kidding! We are already making 32. You have to negotiate for 35."

I got mad and quit the union because the best they could get was 26 cents. I just pulled out the whole Brooks laundry. We walked out of the goddamned union.

The guy came running after me, "You can't do this. You have to come back." "I'm not coming back because you had no business to negotiate the contract. You should have brought it to us first." They had signed the contract and it was a closed shop and eventually everyone had to join the union. So I quit the laundry.

I was still in the laundry when the war came. My friend Martina and I decided we were going to go to work in a war plant, Martina and I both, so that we could earn some more money. And we were sick and tired of working in a laundry.

We went over to Wilson Jones. That's a place that made notebooks and papers. There I learned to run a punch press. Then

I heard about Bendix Aviation that made carburetors for airplanes. It was right around the corner from where I lived. They used to wear blue uniforms, pants and a blouse, and I loved it. The black gals would put on a white shirt under the blue and they'd bring the collar of it out. They'd wear white socks and they'd get blue sneakers. You really had an outfit. You had the cap. "I've got to get a job in there!"

So I went to Bendix looking for a job. I used to go about three times a day. I would go in the morning and they would tell me I was too fat. Then I'd go home and put on a hat and I'd go back in the afternoon and they'd say, "Well, we're not hiring right now." I would sit there and hear them begging white girls to take jobs, so I picked a fight with them. I said, "What do you mean you're not hiring? You were begging that woman. You told her you had a job at nights on the punch press, and nobody can operate a punch press better than I." He said, "We don't have punch presses here." I said, "Whatever you have, I can do it." But I didn't get hired. They had their quota.

Finally they wanted to give me a job. What is the job doing? Cleaning up the bathroom. I wasn't taking no washroom job! "I want to work on a *machine*." Martina took the job, which was good because otherwise I never would have gotten in there.

One day she called me up at home. "Hurry up and come on over here. There's a man here says he'll hire you." We always thought that this guy had some connection with the Communist Party. He hired everything black that came in. Martina went to him and she said, "I have a friend who wants to work in the factory and she's been coming and coming and they never will hire her." He said, "Tell her to come. I'll hire her." So he hired me. When I walked in the door of the plant I said, "I'm going to make you sorry for every day that I walked around to this shop hoping to get hired!"

I worked on the carburetors. I was on an assembly line that had two sides and a belt ran down the center and I was burring—taking all of the burrs off the carburetor. Right across from me was a young Polish woman named Eva. She was going to show me how to do it. We did about ten of them. Then I said, "You don't have to

help me any more." She said, "Do you think that you can keep
up with the line?" "I can keep up with the line." So I did. Eva
and I became real good friends because when she got stuck I would
reach over and help her.

One night she said, "There's a union meeting tonight. Will you
go with me to the union meeting?" And I said, "Ahh, I'm tired."
She said, "Aw, come on and go." She said, "I want to buy you
a drink anyway," because I had helped her. I said, "OK, you can
buy me a drink but I don't want to go to a union meeting."

So we went to this tavern and then we started talking union. I
got kind of high, you know, and "OK, we'll go to the union meeting."

This was United Automobile Workers. I was the only black there.
All the stewards were coming in and saying how they couldn't
organize the workers: "I can't get anybody to join"; "So-and-So
said the union is no good . . ."

I said, "You know why you can't get anybody to join? Because
you don't have anything to sell them. You aren't selling them union.
You're letting them sell you non-union from what I hear you saying
here. You'll never get the workers to join the union if you let them
tell you the union isn't any good. I wouldn't join a union that's
no good either." A steward must sell the union, telling the workers
how much strength they have when they are organized.

I looked at this guy who was the organizer and his face was just
lighting up. "Union! What do you mean? I'll bet you if I was the
steward I could sign them up." The next day I was elected steward
of my department. Two nights later everybody in that department
was signed up.

I only joined the union for what it could do for black people.
I didn't care anything about whites. I didn't care if they lined them
all up and shot them down—I wished they would! I had no knowledge of the unity of white and black. I had no knowledge that you
can't go any place alone. The only thing that I was interested in
was what happened to black people.

Of about three thousand, twenty-five per cent were blacks. Ninety
per cent were women. I was making ninety cents an hour—great
big money! I never thought I would live to make that much money.

When the union thought they were ready they notified the Labor Relations Board and an election was held in the shop. The union won. Then we were going to have an election of officers for the union. I was nominated for financial secretary. I didn't know how to account or keep books and I didn't want to be bothered but I accepted the nomination.

Then Mamie Harris came to me and tried to convince me that I shouldn't run for office. I said, "What do you mean I shouldn't run for office?" (She had somebody else all picked out to be financial secretary.) "Why shouldn't I run? I have been nominated and I have accepted and my name is going to be on the ballot and why in the hell should I take it off?" She said, "Well, do you know how to keep books?" I said, "No, I don't know how to keep books? Do you?" She said, "Yes." "Well, didn't you have to learn? So, I'll learn." She never got around to telling me why I shouldn't run.

Then I went back and told the guys Mamie Harris had told me not to run and that did it! "Discrimination! We got to get her!" From then on the campaign became black against white.

I probably would not have won except that everybody on the night shift was going to vote for me because I was known. I became shop committeewoman when I was working nights and I never lost a case. I settled almost every case on the first phase of the grievance procedure because the foreman knew that I wasn't going to let up. I was going all the way up to the top—arbitration, anything. We always took the worker in when there was a grievance they brought. They saw how we fought. They'd come out and tell it. "You better join the union. I mean because if you get in trouble, Sylvia goes in there and wrecks the place. You better join." So everybody knew me.

The night shift was smaller than the day shift. If everybody on the day shift had voted, they probably would have beaten me. But the day shift didn't come out to vote in as large numbers as the night shift. The night shift didn't have anything to do but go to the union hall. They couldn't go home washing and ironing and cooking and scrubbing at that time in the morning. They had plenty of time, so they all came to vote.

I won by two measly votes. Then they demanded a recount. I won by one vote. The director of the region took me under his wing.

I didn't know what to do and they were sending guys in from downtown to help me.

We had the reputation with the international for being a good local. In fact, the region gave a party for our local because we kept 90% signed up. With the turnover being what it was in those days, we still kept 90%. We were a well-organized local.

We never had check-off. We didn't want it. We said if you have a closed shop and check-off, everybody sits on their butts and they don't have to worry about organizing and they don't care what happens. We never wanted it.

One day a black guy came there looking for a job—one of the skilled jobs. Mamie was called because they were going to hire him. If they hired him, the guys said, they would walk out. But [the company] wanted to hire him because they needed him and he came well recommended. Mamie said, "Fine." So she went back in and said, "He's coming here to work. Anybody that doesn't like it if a black person comes in this shop can leave right now. Turn in your union cards and get the hell out. Go." But nobody left. The guy came and he worked. Two days later he was friendly with one, and the next day with another. Soon he was getting along very well.

So this made me take a little notice of Mamie. She wasn't so bad. She was fighting for the black people so I said, "That gal is all right."

Then another thing came up with another young woman, Selma. They were having a cutback. In our contract it said that you could be cut back to the highest skill and nothing more. The highest skill for Selma was in a department where there had never been any blacks. Selma was a fiery little thing and she was single-minded that she go in there. Here too, they said that if Selma came in, they would walk out. This was on the night shift. I went down there and I said, "If you walk out, fine. We'll fill your places before you get home." They were going to wait and see Mamie in the morning. Mamie told them the same thing. They stayed. Nobody left. About two weeks later, there was an opening for a steward and they nominated Selma to be steward. Selma was elected.

The night Selma was elected I was really tired. I was sitting in the office waiting to go and Mamie came over and said, "I have a friend who is having a party. I'd like you to go to the party with me." I wasn't going to go to a party with white folks! She had to be kidding. I said, "I don't want to go." She said, "Why not?" I said, "I just don't go to parties with white folks. I've never been to one." She said, "But there's going to be colored people there too." I said, "This I have to see."

We went to the party and I enjoyed it. They were writing a letter to someone's husband who was in the Army. Everybody had to sign it. "Well, he won't know me," I said. So Mamie said, "Put down that you're Sylvia Woods and he doesn't know you but he's going to know you when he comes home."

Mamie had done these few things and I had begun to like her. She got in my good book. From then on she was instrumental in teaching me the need for unity between black and white, who was the enemy, because I thought the white people were our enemy —every white worker in America. And she taught me that that was not so. My attitude about black and white changed when I saw what Mamie was doing.

The next year when election time came up nobody ran against me but somebody ran against Mamie and I got more votes than she did. Then I began to see that if I could win an election and get more votes than Mamie with only twenty-five per cent blacks in there, if every single black person voted for me I still could not have won the election, no matter what. So all these white people had to vote for me. Now this is something. I began to think "Now why are they voting for me? Why?" And then, "They're voting for you because you're fighting for them."

We had one guy from Tennessee who went down south and over-stayed his vacation. He didn't send a telegram. He came back and the company fired him. We got his job back with back pay. Then after the union got him back in the shop, he didn't want Selma in this department. I was for going down there and throwing him out bodily and Mamie said, "Let's not do it like that." (We became a really good team. I would fly off, she would rub me down. When she would get mad, I'd say, "Just a second, Mamie . . .") Mamie said, "I'll write him a letter." She wrote him a letter and she said that the union spent half of whatever the arbitration cost was to get him back in the shop. . . . Well, that guy changed and he worked for Selma. He became one of the best union members in the shop. We threw a party one night and he came—this southerner who didn't want a black to do anything—he brought his wife and children. We used to call him Tennessee. I danced with him that night. It was really something.

We used to have a lot of absenteeism and we took the position that you can't fire anybody for being absent. We would tell them, "You don't have to tell any lies. You don't have to make up any excuses. If you're tired and you are absent, you just put down 'Tired.' " The foreman would say, "But you can't say . . ." "But, that's the only reason I was off. I was tired. I worked seven days straight for three months without a day off, so I am tired."

Every night I would have departmental meetings. The women were coming off the night shift at three o'clock in the morning. They didn't have to go home, so this was some recreation for them. We'd have beer and sandwiches and coffee and cake or whatever. We'd sit there and eat and talk. People would voice their grievances about the shop, home, family or whatever. They'd love to come. Every night we met, department by department. This kept us organized.

We had good union meetings too. We would have speakers. Either I would speak or Mamie would speak or we would invite a speaker to come in. We would talk about trade unionism. How were trade unions organized? What was the very beginning? How come they were organized? We would talk about the structure of the international union, how it was set up and how it worked and why it worked like it did, how the CIO was born. We would have a question period where the workers could ask questions. We would discuss current events.

We had social things too. We had a picnic and a big Christmas dance every year. We organized a horseback riding team.

We stayed there until the day the plant closed down. I'll never forget the day the plant closed down. Everybody came to work and there we didn't have any job. I wasn't so worried about my not having a job. I wondered, "What am I going to do without these people?" Everybody just stood around the gate.

Two years after the plant closed up, we still had union meetings.

We would have full crowds. We were fighting for [unemployment] compensation. We made ninety cents an hour and some, of course, made more. You would go to get your compensation and they'd offer you a job. You weren't supposed to take a job that was less than the rate you had been getting. We would fight these cases. They would throw them out and we would go down to the arbitration board and fight the cases and win them. We could call a union meeting and bring in maybe seventy-five per cent of our plant two years after it closed down. We had representation in the international because we still had the workers together.

The main thing that I would say is that you have to have faith in people. You know, I had very little faith in white people. I think that I had faith in black people. But you have to have faith in people, period. The whites, probably a lot of them feel towards blacks like I felt. But people, as a rule, come through.

You have to tell people things that they can see. Then they'll say, "Oh, I never thought of that," or "I have never seen it like that." I have seen it done. Like Tennessee. He hated black people. A poor sharecropper who only came up here to earn enough money to go back and buy the land he had been renting. After the plant closed he went back there with a different outlook on life. He danced with a black woman. He was elected steward and you just couldn't say anything to a black person. So, I have seen people change. This is the faith you've got to have in people.

The big job is teaching them. And I was not patient. That is another thing, you must be patient. I just didn't have any patience. If a worker did something, "To hell with you. You didn't come to the last union meeting, so don't tell me when you have a grievance. You just handle it the best way you can by yourself." But you can't do that. "You better go talk to Mamie Harris because I don't talk to non-union people and folks who don't come to the union meeting. Don't talk to me." This I learned was wrong. You have to be patient with people. People have to learn and they can't learn unless we give them a chance.

ᒐᒐ
ᒉᒉ
ᒐᒐ

MARIO MANZARDO

MARIO MANZARDO'S parents came from northern Italy. They brought with them to the United States a rich working-class culture. Among its heroes were the sixteenth-century philosopher Bruno, burned at the stake for affirming that the universe was infinite in extent, and Garibaldi, who led the nineteenth-century struggle for the unification of Italy. The family settled in the community of Pullman in South Chicago, Illinois, where the 1894 railroad strike led by Eugene Debs had originated.

In Pullman, Manzardo's father, together with his fellow-workers, friends and *paesani* (immigrants from the same region of Italy), continued to express joy and longing for social justice through cultural events of deep meaning to them personally and collectively. The meeting places of their fraternal societies often also served as headquarters for successive waves of working-class struggle. Christine Ellis, Stella Nowicki, and Nick Migas touch on the importance of this nationality group solidarity, but Mario Manzardo most fully describes the sense of roots, the atmosphere of trust, and the ready help which it provided.

Manzardo's account is also notable for its portrayal of the redbaiting in the union movement which followed World War II. He responded in a principled manner, yet without losing contact with the rank and file.

This account is drawn from three sources: two interviews we made with Mario Manzardo; an essay, based on similar interviews, by Gary Antlept; and an essay by Mario himself, entitled "For My Father—A Requiem."

MARIO MANZARDO

Liberi Cuori [Liberated Hearts]

I

I WENT TO WORK in 1927 for the Pullman Car Shops. My father and my brother worked at that plant. There I found out what it was to be a worker. Around 1880 the giant Pullman Car Works and the surrounding town had been built. The architecture was beautiful and the homes comfortable, but behind the facade of the buildings of Pullman the 12,000 people of the town were living in a paternalistic society created and controlled by George M. Pullman. He acted like a feudal baron. He selected his superintendents and foremen and also most of his workers from those ethnic groups which he considered the most desirable — primarily Anglo-Saxons.

When I worked in Pullman, there had been some changes. A few of the Polish, Greek and Italian workers had been made foremen, but one could still feel the aura of discrimination. The Pullman supervisors were still expert at weeding out the so-called malcontents.

It was the period when everybody was going for employees' representative plans [company unions]. They called it a union, but it wasn't. And I spoke up, without realizing that I was sticking my neck out: "Why don't we have a real union, from the outside, here?"

In this plant I realized what I had learned from my father, when I was a little kid. When I was young I didn't realize what was going on. But now it was beginning to catch up with me, and I had some talks with him. I began to realize that he had gone through many of these same things when I was just a youngster, four, five, six years old.

His father had been a Garibaldini. Grandfather was one of "the thousand" who had gone through all the campaigns of Garibaldi as a soldier. As an old man he'd sit in front of his door, in his chair, wearing his red Garibaldi shirt. He was senile, and he'd have tobacco juice and what-not on the shirt, but he wouldn't take his red shirt off—he was so proud of it. And he taught all his sons to be ardent fighters for freedom and equality in the spirit of Garibaldi, the great Italian emancipator. This was the tradition my father came from. I remember my grandfather in Italy, but I was only four years old.

My father worked in the paper mill in our town in Italy as a boy of twelve. He was a rag sorter. Later he worked with my uncles in his father's vineyards, and when *nonno* [grandfather] received a contract to haul the big heavy rolls of paper to Vicenza, Verona and Padova in the horse-drawn two-wheel carts of the period, my father then eighteen or nineteen became a regular driver.

A few years later he married. Mother, his childhood sweetheart, had also worked as a rag sorter at the age of eleven. Before leaving for America, my father was working at a small hydroelectric plant on the Astigo River. The pay was low. Times were bad. He dreamed of the New World and its promise.

In Chicago, Father worked in shops as a laborer, hauling material and sweeping floors; later, as a night watchman, and still later, an apprentice in a forge shop. Summers, often he would leave the shops and work "outside" in the building trades as a cement finisher. Sometimes he would leave home, joining a gang of Italian workers who spent a season or two working for contractors in Iowa or Minnesota paving the streets of an entire town. One time I went along as water boy. I will never forget the adventurous summer of 1920 in Pomeroy, Iowa: a boy and his father.

Eventually he settled down in the forge shop of the Pullman Car Works, a worker with three growing children, a mortgage on a Pullman house, a golden voice and a great love for opera.

Most of our *paesani* and friends were music lovers. They had formed amateur singing and dramatic groups, and performed in the local halls for over a quarter of a century. Often the proceeds of the singing and dramatic "festa" would go to labor causes: the Ettor and Giovannitti [leaders of the Lawrence, Massachusetts textile strike of 1912] defense; Sacco and Vanzetti; Tom Mooney, others.

Father sang baritone, a sweet, lusty voice. He could sing the entire role of Rigoletto and performed duets with his friend, Gildo Padovan, a tenor. They sang from the music of Puccini, Donizetti, Verdi. Also I recall the clamorous applause received for the operatic or popular arias the other singers rendered. Together they sang beautiful stirring Verdi choruses as well as melodic mountain tunes of the Veneto [in northern Italy]. How well I remember the glorious workers' songs they sang: the "Inno dei Lavatori" ["Workers' Hymn"] and other union and Socialist anthems, the old patriotic "Inno di Garibaldi," "Fratelli d'Italia." These, my father sang together with his *paesani* and friends.

But more often they would get together in a home—many times ours—on cold winter Saturday nights. There were songs, new and old; chestnuts roasting in the oven; the Zinfandel wine flowing; black bitter coffee laced with *grappa* [grape brandy] and often a surprise: *Spaghetti al olio e sardella* at midnight.

My father was part of a vocal and organized minority in the Pullman community. Even the priest had to respect them. In the pre-World War I days, and during and for a little while after the war, the local church used to have a church feast every spring. This included the carrying of the saint on the shoulders of the devoted ones in a parade through the town, with the priest in front, and with firecrackers, and with all the sinners following, some of them walking on their bare knees to do penance. And my father and his bunch used to scoff at this. They would stand in front of their hall and hold up a big portrait of Giordano Bruno as the parade went by. The priest's face would show annoyance and anger but he didn't dare say anything, because this was a significant section of the community. My father and his friends didn't mind certain things about the church but they were anti-clerical. I remember my father being invited to sing a requiem in the church. He accepted, but he didn't like that which was medieval and out of touch with reality.

It was a period of struggle and change. My father and most of his friends were workers and trade unionists: a few apolitical, some religious, some Socialists, some anarcho-syndicalists, and later, some Communists. They had witnessed much history together. On the issues growing out of this history, my father and his friends did not always agree. In fact, they often argued vehemently. Sometimes they were split into several groups, each supporting his favorite cause with time, energy, and money. However, there was always general agreement on support of labor struggles in the United States. On one question there was no disagreement: *Noi siamo antifascisti* ["We are anti-fascists"].

In the spring of 1936, on the first day of May, my father joined the Italian chorus on the stage of the Venetian Hall in Kensington. On this gala occasion they sang:

> *Vieni, o Maggio; t'aspettan le genti,*
> *Ti salutano i liberi cuori,*
> *Dolce pasqua dei lavatori. . . .*

> [Come, oh May Day; the people await you,
> The liberated hearts salute you,
> Sweet Easter of the working class. . . .]

This was the last time my father sang in public.

It happened at work in the shop just before the noon whistle. They carried him home on a litter. "Cerebrovascular hemorrhage," the doctor said. "Keep him quiet. Don't waste your money on a hospital. Nothing can be done." We propped him up in bed to make him comfortable. His mute mouth attempted a twisted smile.

We rolled the old victrola to the door of the bedroom. After winding the old spring motor I carefully placed the needle into the groove. The record was a favorite operatic aria. Tears welled up into his eyes. We turned off the disc fearing we had caused trauma. He moved his good arm up and down, beating against the mattress. His intelligent eyes became opaque as with anger. I placed the needle back in the groove and the music started again. His eyes cleared. His lips attempted to form the words he had sung numberless times. But no sound came out of his mouth.

II

During the early 1930s, I was part of the time in Wisconsin and part of the time in South Chicago. My parents had first sent me to Wisconsin during the summer when I was a boy, to improve my health. They sent me to a part of Marinette County where there were other Italians with whom my father had once thought of buying land.

The farmers set up roadblocks on highway G between Loomis and Marinette when there was delivery of milk to the condensery. The family I stayed with was not involved because they made cheese out of their own milk. But I would go along with the other farmers.

You had this kind of situation. When I went up there I had some stickers which said, "Save the Scottsboro Boys," and I put them around in different places. They condemned this. They didn't want anything to do with it, or with some of the other things that were going on in the cities. But when it came to their own struggles even the most conservative were militant. They would have their meetings in the Grange Hall, or one of the other halls. And they would discuss the problem of stabilizing or increasing the price of milk, because in some cases they weren't even making the price of the feed which they gave the cattle for the milk.

They formed a very loose organization, but when it came to setting up these roadblocks, they were there. They even brought guns. They were that serious. They had cars and trucks by the side of the road, and when a milk truck came by it was "Stop! Where are you going? What are you doing?" If the driver didn't turn right around and feed the milk to his hogs, it was dumped on the road. In a majority of cases they turned around.

This only lasted a few weeks, because the government began to respond. Traditionally most of the farmers had been followers of LaFollette but now they supported F.D.R. and the New Deal.

When I came back to Chicago I got involved in the unemployed struggles in South Chicago. All over the area are halls which had been the headquarters of many organizations, many struggles, which the unemployed now used. At 8743 Buffalo Avenue is Linnea Hall which Foster used as his headquarters for U. S. Steel South Works

during the 1919 steel strike. In the '30s it was in turn a headquarters
for the unemployed, and a headquarters for the Steel Workers
Organizing Committee until shortly after the Memorial Day Massacre. Right now it's a Baptist black church. Then there is the famous Turner Hall, where Debs spoke, where Carlo Tresca spoke,
where Elizabeth Gurley Flynn spoke, where a whole series of people
spoke up and down the history of the last hundred years of labor.
Right across the street from it used to be the headquarters of the
American Railway Union during the Pullman Strike of 1894. That's
gone now, torn down.

Then there's the sFBI hall: Societa Filarmonia Bel' Italia. They
sponsored a brass band. We had parades in Roseland in '32, '33,
'34, '35, '36, five years of parades on May Day, and they were
always led by this band. It's now reduced to a coffee club of a few
old-timers. But in its day it was a very important organization among
the North Italians and the headquarters of many other smaller organizations, mutual aid societies from each area of Italy. The Italians
were organized in the form of these societies, 200 to 300 persons,
50 to 60 families, which would give out a little money when they
were hospitalized, maybe a little money when they died. About half
a dozen of them met in the sFBI hall.

The largest of these modest organizations was the Liberty Club.
Later on, some of the members of this club formed the Matteotti
Society which was Socialist-dominated. However, the giant among
the mutual aid societies was the Venetian Union. In the 1920s they
built their own large hall. With 2000 member families it dominated
the area. They even rented space to a rival organization which had
national ties, the Order of the Sons of Italy in America. Both were
apolitical though some leaders were openly pro-fascist.

For a few years in the 1930s there was also formed the Centro
Operaio di Roseland (Worker's Center). This became the anti-fascist
headquarters, uniting workers under the influence of Socialists,
Communists, and anarcho-syndicalists.

Through their language organizations, the workers donated halls
for meetings of the unemployed. Some of the halls were even soup
kitchens. The one at 104th Street and Michigan Avenue, headquarters of several Lithuanian workers' cultural societies, became a soup

kitchen, where, through the administration of the language organizations and the unemployed councils, surplus food from the government was distributed to hundreds of people every day. Whole families would come over for their main meal of the day.

That's how we got to know people, including the people who later became the leaders of the Farm Equipment Union out that way, and the people who got on the staff of the Steel Workers Organizing Committee in that area. One fellow in particular was very active in the Public Works Administration. They were paving streets, a government project. He and others led a strike of the workers for better conditions and better pay. The strike was won. His name became quite famous. He was a left-wing radical. Later on he got on the staff of the swoc, and he was one of the fellows that got hold of me and put me on the staff, too.

III

There were about twenty or twenty-five locals of the Steelworkers Union in the Roseland-Harvey-Chicago Heights sub-district, just west of South Chicago, I helped organize during 1936, 1937, and part of 1938. There was the Pullman Manufacturing Company where I had worked in the 1920s. There was Acme Steel in Riverdale; Buda; Bliss and Laughlin; Brassco, and the stove works; Western-Austin and Perfection Gear; and some others I can't remember in Harvey. Also Calumet and Inland in the Heights; International Harvester's West Pullman Parts plant, Chicago Malleable Castings, Allied Castings; these are some of the shops and I could name a dozen or so more around Blue Island, Roseland, Pullman, and so on.

I remember those mornings in the spring of 1937. Three, four cars would start from the old headquarters on Michigan Avenue in Roseland. There would be about six organizers from the union and six volunteers. We broke open the bundles of *Steel Labor*, inserted the leaflets and retied them with twine, placed the bundles in the trunks of the cars and off we'd go to the plant gates to catch the day shift going in.

We'd park on 155th Street and after a short consultation among ourselves we'd go to the gates, two at the stove works, three at

Bliss, three at Western-Austin and four at Buda. We'd catch a few going out and the main shift going in. Most would smile and take the literature. A few would look angry or cuss and say, "Keep it, we don't need you," but most of the fellows were eager for it and would holler, "Good work, boys!" Volunteers never distributed in front of the shop where they worked. That way the company men could not report them. When all the literature was distributed, back to the cars and breakfast at the Swedish restaurant in Roseland.

We followed up the distribution of literature by meeting with key workers from inside the plant. Naturally the very first meetings were secret. Maybe only five or six people from a department met to discuss how to get the whole department to join the union. We would get together in homes, basements, in the back of taverns.

We designated certain key workers as officers of a new local. They then asked for, and signed, a charter. Then we began to coach them on how to conduct a meeting, how to keep track of their records, how to send in their reports, and so forth, just the servicing work of an organizer until they stood up on their own feet.

The local to which I later belonged was called Security Lodge of the Amalgamated Association of Iron, Steel and Tin Workers of North America. How do you like that for a name? I might explain that in the early days of the swoc we used the old Amalgamated Association's charters, also their recruiting cards and meeting manuals. In those days, the meetings had to be conducted according to the ritual in the manual. Everything was stiff and formal. The meetings were called to order by Jordan Perry, the first president. He wore a derby and often would forget to remove it. I got a big bang out of watching Jordan up there, flustered and embarrassed and stumbling over the words. One time, he put the manual down, glared at all of us in the room, turned to the sub-district leader and said, "To hell with this crap, this meeting's open."

With all our inexperience with unions, locals were organized, officers were elected, and dues were collected. The stewards did that job once a month and, by George, most fellows came across with their dollar. A few would give us trouble, but the great majority saw the benefits the union brought into the shop with their own eyes.

Where the locals had people who had been apolitical in the past or who were interested strictly in what was going on in the shop, their activities were restricted to that. But in some cases locals had within them people from the various language organizations that had been influenced by radicals. They would sing labor songs. One of them wanted the union to learn how to sing "The Internationale." We had to tell them, "Look, let's keep that out of here." But they sang "Solidarity Forever," "Hold the Fort," and a lot of other union songs.

Local leadership was coming forward. A few of us attempted to get hold of some of these leaders and give them an idea that what we were trying to do was not just build the union, but build a movement of the people—a movement that affected all aspects of their lives, and also their whole outlook, their philosophical outlook. In short, we tried to radicalize some of these people, to a greater degree than union life had radicalized them.

In this we weren't too successful. We had a few successes. Some of them remained honest, sincere workers who knew what the score was for the balance of their lives. But some of them would not go along with this kind of thinking and would go back to their narrow, trade union, bread-and-butter type thinking, and looked upon trade unions as a stepping stone to personal success. Our main concern was to make radicalism, or progressivism, or whatever you want to call it, a way of life for these union people.

We would have, let's say, a half a dozen of these people together in a circle. On a couple of occasions I thought that the people who helped me organize these things would back me up, but they didn't, they backed down, which left me holding the bag as the alleged theoretician of the outfit, which I really wasn't.

I think one mistake we made was in trying to disillusion them with existing status quo politics, at the same time not pointing out clearly the steps that you could take from status quo politics into a more progressive kind of politics. Instead we said, "You've got to jump from one to the other," and people didn't know how to make that jump. You've got to have highways, you've got to have bridges, from one point of view to another point of view. The bridges have to be well laid out, so that people can walk over them calmly, without too much emotional strain, without feeling that they are getting into something where the Un-American Committee would be after them and the FBI would start chasing them. "Yes, at a certain point there is a chance that, if you become a well-known leader, some of the monitor groups may try to see what they can do. But don't be frightened. This happens all over." We could have talked to them this way. But somehow we didn't do it right. I think that if we had it to do over again, we could find better ways.

I was laid off by the Steelworkers Union after the Little Steel strike. During the next few years I had many jobs. For instance, a young man got me into a book bindery, on 13th and Michigan Avenue. They were all kids in there, young men and women. We learned how to bind books with the bone, and the glued paper. I ran the paper through the glue machine, let it lay there until it hardened and got tacky, and they used it to cover the boards of the books.

They were ripe for a union so we contacted a union in Chicago, the United Paperworkers Union. I got into a little trouble with those union fellows. Right away they wanted dues. I said, "First let's organize, then we'll talk about dues." So we got in cards and about five of us organized the place in two weeks time. At the end of the two weeks I was fired. They made a Labor Board case out of it and I won the case. I got something like $350 back pay, and the right to go back to work in the plant. I had already gotten a job so I didn't go back. But the Paperworkers Union sent me a bill, for dues! I was still paying dues to the Steelworkers. So I wrote to them very scathingly and said, "How about organizing pay?"

Then I had some experiences in organizing Campbell Soup for the Cannery Workers. There were a lot of women working there. They had a lot of wildcats before the plant was even organized. I was in charge of getting out their bulletin. And I remember one particular issue where I made a big article on "Sweat-Sweetened Soup." When they opened up the big pots they made the soup in, the workers were so hot the sweat would go from their brows into the soup. And the workers told us that when the tomatoes would go through the belt line, they couldn't clean out all the bad tomatoes: they could only do it now and then. As a result, many worms, and bugs, and even mice got into the soup. So Campbell's Soup was not the pure soup that you read about. Shades of *The Jungle*!

In 1940 I went back to work at the Buda plant. This was a Steelworkers local which I had helped organize back in 1937. I remained there until I got out on pension in 1970. I was financial secretary of my local, I was recording secretary, I was on the grievance committee, and often on the negotiating committee. I was among the leaders of that local since its inception, as an organizer, then servicing it and later as a worker in the shop. In those thirty years I've seen executive committees come and executive committees go.

During the war, I was a delegate to the state CIO convention. It was 1943 and I was elected to the state executive board. They wanted two people from steel. Four people were nominated; I was one of them and I accepted. Somehow the forces representing the district leadership got confused and I won. The district leadership was mad as hell. I only served on that board about four months and then was drafted into the Army where I remained for two and a half years. What happened right after the war was already laid down in the minds of some of the people at that time.

After the war, against the advice of my family I went back to the plant. I had the opportunity to do other things: go back to school on the G.I. bill; or go into business with some wealthy relatives. With my eyes wide open I chose the role of a worker in the plant and playing there a part in the local union.

We had a progressive local. At that time we formed a council of Steelworkers locals in Harvey, but they would allow only one council for a county so the Chicago council took over. We had a strong womens' auxiliary, which played a strong role in the strikes of 1946 and thereafter, and there were also women in the plant. It was a local that would send delegates to many things that other locals wouldn't. For example, I went a couple of times as a delegate to get-togethers of the National Negro Congress, which was a forerunner to many of the present organizations.

Of course, later we ran into trouble. I ran into personal trouble, too, where I was brought up on charges for being too far out in left field. The staff man assigned to my local—it was the same man who had led the sewer workers' strike and recruited me for the SWOC—put me on trial for running for office in the local when the constitution of the Steelworkers Union says that no Communist, fascist, or what not, can be an officer in this union. He said, "You can't be." I said, "Why?" He said, "You were in the YCL [Young Communist League]." I said, "But you were a well-known member of the CP." "Yeah," he said, "but I am no longer." "Well," I said, "you want to know if I'm still in the YCL? I'll tell you. I'm too old." Anyway, he put me up on charges and we had a trial. The executive board supported me. In fact, I became financial secretary of the local.

But aside from the question of our political outlooks lay the deeper question of what was going on in America. My father's generation had gone through some rough times, especially during the Sacco-Vanzetti days and the Palmer raids when immigrants who subscribed to socialist or other radical papers or who voiced anti-capitalist opinions were hounded; some were deported.

In my generation we often faced red-baiting, but the creation of second-class citizenship for radicals within the unions and the signing of non-Communist affidavits were no ordinary "contratempo," as the Italians would say—not ordinary bad times, but a time for clear thinking.

As I saw it, unionists should reject the whole idea of two types of membership, one from which leadership would be chosen and one that could only pay dues. Also, the charge that radicals were working against the interest of the unions had to be rejected. When John L. Lewis formed the SWOC he hired the men and women necessary to do the job regardless of their political background. All made many contributions, some of them at great personal sacrifice. The Communists were among the most dedicated. As I saw it, neither the Congress of the United States, nor the union leadership through a steamroller at a convention, had the moral right to pry into the political philosophy of workers.

This is an inalienable right which my friend, the organizer, couldn't see. He figured he had cleansed himself by washing his linen in public. Cleansed himself of what?

It seemed to me further that union leadership should be judged on the basis of work done to promote the welfare of the union membership, and not on the basis of an individual's politics.

I remember how within three, four weeks the atmosphere changed. A delegation of CIO leaders led by James Carey came back from a trip to the Soviet Union for the CIO, and put out a report. They didn't say it was a workers' paradise but presented it as a country that was doing something for the people. They had some good words to say about the unions there. We distributed the report in our local union meetings. And then, about a month later, we had a banquet and Van Bittner from the Steelworkers Union got up and attacked the Soviet Union and every one gave him a big hand. The climate changed overnight. This was in 1948, when [Henry] Wallace ran for president.

Then came the Taft-Hartley Act. It required that the officers of trade unions, including local trade unions, sign non-Communist affidavits. I was an officer of my local, and had been active in the Wallace campaign. I felt that none of us should sign and I got some of the other officers to go along with the idea. But they changed their minds later. Only the top officers were required to sign: if it had extended to grievance men and stewards, there were plenty that would not have signed, and would have gone along with me. The district laid down the law that it had to have the signatures of the three or four top officers. "We're waiting for them," they said. "We've got to have them. Send them in." And I was delaying it.

Finally, I said I wasn't going to sign. It was just stubbornness. I made a statement to the executive board of the local, which passed it on to the membership, that I wouldn't sign a Taft-Hartley affidavit because it was impinging on my freedom of association, my freedom of thought, that I would be tying myself down because I think certain ways and I would have to sign that I wouldn't think those ways, and I can't control my thoughts. Thought control I wouldn't go for, and that's why I wouldn't sign. I said, "I have nothing against those who will sign, because they're doing it for the practical purpose of maintaining a consistent leadership in the local union." I said, "I feel that leadership is a good leadership, and at this point, if I have to sign something against my conscience to remain in this leadership, I'd rather not remain in the leadership and play a role lower down in the organization." They accepted that.

I assumed the leadership at the lower level where I didn't have to sign. The officers invited me to all executive board meetings, and I played a role among the stewards. Later on the Taft-Hartley

affidavits became unimportant and were no longer enforced, and I
ran for office and became part of the executive board again until
I retired.

IV

The leadership of the unions today is not the same type of leadership
as in the 1930s. In fact the union turned out to be the training ground
for some of the supervisors and some of the superintendents and
some of the foremen and even some of the engineering people. They
first worked, and they became stewards and grievance men, and then
later on went on to jobs with the companies. Many times the companies will take aside the strong members of the union and say,
"Look, we've been watching your progress and we think if you keep
it up you'll make foreman or superintendent within a year." Now,
this offer of personal advancement many times can affect how hard
this union member will, let's say, push a grievance. After all, the
company may not give him this job if he fights too hard. Many
times the company will do this to weaken the union.

You come across workers who will say, "You know, we ought
to eliminate the dues check-off because dues check-off puts the burden of collecting dues on the company, and the steward doesn't go
around and talk to the people and find out their gripes."

My answer to that is, you should have stewards at a departmental
level always available to the workers. In the plant where I worked
we never had more than twenty-five or fifty workers without a steward. Each shift had a steward for each particular line or group of
workers. When you had 1500 workers and you had thirty or forty
stewards you had enough to take care of the situation. So that a
worker couldn't say, "I can't see a steward for days at a time."
You could see him.

And we had a separate steward body that ran independent of the
officers. They used to call their own meetings at their own time.
We requested grievance committeemen to volunteer to attend the
meetings of the stewards, not to dominate, just to listen and to
answer questions whenever called upon. But the chief steward and
assistant chief steward ran their own meetings. They would meet
once a month or sometimes more if necessary and they would order

their own refreshments and sometimes even have their own little stag party.

Capitalism has a way of influencing people and buying them out, whether they're bought out with cash or prestige. There is an English movie, "Fame is the Spur." It's the story of an English labor leader [Ramsey Macdonald] who was an honest labor leader until he started rubbing shoulders with the elite in the country, and he ends up being given a lordship and having sold out workers all the way down the line. He became isolated, his wife left him and his children hated him, his friends he had no more. What did he have but a peership and the love and admiration of the lords of the clubs? He didn't have anything else, his life was empty. And he became aware of it. In the end he realized what caused it. Most of them don't.

Take David J. McDonald, the second international president of the Steelworkers Union. He was an assistant to the first president, Philip Murray. Murray was quite an honest guy, a good leader. Unfortunately, near the end of his life he fell for the red-baiting business, too. That was the way of the times and he went for it. Well, David J. McDonald took over and the first thing you know McDonald started developing what we called "tuxedo diplomacy": rubbing shoulders with the big corporation owners, visiting in steel mills together with the president of U. S. Steel. They voted him out of office. Everybody did.

But David J. McDonald went on to write an autobiography that was out of this world. He claimed everything in the first person: "I did this, and I did that, and I did the other." He didn't do any of these things. It was all done by other people, mostly local leaders, rank and filers, radicals among them. He didn't single-handedly organize. This is history twisted around, history which is written from the viewpoint of: "I walked into the room and I looked at these corporation heads and I had anger in my eye and they saw it. And they then knuckled down and signed this contract. I went out of that room and I went to the workers and I announced, 'They signed. They gave in.' " Is this history? He went in and terrorized them and they gave in and signed. That's not history, that's egotism. History is where you show that workers through their militancy, their

picket lines or their demands or their continuous agitation, forced
an issue.

I was just a guy at the level of the local union or at the level
of a staff organizer, and briefly on the state CIO council. But I think
it was guys in the position of myself, hundreds of thousands of guys
in the position of myself, who helped establish these unions. For
that I take a little credit, but only to the extent I was able to, not
any more than that. I don't want to exaggerate my role or that of
any of the people I worked with.

BURR McCLOSKEY

BURR McCLOSKEY came to the conclusion that workplace organizing around economic issues could not in itself produce a political movement for comprehensive change. In 1946 he joined with John C. Green, an elderly agitator who had been a delegate to the founding convention of the IWW, to form the United Labor Party.

The United Labor Party was based in Akron, Ohio, where the first sit-down strike took place in the rubber plants in 1936. The party ran working people for City Council and Congress on a platform which opposed racism and the Korean War, and called for nationalization of basic industry. At its height it received about 10,000 votes in Akron. It had branches in several other communities, and had given a certain impulse to a national movement for libertarian socialism, before it died in the early 1950s.

The ULP is described by John Barbero, Ed Mann and others (pages 265–284. John Barbero and Ed Mann were members of the ULP). The present account describes Burr McCloskey's personal development.

There is a good deal of kinship between the approach to action of Burr McCloskey and his friends, and that of the New Left of the 1960s. The ultimate value was not to be pushed around: to take shit from no man, as Burr McCloskey puts it, or in the language of sds, to participate in the decisions that affect one's life. Central both for McCloskey and the New Left, as for the iww before them, was the notion that the best way to communicate an idea is to act it out.

I Appeal the Ruling of the Chair

SOMETHING MAKES A RADICAL, in every time and place. You can't be for any kind of a program different from the prevailing main stream unless you have the capability to resist the status quo. You don't have the right to a dissenting point of view unless you're prepared to fight for it. That was the main thing in our militant history. I think it's mostly a matter of chemistry, but the chemistry, of course, is stimulated by specific events.

I learned how to fight as a wee boy because my name is Burr, and my father's name was Burr. The popular cant is that Aaron Burr was a traitor, and my lovely chums in grammar schools across the country used the cant to malicious advantage. I had to fight because I knew better. In my family the saying around the Sunday dinner table was that the only mistake Burr made in killing Hamilton was that he should have done it twenty years sooner. I still believe this. There was a national debt, an Eastern establishment: it all goes back to Hamilton. He was a pimp for Washington at Valley Forge. He should have been killed twenty years sooner. American history is so distorted that it still isn't nice to say this in polite society.

Akron, Ohio is a very important part of the story. It represents one of the mythologies of America, the melting pot. Nothing ever melts, you see. Because of its hillbilly tradition, Akron had the strongest, most militant, unadulterated strain of Protestant Anglo-Saxon whites in a very, very difficult industry. I've worked in rubber and I've worked in steel, I've worked in the Teamsters and I've worked with District 50 of the Mine Workers, and nothing touches the rubber shops in those days for what we used to call "rawhide" labor.

I grew up with an uncle who was treasurer of the Goodyear Tire and Rubber Company until it was reorganized, and the banks took over, about 1924, and I resolved never to go into the gum mines. When I ran into the (what I considered) middle-class radicals in the early '30s, who almost idolized the working man and whose goal was to get into industry and become proletarianized, I said, "Bullshit!" I couldn't stand the smell of soapstone. I vowed when I was eleven years old that I'd never go into a rubber shop. Never wanted to. Never saw any great distinction in it. But I did. The current of the times pulled me in, just as it was going to pull me into the infantry later on.

I went into Goodyear. As I say, my uncle had been treasurer of Goodyear. My uncles, my father, my mother, my sister, all worked at Goodyear. So I ended up at Goodyear.

But my feeling toward Goodyear was not the same feeling that the hillbilly kids had, coming in from out of town and standing in line to get a job, making a dollar an hour for the first time in their lives. I was full of contempt for it from the very beginning. I knew, for example, that my mother never could keep a clean table because Goodyear was burning its filth and blowing it out its smokestacks right into our kitchen. I can't get excited about the newfound discovery of pollution because I grew up in it, and I knew who did it, and I knew why they did it, and I knew what it was doing to me, and my mother, and our food.

Goodyear, like all basic industry in the '30s, was waiting to be blasted out of medieval baronialism and my particular "sense of awareness" gave me a different point of view, for better or worse. Have you ever heard of the College of Complexes here in Chicago? I used to make it a practice to debate there once a year. And on one occasion my topic was "The Day American Labor Died." My oversimplified thesis was that American labor died the day the check-off went in, that once we lost the voluntary principle we were screwed like a Christmas goose. No way out. Unionism became an adjunct of the company, lock, stock and barrel, once the automatic check-off went into effect. During the session, the priest with whom I was debating, who had been working with the Chicano fruit pickers out West and was very much enamored of the class struggle as he was engaged in it, stopped in perplexity and said, "I have never met any one who was as disaffected as you are." Well, my alienation has always been the same since I was a small boy.

The thing I believed in, and the reason I've been in the anti-Communist Party faction from the time I drew a political breath, was the old American "Don't tread on me" tradition. My Uncle Charley was an alcoholic follower of Gene Debs in Canton, Ohio. He rode the Red Special [the train Debs used in campaigning for president of the United States]; he had the greatest socialist library in Canton, which was a Socialist town. He was a reporter there when Debs made his famous speech which led to his imprisonment for opposing World War I. And Uncle Charley was always a hero of mine. The big thing about Uncle Charley, and about Debs, and about that whole tradition, was that you took shit from no man. And when the monolithic political movements came along, and you had to take a party name, and you spoke only when the chair recognized you, and you had to follow the party line, and you had to worship the shibboleths that they pre-fabbed for you, I was again alienated. There was no place for me in such a movement. It didn't matter to me whether it was Goodyear telling me how to vote or the break-off faction of the CP telling me how to vote.

My grandfather had run for councilman during the big Socialist upsurge of, I think, 1916. He ran as a Democrat and was defeated by a Socialist. And he was the kind of man that when the Ku Klux Klan marched down East Market Street, and we stood there watching it, all of them with their sheets on and the burning cross, he'd say, "Look at the shoes." I said, "What about the shoes, Granddaddy?" He said, "They're riffraff. You can tell by their shoes." So I was alienated even from that kind of proposition.

My father, who was crippled and alcoholic, wouldn't go on WPA. He was too proud to go on WPA. He didn't believe in taking help. He had been a salesman; he sold tires. He was a good salesman but he was pushed into the sales mold because he had a club foot. Alcoholics Anonymous started in Akron, and my father was one of the early recruits—prominent in AA until he died. He always regarded the Depression as his own personal fault, and refused to lump himself into an abstract statistic. We fought industrial fingerprinting at the beginning of the War for exactly the same reason.

My rebellion, if you want to call it that, began against the schools. I believe in nine-tenths of what Ivan Ilyich says about deschooling society. It's a horribly manipulative institution. And I led two school strikes before I was fifteen. I could do it because I was in a position of leadership, editor of the school newspaper, and so on. I confess that we used the fire alarm bell to get everybody out. We figured that once we got them out, we could keep them out. I was expelled. In fact, I was expelled several times. I wrote an editorial on syphilis, because a young freshman girl in our school developed syphilis when she bought an apple from an old vet in front of the school who was spitting on his apples to make them shine. I devoted the school paper to the signs and symptoms of syphilis, opening the door to sex education, and demanding that it be established as part of the regular curriculum. They wouldn't publish the paper. So I went down to the print shop—it was a contract shop, not a school print shop—and got the paper out, and bootlegged it.

One of the demands in our high school student union was, "Ask your teacher for his union card." I was a delegate to the Central Trades and Labor Assembly, representing a student union.

I joined the Young Peoples Socialist League. As a result, Akron was to have the largest YPSL group between New York and Chicago. I was recruited by a school teacher, Chalmers Stewart. He was one of three—another was B. J. Widick, who wrote the Reuther book and is a kind of mouthpiece for the UAW—who were very active in educating the first group of Akron labor leaders, when the CIO was first formed. They were the young intellectuals who went in and gave them classes on the labor theory of value, and the class struggle as the locomotive of history and so on. Along with Cannon and Shachtman they helped to set up the Socialist Workers Party in 1938. They were the so-called adult group in the Midwest. They got me, and I got the rest. Our membership was very bright, very brave. They came from a variety of family backgrounds—hillbilly, foremen's children, Jewish—the whole spectrum. High school, university, and dropouts, too.

I got the rest on the basis of militant activism, because we were going to do things. For instance, we agreed with the IWW in its free speech fights that the way to fight for free speech was not to talk about it but to do it. We did things in our own smart-assed way. The American Legion was sponsoring the head of the Un-American Activities Committee in Akron. We wanted to picket against it. The police refused us a permit. They said, "Look, the American Legion will crack your skulls, and after they get through the Akron cops will crack your skulls." We said, "Do we have a right?" They said, "Yes, you've got a right, but we're not going to give you a permit." So we said, "All right, we'll picket." We got our heads broken a little bit.

I was a senior in high school when the sit-down strike of 1936 happened. It was winter, Akron's coldest winter up to that time. They had shanties set up along the "longest picket line in the world," built out of waste wood. They each had a name: "Mae West," or "Orphan Annie," or "Toonerville Trolley." We used to sit in the huts and drink Dago Red and coffee with the guys on strike. And they held a mass meeting in Central High School auditorium. This was in my high school. And I'll tell you, watching them pour into that auditorium was like watching the storming of the Winter Palace. We had a lot of physical evidence to make us accept the doctrine of the class struggle. The only catch was that we wanted it to be *our* class struggle, not the property of a commissar.

And when they came down the street for a collection for the striking rubber workers, they went to the pool rooms, they went to the butcher shop, they went to my grandfather's store, and they went to the whorehouse. Everybody chipped in. Everybody knew, "These are our boys. If they don't make it, we don't make it." The idea of community solidarity was pretty well impressed on me at that time. In those days, when somebody carried the title of "committeeman" it had all the weight, in our neighborhood, of "councilman" or "alderman" today.

The big riot, where we took the bad licking, occurred in 1938. It happened on a Sunday at the Rialto Theater which was right across from Goodyear's one entrance. My father, my mother, my sister, and I were driving in from the country and when we got to the stop light we saw all these women running, with their heads flopping, because they'd all been billy-clubbed. My father and I got out of the car. We both were teargassed that night, badly. The battle was waged all night. Three were killed and hospital arrests numbered something like seven hundred. I did a couple of things that night that I'm quietly proud of. When we found out that fire engines were being used to bring in more tear gas and ammunition, we set up a barricade and stopped the fire engines. All through that night, my father said it, I said it, and I could hear all these rubber workers saying it: "This can't happen in America."

At that time there were men marching and drilling in basements all over Akron. We believed there would be armed civil war. You made no long-term plans. You never worried about family, you never worried about retirement. There was no point in thinking about college.

We didn't even worry about war. We knew the war was coming. From the time that the gunboat, the *Panay*, was sunk on the Yangtze River in 1937, we were saturated with a sense of inevitability about the second World War. There was no way to do anything but make a hopeless, desperate protest against it, because you knew it was a juggernaut that could not be stopped. We felt—I'm speaking for my peer group—that it was important to be your own man, to believe what you believed and speak out when you felt like speaking out; that in this terrible, suffocating cul-de-sac it was important to find something meaningful to do, that you planted your own garden even if the bombs were coming.

I decided to go into the rubber shops but I had a hard time getting in, because I was pretty well known. Since we believed in "open struggle," not conspiracy, we always had a good press in Akron and my file was voluminous. I got into the tire department at Goodyear by a fluke. Our whole fight then was to hold the meager advances that had been made. The six-hour day, for example—this became our major battle, lasting right into World War II. They put us on an eight-hour day without consulting us. We went in at the beginning of the shift and left two hours early. The next shift came in two hours late, so that there was a four-hour gap when the factory was open and nothing happened. Then they locked us out. So we set up our picket lines: "When one is locked out, everybody's out until everybody's in." In the papers we were Hitler's agents.

Along with trying to hold on to the six-hour day and these auxiliary privileges, I had another problem because they came around and wanted to solicit for war bonds. They got the union to be their collection agents. And I said, "I don't buy war bonds." They said, "We're going to have one hundred per cent." I said, "Well, you can lie about it but you're not going to have one hundred per cent." All my friends took the same position. "Are you a Jehovah's Witness?" they asked. "No," I answered, "I just don't believe the government's going to last." It was more than ironic when my own union brothers formed a "gate party," using goon squad techniques to try to force me into buying war bonds. They failed.

Finally Goodyear refused to let me work. They insisted that the union put me on trial, under the clause of the contract that read that the union will not open its membership to any "Nazis, Communists or others." I was an "other." I had to stand trial. The executive committee tried me without permitting me to appear in my own defense, and found me guilty. So I had to get the tire room out to the mass meeting which would ratify or overturn the executive committee's ruling. And they did overturn it. But by this time, because the executive committee had expelled me from the union, the company shut me out. And that night the draft board called me and said, "We understand you're not working." I said, "That's a contentious point. The company says I'm not, but I say I am. If you take one side or the other you're interfering in a labor dispute." That held them up for about four months. But the union bureaucracy failed to follow the membership mandate and refused to negotiate sincerely for my re-employment. So I was "out for real," and shipped for cannon fodder without as much as an Army induction physical. On a small scale, it reminded me of what happened earlier to a good buddy of mine, Clark Culver.

Culver was Canadian-born, a strong, laconic man. He had a massive forehead, inset eyes, and a muscle-clamping jawbone. He was a tire builder.

He was building passenger tires when Roosevelt's Section 7(a) came along. There wasn't anything like a union at Goodyear at the time except the company union, the Goodyear Assembly. Culver happened to know Stanley Denlinger, an Akron criminal lawyer who later went on John L. Lewis' staff. They got together and Culver said, "Stan, tell me what this 7(a) means." Denlinger studied it a day or two and then he said, "You can organize, the government *wants* you to organize." So Culver rented a basement hall on Goodyear Boulevard in East Akron and put out a call. Something like a hundred tire builders showed up. Denlinger was there to tell them what he had told Culver. They signed up.

The union kept multiplying, until finally they held a mass meeting and elected Sherman Dalrymple as president, and Clark Culver as secretary. In those days the secretary ran everything. The secretary took their dues, had their names. The president just opened the meetings. Culver quit the plant because it was a full-time job. He was the first full-time officer in the Akron rubber union. He gave up ten years' seniority because the boys voted him to take a full-time job with the new union.

After a few months the rubber workers felt ready for their own international union. A meeting was called in Indianapolis to consider getting out of the AFL. Culver was the delegate from the Goodyear local. The local paid its per capita tax direct to William Green and he loved all that dues money coming in from thousands of rubber workers, so he said, "No, you can't have your own international." The meeting in Indianapolis was supposed to be secret but all the wire services were there, and when Culver got back to Akron the shit had hit the fan.

Green sent a hatchet man named Coleman Claherty into Akron. A mass meeting was called in the very hall where Culver had set up the union and Culver was expelled for having been a delegate to Indianapolis. The same men who had stomped and hollered when they made him full-time secretary packed the hall to hear Green's motion to expel him. Claherty said, "Clark Culver is as far out of the American Federation of Labor as a Chinaman walking the streets of Hong Kong." Culver waited for his chance to speak. He'd stayed up all night planning his speech in self-defense. His wife, who had been to high school, helped him. But they ruled he couldn't say a word. A vote was taken with none dissenting, and he was out. After the meeting the guys were still coming up to Culver to pay their dues. They didn't know what had happened.

Because he was expelled he was out of work. He sold insurance for a while, and he didn't get back until the latter part of 1937. Because he was a new man, and had no seniority, he worked the night shift. His second night back on the job he heard that there was a big strike at the city waterworks. A CIO committeeman came down the line and said to him, "All union men at the waterworks first thing in the morning." The committeeman didn't know him from Adam. He was saying the same thing to everyone.

Culver hadn't been signed up yet in the CIO but he thought, "Well hell, I'm a union man, card or no card." So he drove up to the waterworks. It was still dark, but he could see a mass of men already there. A voice yelled, "CIO?" Culver yelled, "Yeah." They broke his nose, four of his ribs, shattered his collarbone, gave him a rupture and concussion of the brain. Only two CIO men had showed up, Culver and a man from National Rubber. The rest were all sheriff's deputies.

They took the two men down to the station and Culver demanded medical treatment. They said, "Sure." So two cops ran him up and down the three-story stairs of the city jail until he blacked out.

Then they brought down Denlinger, the same lawyer Culver had gone to about Section 7(a). The lawyer sprung the other guy, and then he said, "Clark, I can't touch you because you're not a member of the union."

He was one of my best friends in the Rubber Workers. I kept nominating him for president and he kept declining. He kept pushing me for president and I kept declining. Neither one of us would take the top job, or even run for it. When Clark and I went to union meetings we'd sit alone, because every man who had been in the union in the early days and knew what had happened to Clark, just didn't know what to do about it. He's not in labor's history books as a hero of any kind. He's just one of the anonymous guys who got every bone in his body broken. And his own men wouldn't help him. Clark died a premature death, the delayed effect of the awful beating he took at the waterworks.*

There was not the maturity in the CIO for any ideological organization, that I can see. Industry was so highly organized, and the humankind involved were so not-ready-to-be-organized, yet we were forced into it. Union meetings were absurd. I can't tell you how many times I've appealed the ruling of the chair. Some stumpjumper would be up there shaking a gavel like every bureaucrat that'd ever preceded him, and people would be saying, "Isn't this a lovely meeting?" And I'd say, "I appeal the ruling of the chair." This wasn't always a safe thing to do. On one occasion the president came roaring down the aisle to attack me with the presidential gavel.

The real militants like Clark Culver ended up on the grievance committee. They were the job stewards, shop committeemen. The few, such as C. V. Wheeler or Ike Watson, who became local union presidents, were eventually torn apart by the tensions of an administration it was impossible to administer. With their help, however, we tried a good many thrusts to keep the union structure democratic. For example, we advanced the concept of rotation of officers: that you couldn't be out of the shop for more than eighteen months, because you'd forget what it was like unless you went back in. It failed utterly. The rank and file said, "What the hell! We train a man to be president, he might as well stay there. Why bring him back?"

To give you another example of the things we fought for, there

---

*Clark Culver is in labor history books but what they say about him is so incomplete that it is actually misleading. Harold S. Roberts (*The Rubber Workers*, pages 108–109) and Irving Bernstein (*Turbulent Years*, page 102) tell the story of Culver's expulsion, and then state that William Green restored him to full membership privileges in his local. This statement leaves out the fact that "Culver was accepted into the union and promptly suspended again by the executive committee." (Federated Press dispatch, Feb. 15, 1934, Special Collections, Columbia University.) The statement also fails to consider that Culver had given up his job at Goodyear in order to work full-time for the union. Even had he been restored to membership in the union, unless he had also been restored to his position as secretary of the local he would have been out of work. As it was, having lost his seniority he was not called back to work (says McCloskey) until late in 1937.

was no smoking in the shop. I worked in the fifth floor tire room, and you had to go all the way down the stairs and walk about two city blocks to a railroad siding, where you could smoke. And we were all on piecework. The only way you could afford time for a smoke was if you had rates good enough to allow you to take the time off. You had to pay for your own sins. They sent around chow wagons, packaged foods. We never touched them. We'd shut our machines down, wash our hands and faces, go out of the plant and across the street and have a meal like a human being. We were allowed twenty minutes, but we took fifty and paid for it.

It was at that primitive level. You could talk to them about a lunch wagon, but on the political end of things, the sociological end of things, there was no dialogue. The night of Pearl Harbor, Sunday, December 7th, I was so goddamned mad that I said, "Remember the Maine." And my boys turned on me and almost killed me. When big guys like that get mad at you, you're in trouble.

I'd argue economics. I'd say, "I'm building the goddamned tire and the salesman that sells it will never see it and he's going to make more than I do. Something wrong with the set up, that's all." They'd say, "You're making enough, you're making more money than the guy down on the other end." I could never get it beyond that level. Later, we'd bring scores of the best men down to the United Labor Party hall for a beer party, and we'd have a hell of a beer party. But the ratio was about one to a hundred in making a ULP-er out of them.

From this experience, I came to the conclusion that the Trotskyists were wrong in thinking that everything was going to be solved by economic organization. I and my confederates said, "No, it's going to be solved politically." We hoped for a populist organization with a labor-anchored base. That was our theoretical platform. But it takes independent politics. You can't do it by a Political Action Committee. We pushed and pushed within our local unions for independent political action. Finally we decided it was like the free speech fights: there's no use talking about it, do it!

After the war I went back in the plant, at Firestone Steel. At the same time that we set up a credit union we demanded a sliding scale of wages and hours: as the available hours of work were reduced, the work force should be divided into those hours. We regarded this as a transitional demand. But Jesus, this threw you in the face of seniority. Our battle cry was "Solidarity Versus Seniority!" They said, "You youngsters don't have obligations. We gotta work more hours." We said, "Piss on you, we got the credit union for you. If you can't pay it back, we'll pay it back." But it didn't work. It was too divisive, too stratified, but we tried it.

I always knew in a fight—a picket line, or a union meeting, or a political faction struggle—whether somebody was on my side or not. You learn to recognize the cohorts who will be there when the chips are down. The chips were down about all the time. I'm proud to say that my closest friends today are men and women who were with me in these struggle situations thirty-five years ago.

They always said that anybody from the radical movement in Akron had a certain look around their eyes. We were mavericks in the radical labor movement. We were intellectualized activists. We fought every battle there was to fight. Student fights. Unemployed fights. Anti-ROTC fights. Anti-conscription fights. Anti-Legion fights. Anti-management fights. Anti-Union-boss fights. Anti-CP fights. Anti-Jim Crow fights. You name it. We were there.

NICK MIGAS

IN HIS AUTOBIOGRAPHY *Union Man*, David J. McDonald (then secretary-treasurer and later president of the United Steelworkers of America) gives the following account of the climactic incident at the 1948 Steelworkers convention:

> That convention was kept in an uproar most of the time by a handful of left-wing radicals who were angry with Murray for deserting Henry Wallace. They badgered Murray constantly from the floor until some of the Murray supporters finally took matters into their own hands. A delegate named Nick Migas made a vicious attack on the union leadership, and as his language became steadily more violent, a group of angry members formed spontaneously on the floor and began to move menacingly toward Migas. Several ushers got there first and removed Migas for his own protection. In the scuffle, a .32-caliber revolver fell to the floor. Migas was escorted to the door and turned loose on the street. The next morning I read in the newspapers that he had been beaten up a few blocks from the convention hall. Feelings were running high among the steelworkers.

This is the view from the rostrum. The following account presents the view from the floor mike. It includes the text of the leaflet which Nick Migas and his supporters circulated during the luncheon recess after Murray had refused to recognize Migas during the morning session. Circulation of the leaflet obliged Murray to recognize Migas when the afternoon session began, although Migas was continually interrupted and unable to present his point of view fully.

Nick Migas was an open Communist with deep roots in the union movement and strong support from his own local. This account makes clear why he had that support. Unlike many other locals in the steel industry, Local 1010 at Inland Steel in East Chicago, Indiana was organized by the men in the mill and had to struggle for years to achieve recognition. It had a tradition of departmental wildcats and aggressive handling of grievances (see, in addition to Nick Migas' account, the account of Local 1010's first president, John Sargent, pp. 105–110). As a grievance committeeman for the open hearth, staff man, and local president, Migas had won the respect of his fellow-workers. The demands he presented at the 1948 convention were demands he had been instructed to make by the membership of Local 1010.

As Migas explains, the confrontation at the convention was part of a larger process through which the international union took over and tamed a vigorous local. The same process took place in many CIO unions during the years after World War II.

Late in 1948 Nick Migas left the mill and settled on a dairy farm in Wisconsin, not, he states, because he had been driven out, but because he had always wanted to own a farm of his own.

NICK MIGAS

How the International Took Over

I WAS BORN in McKees Rocks, Pennsylvania and raised in the coal
fields of West Virginia. My dad was very active in the union
and especially in control of the union by the rank and file, by
the members themselves.

Before Dad came to the coal mines he worked in Pennsylvania,
in the mills there. He was in a big strike there [the McKees Rocks
strike of 1909]. It was a vicious strike. I remember him talking about
the police on horseback and the Pinkerton detectives. In fact, he
was blackballed and that's why he had to go to the coal mines. He
couldn't get a job anywhere in Pennsylvania.

My dad was a member of the United Mine Workers. This was
a small mine. They had their own small local there. He was a pit
committeeman. He was looked up to as a good representative
because of his position for the rank and file, for the average miner.
I listened to him discussing grievances with the miners who came
to our house: Poles, Italians, Ukrainians like ourselves. He would
always stick to the men's version of the grievance. There was a
no-strike clause in the union contract but that didn't prevent the men
from striking when they had to. Some safety violations were settled
that way. I know of a number of occasions when the miners came
right out of the mine with my dad in front of them, walked into
the superintendent's office and got a grievance settled.

There was a big coal strike when John L. Lewis became head
of the union. Many miners were in a pretty tough position because
the coal companies imported scabs and especially Negro people, to
try and break the strike. Many of the black people were not aware
of this until they were brought in and then, to the amazement of

many white people, the black people supported the strike, would work with the white miners and help them out. That's where we gained the experience of labor and of the control of unions by rank and file.

My dad was a member of the ıww way back and then he joined the socialist movement, and I guess he went with the left wing when the Socialist Party split up. I remember him talking to me about Debs. One of my big heroes was Big Bill Haywood. I heard him speak in Rockford, Illinois when I was attending workers training school. He was a wonderful man.

In the early 1920s the mine closed down and we moved to Hammond, Indiana. Quite a number of relatives from the old country lived there. There was a big car shop in Hammond, and in corresponding they told him that jobs were available, and so we moved. He got a job at the Standard Car shop in East Chicago. I was fourteen.

When the Depression came, my dad was laid off because he did not have much seniority, and went on wpa. We almost lost our home. My brother and I got jobs after school in a bowling alley, setting pins. My mother went out to do housework among the rich people in that area. That way we were able to pay interest on our loan. In fact, I was involved in an accident which enabled us to pay off the mortgage. I had just pulled out of a neighbor's yard where a Serbian orchestra I belonged to was practicing. I was coming out of the yard across some railroad tracks, and another group of kids were trying to beat a train. There were no blinkers. As the train came by they had to pull over to my side to avoid the train and we crashed right in the middle of the tracks. The cowcatcher picked up my car and slid me for about three hundred yards. My wheels collapsed. I tried to get out of the car but the cowcatcher caught the door and my leg, and crushed them up against the car. We settled with the railroad and were able to pay off the mortgage. We were lucky. Many people lost their homes, their bank accounts and life savings.

My dad was active in the unemployed councils at that time. There were meetings at the little red house which was owned by the Hungarian Fraternal Society. The ıwo and the ycl also used the Hungarian hall. I remember parading in Hammond, going from store to store, asking for donations to help the hungry people. Most of the grocers would give small donations, although they were as bad off as the rest. There were demonstrations in Indianapolis, and I remember one time the police and fire departments in East Hammond tried to break up our car caravan as we were getting ready to go to Indianapolis.

After graduating from high school I thought of going to college. But financial conditions being what they were I was unable to go to college. I could probably have worked my way but a job came in the offing at the steel mills and I thought, "Well, I'll make some money"—get started, you know. So I took this job at the Inland Steel as a stocker in the scrap yard, loading scrap on little pan cars and hauling them up to the furnaces. That was in 1933.

From stocker I was promoted to switchman, and from there to conductor. That's when I became involved in union activities. I was a steward in my department, the No. 1 Open Hearth. That was the stronghold of the independent union. The president of the company union was a first helper in No. 1 Open Hearth. And so the fight against the company union wasn't something remote. It was right there.

When I saw how the company worked against the workers, especially against the foreign-born workers who were in no position to defend themselves, it kind of roused my feeling about those people not getting a fair deal. At that time a foreman could easily say, "You don't like it? Go on home. Take three days off. Take a week off." And there was nothing you could do about it. And so when the Steel Workers Organizing Committee came in to organize the CIO, we were pretty ripe for organization. I suppose being connected with labor unions through my father pushed me right ahead.

We had a lot of Mexican workers in my department where discrimination was practiced. They were constantly kept on small, menial jobs—scrap yard, labor gang, furnaces—dirty, menial, hard work. And no chance of promotion. That's why the union swept like a wildfire through the steel mills. Every place you looked you saw, "CIO, CIO, CIO," in spite of everything that the company would try to stop it.

During these early years Johnny [Sargent] was president, we had a progressive leadership, and that made a world of difference. We were encouraged to work with the rank and file, with all the people that we represented. We organized departmental meetings. Every month the department would meet at the union hall and discuss their immediate problems, work things out, and decide what to do about it. You had a sympathetic leadership to work with you. Whereas now, departmental meetings are discouraged, you're discouraged to put out [departmental] newspapers reporting to the membership what you're doing as far as their grievances are concerned. A man will file a grievance, the steward will take it up, and that's the end of it. If it goes to the international, the member himself doesn't know what is happening.

In those days, the man who had the grievance came right along with me. We discussed it right in front of the foreman. He went with me to the next step, the superintendent. We discussed it there. If we couldn't settle it there we went to the industrial relations department, the third step. He was always involved, he was always there, he knew exactly what his case was, he knew exactly what position the company was taking.

There were times, I remember, we'd take a man into the superintendent's office and the superintendent would try to browbeat the man involved, give him a little scare. It was then that the union made its position felt, by blasting the superintendent for his attitude. We slammed the table. You'd be surprised at the results that would bring. Then they'd say, "Nick, how would you like to be a foreman?"

There was one time when they wouldn't settle a grievance for the charging car operators. They had increased the tonnage on the furnaces without increasing the rate. We discussed this question with the superintendent: nothing doing. So that night it started to slow down, and by the next morning there were two furnaces where they had to shut the heat off. By that evening there were six furnaces that had to shut the heat off. They settled the grievance in a hurry. Nobody told anybody to strike. There was just that close relationship, working with the people, where they knew what was necessary.

It was nice. It was good work. We set up promotional sequences in every department where it made no difference if you were a Mexican, if you were a Negro, what you were. Every step of the way you were entitled to the next position if your seniority permitted. So as a result, my first case was of a Mexican worker promoting to a crane operator. This was unheard of. It happened to be one of my stewards, Merced Velasquez. He was very intelligent. The grievance was taken up, and he became the first [Mexican] to get on a crane.

Same thing on the open hearth. You never had Mexicans as helpers. "First helpers? That's ridiculous. No Mexican can be a first helper." Well, it wasn't too long after that when we had a regular procedure. There was no chance of any real opposition, because that was the procedure, that was the way it was set up, and every person had his rights.

We had a strike in No. 2 Open Hearth when a Negro fellow was refused permission to become a second helper. There were many Southern people who had come in at that time, and were working as third and second helpers. This thing broke out: management refused to give him the job and [management] was supported by the other workers. We held a meeting inside the plant. Gillies, the superintendent, spoke first. He was wishy-washy: "Well fellows, you know what's right and what's wrong, but we can't force you." Then I spoke after Gillies got through. I told them in plain words that this was wrong, that the union would never support them, that this man was entitled to a job regardless of his race. I pointed out to them that discrimination starts, maybe, with a Negro, but next it will go to the Mexican worker, and that it hasn't been long since Mexican workers could not work at this job (and there were Mexican workers there listening), and then it'll go to the Kentuckian, the hillbilly. I said, "Then a so-called hillbilly won't be able to work in a steel mill. And where will it stop?" After that the man was given his job.

Women were brought in during the war and immediately the company began to pay them less wages. The first case I took up was a woman by the name of Delgado who was working in the labor

gang, and was getting less wages for the same work. It took about
six months but the arbitrator ruled against the company. That set
the precedent. The women in the tin mill struck over the same issue.

During the early days, the international wasn't too much of a question. People were involved with their immediate problems in their
own localities, their own local unions, and they felt that here was
where they had to settle their problems. It wasn't until the international came in, and dictated a contract with a no-strike clause, that
it became a matter of what kind of leadership you had in the international.

When SWOC became the Steelworkers Union, it became a top-
heavy organization. Before that the local union leadership did its
own negotiating. A contract would be read clause by clause at the
local union meeting, and then voted on, and adopted or rejected.

How did the international take over? It was very much like the
political situation now. Look at the trend in this country with Nixon.
He goes into Cambodia, he goes into other countries, doing what
he pleases, and people feel that they can't do anything about it. It
was just the same way when the international came into the local
unions. Hedging here, hedging there, getting people under their
influence in the local who were ambitious to become foremen or
to get on the staff, spending money just before an election: that way
progressive leadership was broken up in the plant, in the union.

It was a gradual process. You had elected representatives in the
different departments. Maybe for a period of time they were sincere,
and they worked hard to get grievances and problems settled. But
generally, they did not work closely with the membership. They
didn't report to the people they represented. Eventually, maybe some
people broke away, got disgusted, and new people were elected. Or,
if you had a good man as grievance committeeman, and the international didn't settle his grievances at the third and fourth steps, then
the people involved thought it was the grievance man's fault [and
voted him out of office]. That's how the international took over.

I was a staff man myself for a while. They wanted Sargent, and
he turned them down, but he urged me to accept it because it was
a position from which I could help the rank and file. It was good
work. You got into contact with more people that way. Even as

a staff representative, when a grievance man had a grievance that was perplexing him I would go with him into the department and discuss it with the men. And while I was a staff representative wage increases were received throughout the whole mill. Every time there was an increase I wrote a personal letter to the grievance committeeman, listing the amount of increase each job was affected by. He had to post that letter on his bulletin board and this brought me almost directly in contact with the people in the opposition's departments.

While I was a staff man, George Patterson [see pp. 89–97] decided to run against Joe Germano [for district director of District 31 of the United Steelworkers of America, including Chicago and northern Indiana]. I immediately supported George. I was the only staff man who did, at least the only one who did wholeheartedly. And at Inland, which was the only place we were in a position to ensure an honest election, Patterson carried the local. But Germano was declared to have won the election and the day after the election I was fired.

[Nick Migas went back into the mill. In June 1945 he was elected president of the Inland local, Local 1010. In 1946 and 1948 he was a delegate to the Steelworkers convention, although no longer president of the local.]

As a delegate to the 1948 convention I was instructed by my local on every one of the issues I raised. Many of Germano's delegates were out playing cards all night. They didn't give a damn. They didn't care. I went up to Murray [Philip Murray, president of the Steelworkers Union] and asked him if he would permit me to get up at the front mike. Murray refused. He said, "You have a mike on the floor," and he said, "If I want to I shall recognize you, and you can speak on any issue that is at that time on the floor." So I walked off.

After Murray refused to recognize any of us who wanted to speak, we put out a leaflet. We didn't want to disrupt the convention. We did it when the convention was not in session, when it was recessed for lunch. I'll never forget the look on the face of Dave McDonald [at that time secretary-treasurer of the union] after he read that leaflet. I was standing there in the hallway and McDonald walked by

me. The look on his face was pure hatred. He never said a word
to me. Normally he would have said, "Hello," or something,
because I'd met him a number of times at conventions in Pittsburgh.
I knew something was up just from the look on McDonald's face.

The leaflet challenged Murray's position and Murray being the
exalted ruler, no one had dared to do that. It said he was working
with the company. That was the sharpest point, that he had
acquiesced in the company's position. The international's position
was no wage increase.

[The text of the leaflet was as follows:]

FOR A 25 ¢ WAGE INCREASE NOW!
STOP THE NO-FIGHT POLICY!

The officers' report shows that the Steel Companies were never
in a better position to grant unions' demand for a wage increase.

—Workers need it—higher prices make it mandatory.

—It is clear that prices are *not* dropping, that they will rise more.
So—we can't wait until next year or until Steel Companies feel
like granting wage increases. Nor can we sit by with mouths
open to take what companies want to give us.

This convention should adopt a stand that:

—We want wage increases NOW!

—We want 25c an hour increase NOW!

President Murray revealed that the Steel Trust did not bargain in
good faith in the wage talks. Not only that: We now see the companies didn't bargain in good faith when they signed the present two-
year contract.

On the other hand, our leadership has done almost everything it
could to please the trust and the powers-that-be:

—It influenced our union to go easy on beefs in the mills.

—It stopped or discouraged departmental stoppages, slow-downs
and other actions against departmental beefs; it permitted staunch
union men to be fired without benefit of union defense for simply
fighting speed-up and other beefs.

—It supported the Marshall Plan.

—It condemned the Third Party and the only Presidential candidate
who supports our wage demand and opposes Taft-Hartley—
Henry Wallace.

—It carried on more and more anti-Communist, red-baiting activity.

This is how our leadership proved its good faith and its confidence in the company's good faith! Only the good faith of the rank-and-file was forgotten.

And for all this, the pay-off wasn't even a wooden nickel pay raise. We got taken in; we got speed-up; we got a weakened union; we got laughed at. We pleased the Company and hurt ourselves.

Never Again! Never again must our union be made a laughing stock! Never again must we be taken into camp by the wily steel trust and a gullible leadership! No more 2-year contracts! No more no-strike clauses! No more free hands for the company and bound hands for the union!

The bad faith of the companies in these wage negotiations is clear. In the face of the companies' bad faith—in the face of a crying need for a wage increase—we cannot let the talk about "sanctity of contract" replace our responsibility for working out a policy to carry on the fight to **win a wage increase now!**

The miners too, have a no-strike clause in their present contract, and a few other rotten clauses. But when the chips were down these clauses didn't stand in their way. It was found that they had to be "willing and able" to work. It is widely known that the miners had good reason to be "unwilling and unable" to work, for certain reasons. AND THEY WON! THEIR FIGHTING POLICY PAID OFF!

The same goes for us: Either we are a fighting union every inch of the way or we go down the road to company-unionism! Let's show some good faith in our membership! Let's respond to their good faith in electing us to this convention. They expect a fighting wage policy—not weasel words, from us.

The Wage Policy Resolution now offered to you by the Resolutions Committee should be sent back to be amended as follows:

1. That we make clear that our demand for a wage increase is 25¢ an hour retroactive to April 30.

2. That in addition to the advertising campaign to win the public there shall be an all-out drive to win the solid support of the steelworkers for this demand. That we shall set aside one day for union rallies in every steel center to show the rank and file support for the demand and to express their determination to win it.

3. That we shall establish closest possible unity with all other
unions which are in struggle or negotiations for wage increases.
Statement of Delegate Nick Migas, Local Union 1010, USA-CIO.

Because of the leaflet, Murray had to call on me. When I got
up to the mike I felt, as I was talking, that the people were listening.
I could have swayed the people. But the damn staff representatives
wouldn't let me. They started hooting. They were there for a purpose: they wouldn't let you talk. And half of the delegates were
staff representatives. So how can you do it? If it had been just the
membership, the rank and file, I could have carried them right along
with me.

Germano took this opportunity to bring up every personal slander
he could think of, to tear me apart. I was escorted by three big,
husky staff representatives right out of the convention, and thrown
out of the door. There was a group standing there, I don't know
who they were, and they started after me. I got across the street
and as I stepped on the opposite gutter I slipped and fell down, and
one of these guys caught up with me and kicked me in the ribs.
Then Ralph and a couple of other friends came up and things quieted
down. We went into a drugstore. Then the police came. I stayed
hid for about three days in a friend's house there in Boston.

Upon returning to our locals we continued to press this issue, and
finally, the wage increase came across. Bill Young got up at the
local meeting and said that it was thanks to me that it had happened.

Elections in our local came up a month later, and I ran for grievance committeeman in my department. I was unopposed. The international had their people in the local prefer charges [because under
the Taft-Hartley Act, a Communist could not hold office in the
union]. A trial committee was appointed by the president: Bill Young
and Merced Velasquez from my department, Max Luna who worked
with the Trotskyites, and Don Lutes and Pete Calacci representing
the international. During this trial, the Trotskyites contacted me
several times and said that they were going to support me because
this was a political persecution. And they did. They supported me
during this trial, so the majority on the trial committee voted in support of my position. The majority and the minority gave their reports

at the local union meeting, and the local union supported the majority. Then the international overruled the local. That's the way it happened.

But I was never removed as a grievance committeeman. I had bought a farm. I had always wanted to own one. While this struggle was going on in the local, my family had moved to the farm. My wife was having problems. She was trying to run the farm with no water, no electricity. She had a refrigerator, a washing machine, an electric stove, but she had no electricity. It was overbearing for her to take care of the two little girls and all this as well. Our political activities, our union activities, had nothing to do with this decision.

I wouldn't change a thing if I had it to do over again. A lot of people feel that the progressive group isolated itself in the steel union by supporting Patterson. I don't think so. We supported a progressive man, and we had to show opposition to a fellow that wasn't doing for the union what he should have been doing.

STAN WEIR

DURING MORE THAN TWENTY YEARS as an industrial worker, unionist, and organizer among seamen, auto workers, teamsters and construction workers, Stan Weir became impressed by the importance of informal work groups. The informal or primary work group is

> that team which works together daily in face-to-face communication with one another, placed by technology and pushed into socialization by the needs of production. It is literally a family at work torn by hate and love, conflict and common interest. It disciplines its members most commonly by social isolation and ridicule, it has a naturally selected leadership, makes decisions in the immediate work area, and can affect the flow of production.

Searching industrial relations libraries, Weir found much literature on primary work groups but only one study that was partisan to workers (Loren Baritz, *Servants of Power*), and he learned for the first time of the Hawthorne experiments. Weir sees the informal work group as the only organizational form opposed to formal bureaucracies which cannot be captured by them.

This account does not present the cumulative life experience of Stan Weir, being highly condensed and ending in 1956. In the late 1950s, Weir went back into maritime as a San Francisco Bay Area

longshoreman. Together with a thousand others hired in 1959, he
was part of a new class of registered longshoremen called B-men.
B-men paid a special form of dues but were not permitted membership in the union and were allowed only the work that was left over
after the union members or A-men took the work that they wanted.
As one of the elected leaders of the B-men, Weir became involved
in a sharp and protracted dispute with the leadership of the International Longshoremen's and Warehousemen's Union (ILWU) headed
by the union's president, Harry Bridges.

After four years of agitation and after a large number of A-men
had retired, the union and the employers decided to take the 1959
B-men into what almost amounted to full membership. All were
investigated and all were promoted but a group of eighty-two which
contained those who had taken the lead in criticizing Bridges'
policies affecting the B-men. The eighty-two, Weir among them,
were fired after a secret trial which was opposed by the local union.
Accusations against them involved late payment of dues for which
they had paid fines, and chiseling in accepting work assignments
out of turn. Ten years later a number of those who were deregistered
were still attempting to get a hearing and reinstatement to their jobs
via the courts.

Stan Weir is at present an instructor at the University of Illinois.
He has written several influential essays based on his experience,
including "USA—the Labor Revolt," first published in the *Interna-
tional Socialist Journal* (Rome, Italy), April and June 1967 (re-
printed in *American Society, Inc.*, Maurice Zeitlin, ed., 1970, and in
American Labor Radicalism, Staughton Lynd, ed., 1973); and
"Class Forces in the 1970's," *Radical America*, May–June 1972.
His articles on longshore have appeared in *New Politics*. There are
substantial similarities in the life events of Stan Weir and Harvey
Swados' fictional character Joe Link in *Standing Fast*.

S T A N   W E I R

The Informal Work Group

I

T HE WHOLE EARLY PART of my life was dominated by the idea that solutions to all that's wrong lie in individual morality. But my life experience, like that of most people, sent me messages which constantly contradicted this idea. I came to have a different idea, that you had to have a cause that was bigger than you because that was the only real freedom—living at one with a total society rather than just for oneself. It's impossible to know precisely where one gets that idea, but I came to know that the corruption of individual humans is the result of corrupt and outdated institutions.

My grandmother was a scrubwoman in office buildings in downtown Los Angeles. My mother quit high school in the tenth grade and became an apprentice dressmaker at fifty cents a week. She met my father when she was working at the Post Office. A year later they married and I was born a year after that, in 1921, the year that women got the vote.

I didn't know my father. That marriage lasted five months after my birth. Both my great grandfather and grandfather died in the early '20s. That left me with a family that was female-dominated. My uncle was an important member of our household, but due to the Depression, his unemployment and resulting alcoholism, he was constantly held up as an example of what not to be. My block in East Los Angeles was made up of close and long-time neighbors. They worked hard. They were poor, generous, warm and at the same time petty and suspicious of anyone not like themselves; that is, not of English, Scotch, Irish, or German stock. Most of all they wanted the happiness they felt could come from obtaining "a steady job." When two Armenian families moved in at the bottom of the block there was a temporary but noticeable resistance. Real socialization and integration did not materialize. In 1944, a freeway cut through and made the separation of the lower part of the block permanent.

All through school there were not more than three teachers who related to me on my own terms—really only one, a young Armenian substitute teacher. I was to give one of the speeches at the graduation ceremony from junior high school. My speech was called, "Our Flag, the Star Spangled Banner." In rehearsal, I walked up onto the stage to give the speech in a very sloppy manner. The teacher in charge of the ceremony had a fit of anger and in front of everybody told me off and said, "If ever I see you walk up there like that again, that's the end. You're not going to give the speech." One of the big tough ball players on the team that I played second base on came to me at noontime and said, "Mr. Dingilian was talking about you. He said you did that because you didn't want to lose touch with us regular guys."

In the first year of high school I completely stopped attempting to participate in official school activities that were connected with the administrative establishment. I began to see that they were part of a system of favoritism and I was one of the beneficiaries of that system. However, I was opposing it individually, without organization, not effectively. I can remember I cut school one day, left the school grounds in my '29 Model A Ford with five others. We drove to the beach and spent a great day body surfing. The next morning I had to face up to the fact that I had been seen ditching. I walked in to get my demerits with everyone else and I was told by the registrar to report immediately to the vice principal's office. The vice principal explained to me that he couldn't give me, one of the leaders in the school, demerits like anyone else. That was impossible. "Just watch your step and don't get caught like that again. Get back in class." That had a great deal to do with opening my eyes.

Out of 323 seniors graduating in February 1940, the same man (who thought he was doing us a great favor) invited the five boys who were known to be going on to college to his house for dinner. He explained to us how to get a commission in the Armed Forces when the U. S. finally got into the war. He told how he had gotten a commission in the Army as a young man in World War I and how we could do the same, that we should not get caught being privates in the Army. He told us how to work the angles through Congressmen.

It was very oppressive for us to know that the war was going on in Europe. I think this is one of the reasons why we threw ourselves into the "swing era" so hard. That was a big part of my life. Dancing and listening to the swingbands, and the security of the group that was doing it, was a way of putting behind the thought of that oncoming war. We all knew one another and all the males wore suits that were at least slightly zoot.

I always thought in grammar school that it would be different in junior high—we'd start learning the truth. In junior high I thought it would be in high school. And in high school I thought it would be in college. I went to Los Angeles Junior College in February 1940, and it appeared to me that that was finally going to be so.

I had a professor of English named Richard Lillard. He was a liberal from the John Dewey tradition and he provided an analysis of society and the world around us that made sense to me. It was liberating and I listened hard to every word he spoke. But toward the end of the semester I asked him, "This is all fine but where does one go to put into practice these ideas?"

The following semester I went to UCLA. I was in the Westgard Co-op. It was a co-op eating group. I was introduced to it by a friend of mine I had gone to high school with named John Slevin. He was a Molokan, a member of a fundamentalist Christian pacifist sect from the Ukraine near Armenia. His pacifism hadn't had a great effect on me until the war got very close. Then it became apparent that he was going to be a conscientious objector. He was in conscientious objector camps for four years and he led a strike as a CO. That made him a felon and for life he has literally been blackballed out of any career because of it—and he is a great human.

I didn't finish my third semester at college. I could see no point in it. I had had a philosophy course in which the professor effectively tore down what he called the metaphysical temple and philosophically destroyed any basis for my belief in God, and I went with

Professor Piatt every step of the way. But he had nothing to supplant it with. At this point I was developing a lot of cynicism about the world around me. I was despairing about ever finding a way to pursue a good life.

I seriously considered being a CO myself and I went and talked to Richard Lillard about it. He said, "Well, there's just one thing about being a conscientious objector. With your particular bent, your personality, it seems to me that you would like to live the social experience of your generation. And if you become a CO you won't, not directly." I wanted to find a way to do that without at the same time becoming a victim of the discipline in the Armed Services. It appeared to me that while the risk to life was greater on merchant ships during the war, if I became a merchant seaman I could then get the best of both worlds.

I became an apprentice seaman in the Merchant Marine. I was then accepted as a U. S. Merchant Marine cadet and midshipman in the Naval Reserve, went into training, and went out on a merchant ship as a deck cadet.

Living with the officers topside, I saw that this was an aristocracy. The contempt that the officers had for the men in the foc'sle (forecastle) was a fact of life. The first day on that ship I appeared on the boat deck with my midshipman's uniform on. The deckhands looked up at me and I saw in their faces that look of pity for the worthlessness of the contribution that anyone could make who would be wearing such an outfit. To them, that uniform symbolized useless activity.

They knew something about the ability they had to make that ship go from port to port with or possibly even without officers. They were a highly conscious group of men from the strikes of the '30s, an experience which was still fresh in their minds. They were involved, even on that ship, in job actions from time to time. Several among them were ex-IWWS; they believed in direct action.

Within three months, I was working on deck with them as a seaman, wearing the same clothes they were wearing which I got out of the slop chest. They saw that I was interested. They went out of their way to teach me all of the skills, the wire and line (rope) splices, the knots and hitches, and to make a deck sailor out of me.

They wanted to win me away from the "topside" for good. So they started telling me the history of the strikes to win the hiring hall, the fights to destroy the "fink hall" and the "fink book," which had been parts of the government-employer controlled hiring system. Prior to 1934 on the West Coast, when you got off a ship, if the skipper wrote anything other than "VG," very good, in your continuous discharge or fink book, then you were marked and couldn't get another American ship. Carrying the continuous discharge book meant you carried your own blackball in your pocket.

So they pumped all this history into me. And then they would quiz me. "What happened on such-and-such a date?" "What's Bloody Thursday?" "What were the big demands?" "What was the 1934 award?" "Why were we able to win victories before getting a collective bargaining contract?" "Who's Lunchbox?" (That was Harry Lundeberg, the secretary-treasurer of the Sailors' Union of the Pacific.) "What's a Lunchbox Stetson?" (That was the sailors' name for the traditional white cap of the West Coast maritime workers.)

On that ship I had finally found a cause and a vehicle for pursuing it. These guys were involved, day to day, in establishing dignity for themselves and thousands of others, and policing all the things that they had done to obtain that dignity. I saw the boatswain tell the chief mate on that ship, "Get off the deck while we're working. Come and see me before 8:00 in the morning and tell me what to do. Come out here after we quit at 5:00 in the evening and find out what we didn't do right, if you think so, and tell me what's wrong. But don't come and stand on this deck while we're at work. Get off the deck and back on the bridge where you belong." I was very impressed with that power. He got away with it. I was amazed he could do that. I knew I wanted to be able to do that too. And I did! The time came when I sailed boatswain and I told the mate, "Get off this deck. Don't stand around us and watch us or else there's going to be no work going on while you're here. Hold everything, fellows!"

When I left that ship I had learned the loophole in Naval Reserve law on how to resign as a midshipman without any penalty, just to get out. So I did that and I went immediately to San Pedro and reported to the port agent at the Sailors Union of the Pacific hall. (We didn't have "presidents" in the Sailors Union—it was a syndicalist tradition—they were "agents.") I went with a letter from the boatswain saying, "This here is to introduce Red Weir. He wants to come up through the forecastle like a regular and he knows the work. Give him a trip card." So I was in the foc'sle as opposed to the "topside" where the officers bunked.

Within a year's time I became a person who was usually elected the deck delegate on any ship that I would hire onto. They don't have union stewards on deck crews because the word "steward" means the person who is head of the food department. So you have "delegates" from the deck gang, black or engine room gang, and steward department. I was extremely and youthfully militant against the officers on every ship, to protect the gains of 1934 to 1937, like I'd been taught on my first ship by that gang of strike men and ex-Wobblies. When the food was not good or the mattresses were bad, and the ship got ready to sail, I several times had the crew standing on the docks and saying, "Until those mattresses come aboard . . ."

We were being trampled on because of the no-strike pledge. We were losing the gains of the 1930s because of the war, and that in particular kept me in political opposition to the war throughout the war. World War II was being used by employers to wipe out the gains made by labor a few years earlier and the democratic gains previously won by the general citizenry. When I finally became political it was through the only socialist organization that maintained political opposition to World War II. This was the Workers Party, later renamed the Independent Socialist League, whose leading personality was Max Shachtman.

One day, still early in the war, I came out on the deck of a Moore-McCormack ship on which I was deck delegate and I spotted a small broad man walking down the dock under a seabag that almost hid him from view. We were short one skilled deck hand [AB] and I figured that had to be him, the last man to fill out the crew so that we could sail. He came up the gangplank and I asked him, was he the AB from the hall? He said yes. I introduced myself, learned his name, showed him where to stow his gear and took him forward and introduced him to the whole gang by name. That kind of impressed him because he was a Jew and there weren't many Jews sailing, on deck in particular, and he had expected a little harder time. We rapidly became close friends. Within two weeks after we left port, he was the authority on almost all subjects in arguments on almost any question.

This man, who introduced me to socialism, was a visionary and had created in his mind a vision of a better society. He was a developed intellectual. He knew music, art and literature and a lot about natural sciences, and he was able to apply all those things to a vision of a better society. That was very attractive to me and many of the men on that ship.

When we got to Australia, he visited one of the famous rank-and-file organizers of the Australian labor movement. From that old man, who was retired, he got a number of copies of *The New International, The Fourth International, The Militant,* and *Labor Action.* He told me to read them, see what I thought. So I read them. I wasn't tremendously impressed with any of them, but there were some good things in them I thought. Trotsky was raising the whole question of democratic ideas and the necessity of democracy, which I was very much interested in. But the Russian experiment did not seem important to me at that time.

It was in the Sailors Union and while going to sea that society at least in part began to become understandable to me. Marxism facilitated that. The term "cause," instead of just being an emotional and simplistic thing where you got an identifiable enemy figure in "the boss," became part of a whole world view. I could see that the great contribution of Marx was that he was paying attention to what people were doing rather than trying to impose a utopia upon them. He had analyzed the French Revolutions, the communes and the forms that people themselves had produced and was trying to systematize it in some democratic way so that they would have some control of their own destiny. Being a militant delegate began to take on new meanings.

I began to understand that the reason why merchant seamen were often in the forefront of militant labor activity or revolutionary activity throughout the world was because, as citizens of a ship after it left the dock, they were really citizens of a molecular state, a total state in which the captain is the dictator. There is the middle class—licensed officers. And then there's the "lower class," the unlicensed seamen. It's a reflection of a class society. Once one can make an analysis of a small state like a ship, one can transmit that analysis to the larger state without even fully realizing it. There's a carry-over. At first I thought that merchant seamen were militant because they travelled and read a lot. But later I was to see that the informal social groups that develop on a ship at sea are in the main created by the formal and official division of labor which operates the ship; that is, the informal and formal work groups are identical so that the social and technological powers of the seamen are merged, thus revealing to them the importance of their role and enlarging the consciousness of their strength.

One of my deepest concerns when I first met a Marxian socialist was the whole question of violence and terrorism, sabotage, all those things I'd read about that radicals are supposed to be "guilty" of. The answers given me were that there is nothing radical or revolutionary about terrorism or any kind of super-militancy. It's essentially a reformist activity in its attempt to change society without changing institutions, merely by removing a person or group of people or terrorizing people through violent methods. Someone who is revolutionary, in the literal sense of the term, is someone who is for changing society's institutions. Socialism, if it's good, is finally for everyone's benefit. A way of saving the souls (if I can use the term) of all, including those who are managers or owners of the forces of production, is to create a society in which no one ever has to make that terrible decision to exploit others.

The question then came up to me immediately, well then why aren't we pacifists? It was explained to me that we cannot be pacifists because at a certain point that is irresponsibility. One has to be prepared, if attacked, to fight to defend oneself, and maintain the right to meet, to talk, to picket, whatever, and carry one's rights as a citizen to full conclusion. But if one ever has to do that, one should be as thrifty as possible, for not only do you want to not take a life but you want to create as few bitter enemies as possible. Those in power always have more arms than you. Those who work, who operate society, make it move, whether they dig coal or write poetry or keep books or file bills, have to be the answer to that brute force. Because that brute force can't stand up finally against the threat of the withdrawal of labor and economic and political power by those who, "from below" so to speak, operate and make the society function in all its ways.

In late '43 or early '44, the Sailors Union of the Pacific, in conjunction with the Seafarers International Union, decided to organize the tankers belonging to Standard Oil of California. [The Seafarers International Union was an industrial union founded by the Sailors Union of the Pacific which was a craft union. The SUP then became an affiliate of the SIU.] The only men who could get hired by Standard with any ease were those that looked young enough not to have had union experience. I was easily hired and I went out to Point Richmond, to the dockside refinery, to get on a ship. The practice was to hire seamen and let them work on the dock, servicing incoming ships, until they were assigned to a crew. I became a member of the relief gang and I was made assistant dock boatswain. That put me in a key position and I soon became head of the campaign on the job. I would assign rank-and-file SUP organizers so that they were not all concentrated on a few ships.

At a point midway in the campaign SUP men began to appear at work who were giving Jim Crow messages to the seamen we were trying to win over. Our opponent was the National Maritime Union (NMU). Their organizers were preoccupied with winning the war, Russia, and maintaining labor's no-strike pledge into the post-war period, rather than improving conditions for seamen in the here and now. We had been doing a good job by openly comparing our contracts with those of the NMU. I could prove to anyone who was white that we had the best union because we had the best contract. I hadn't thought through the whole racial issue but I could see that I couldn't give uncritical support to either [the SUP or the NMU] and neither side would abide criticism of any kind.

The men coming out now from the Sailors Union were saying, "We got to get a white union in here." On that dock, the messmen in the cafeteria and the room stewards in the hotel were Filipinos who were bitterly anti-union because of the experience that they'd

had in the original union organization campaigns years before when
the union had rejected them as members. I grabbed one of the men
who had made some Jim Crow statements and pulled him behind
a shed and demanded to know, who sent him out? It turned out
that he had been sent, not from the Sailors Union hall but from
the SIU tanker office in Richmond, headed by Hal Banks, a man
who was later to get into the news as a strikebreaker in Canada
for the American SIU. He was open about his bigotry. Some among
those he worked closely with said he boasted membership in the
Ku Klux Klan and was often armed. I phoned the head of the SUP,
Harry Lundeberg. He had been challenged about Banks before and to
me, like to the others, he said, "Well, Red, the man's doing a good
job for us over there and we have to overlook some of his faults you
know."

I immediately got myself shipped out on one of Standard's tankers. Two months later the NLRB representation election took
place. I piled off the ship the same day. Eighty-five per cent voted
for the SUP-SIU. Lundeberg signed a contract allowing Standard to
hire forty-nine per cent non-union seamen, but by that time I had
been sent to Canada as a special representative to the British Columbia Seamen's Union to clear up a bad situation created by the man
heading it up.

I hit all the ships as they came in and organized the ranks to take
control. After several months I learned that Lundeberg had armed
the British Columbia union's president with a telegram stating I was
a "Trotskyite," with the idea in mind that this could be used to
keep me from cleaning house too thoroughly. I had learned a lesson
about how control is maintained by bureaucracies. I stayed on until
I had maximum insurance that the ranks could sustain an opposition.
I returned to the states and got the first ship available to the East
Coast.

I would no longer be a staff organizer for the Sailors Union. I
could no longer see my official union as a viable instrument for qual-
itative social change. I was now a militant but without legitimization
from the union. In 1945, when it appeared that the war was going
to be over, the Coastwise Committee in the Sailors Union of the
Pacific held a meeting and came up with a post-war program in

which they said that, "This union does not checkerboard ships," in other words, ship blacks or accept blacks into the union, "because checkerboarding causes racial friction. But we are still a democratic union because the day the membership wants blacks in we will allow it."

I took the floor of the meeting and pointed out that the report of the Coastwise Committee "solved nothing," that it was true that the unions that were in any way Communist-line did utilize blacks as political footballs by patronizing them and then using them, but that no member of the Sailors Union could tell that to a black man and be heard because blacks were allowed some kind of citizenship in CIO unions and not in the AFL unions on the waterfront, and were totally barred from the Sailors Union. And therefore the crisis continued for us as long as we were an all-white union. (We had minority groups in the Sailors Union with darker skins than many American blacks. To this day I believe the bar against American blacks is more political, in the small "p" sense of the word, than it is racial. Confrontation with guilt is feared.)

I was interrupted by the chairman who said, "What would you do, Brother Weir, if you were on the Coastwise Committee . . ." but he never finished his sentence because I believe he realized it would be opening up a discussion on the floor about the whole basis of racism to the ranks present. They had visibly shifted during even that brief exchange on the floor of the meeting.

I think most people were seriously pondering the problem in that key meeting. But bureaucratically the discussion was avoided. One did not pursue questions after the gavel had come down. In those days it meant having to face up to violence and unless you had a caucus or organized muscle going you couldn't stand up to it. I had no caucus. Like all the other dissenters in those war days, I was very much an individual, isolated and alone in that union at that time.

I decided after the war was over that I no longer wanted to go to sea. I no longer was able to do what seamen do when they first start going to sea and that is to "ball it up" in foreign ports, carousing in bars and whorehouses, because finally one sees that the women are only there because of their abject poverty. As a man of twenty-five, and like most seamen, I had become divorced from mainstream shoreside society and I wanted a broader social life. I remember one night I was in Port Avila on a tanker and the moon came up over those California foothills in the east. It was New Year's Eve and I realized how many guys my age were ashore having a good time and here I was with my ass on a cold tank top watching nothing but the moon come up. So I got a ship, a Grace Line run, and paid off in New York. That was the last time I ever shipped offshore.

II

I went to the national office of the Workers Party and Max Shachtman asked me, "What are you going to do now, Red?" I said, "Well, I'm going to go to San Pedro and I'm going to spend three months on the beach in the sun on the sand and in the surf, see my friends, get a job longshoring, work three days a week and do what I want to do."

Shachtman said, "Red, we don't want to miss the boat in auto. A lot of important things are happening. You could do a lot of good in auto." That wasn't what I wanted to do but I realized that I would no longer have legitimization in the Party if I didn't do that. So I went back to the Bay Area, got myself a little apartment in West Berkeley, went out to Point Richmond to the Ford plant, and got hired on the assembly line.

It was chaotic. In those early days after the war they couldn't keep anyone working there. People'd hire in in the morning and quit by noon. Some of them never even got far enough down the line to report to the foreman when they saw what it was like. So every day you'd start off with almost the full complement of personnel and by noon you were already taking over half another man's job. The work was really oppressive. Those who worked any length of time on the Ford line called the place "the prison." I would come home every night battered by the violence of the work.

Every day at quitting time, at the five-minute whistle for clean-up, the men would all line up waiting for the second bell to ring, like at the line in a race. When the second bell would ring they would *run*, as fast as they could go, down the aisles to the time clocks.

During the first few days I thought they were out of their minds. A week later, I was butting them out of line to get my place at the starting point too.

We were always in the hole on that line. One of my operations was to put two bronze screws into the frame of the car that would hold on the hydraulic brake linings or tubings that run to each wheel brake cylinder. One day I was so far in the hole (the man next to me couldn't complete his task because his partner on the other side had put him in the hole) I couldn't reach my electric wrench. And so, not wanting the inspector to spot loose screws, I hit them all the way in with a ballpeen hammer and learned that they would stay in. No one would suspect. I had found a shortcut in the work. Those brake linings would stay on the frame of that car probably for several thousand miles without loosening. But I quit looking at Fords after that when they drove down the street past me because of my guilt and because I knew everyone in that plant was taking shortcuts in some way.

One day they transferred me to another job. A man working near me lifted the motors off the motor line on a hoist and then lowered them into the chassis of the car. He couldn't lift the motors high enough into the air to clear the other men's heads if he was going to make the drop into the car at the right time, so he had to move them horizontally over the men's heads at about a five foot height. He had to yell constantly, all day long, "Watch your head . . . Heads up, heads up." The man was a nervous wreck. He would say after work, talking to himself, "Well, I only hit three men today." "Why don't the dummies get out of my way? They know I have to do it this way to make it on the job."

But then came the day when one of the pneumatic air wrenches hit me on the side of the jaw, because of a faulty clutch, and knocked off half a tooth. I walked out. That was my last day at Ford's.

There I was without a job in auto. The very next morning I went and got a job at Chevrolet in East Oakland where I stayed for two years. Most of the people in that local were Portuguese-Americans from East Oakland. There was a great deal of Jim Crow amongst them because American society was constantly trying to put them in the position of the American blacks. Their way of avoiding that situation had been to say, "Look, we're not American blacks. We're American Portuguese. We have our own Latin culture and we're proud of that culture." So for both good and bad reasons, to express their own culture, they were Jim Crow. The East Oakland, California plant and the Atlanta, Georgia plant of Chevrolet were the last two all-white GM plants in the country.

I pushed a resolution on the floor of the union that we should go to management to bring blacks into the plant. There was opposition to it in the rank and file and the leadership of the shop unit (which was mostly from the then dominant section of the left) went along with those Jim Crow sentiments in order to maintain their hold on the leadership. But then they were in the position of being in violation of the United Automobile Workers constitution. That couldn't go on for too long and I realized that it would come up again.

When I was transferred to another department, everyone in that department was Jim Crow and they wanted me to be the shop steward. I had the choice of either rejecting them because they were Jim Crow or accepting them and dealing with a life situation as it came up. I chose the latter.

We won a lot of conditions in that shop. As a matter of fact, we had a sit-down strike in order to retain the right of having gloves supplied by management. We wore out three pair a week on that particular job. We won gloves in a grievance and then management began to renege on the supply of gloves. The men came to me and said, "We got to do something about this," and half of them were going to the time clock. I got them all back and said, "Look, any man who clocks out . . ." I didn't get to finish my sentence because someone else in that group of about forty men said, "We'll never get back in the plant again." And someone else said, "But if we stay here . . ." and someone else said, "Available to work when they supply the tools to work with, we'll be OK."

It was an outcrop of an idea I'd laid on them very early. They came to me saying, "Look at the holes in our gloves. They're reneging on the supply." I said to them, "Well, gloves are tools, aren't they?" and walked away. I learned that an efficient agitator is not one who talks and lectures a lot, but who simply throws out an idea and sees if that idea is workable and acceptable. We won that sit-down. We were opposed by the leadership of the local for doing that, and they tried to get us for it but we survived.

In all this I was learning from and being counseled by an old-time fighter who had led the sit-down strike at the Richmond Ford plant in the early '30s. His name was Luis Guido. He was one of the greatest men I have ever met—a true yet unsung hero. He would never take a union administrative job. For over thirty years as shop committeeman he fought the Ford and General Motors corporations to create a better life for himself and others. Who will ever record his name as a maker of history?

The second time the question of hiring blacks was going to come up, the men in my department said in effect, "We've got to forgive Red for his strange ideas," and "He needs help on this resolution." The speakers in favor of bringing blacks in were mainly Portuguese from my department and that won the rest of the Portuguese: "If you don't want to do it on a moral basis—the fact that everyone's got a right to eat and work—you damn sure better do it because if we have a strike they'll recruit scabs in West Oakland." It was only a matter of time after that that blacks were on the line and working everywhere in the plant.

I got married while I was working in auto. My wife came out of a West Virginia coal mining family and we had a lot of basic values in common from the first. In addition to developing a career and family, she found no insurmountable problems living a life whose routine was regularly broken by job crisis and economic insecurity.

It was in that period right after I met her that the Oakland general strike occurred. The Oakland general strike was called by no leader. It was unique, I think, in general strikes in this country. There was a strike of women who were the clerks at Kahn's and at Hastings' department stores and it had been going on for months. The Teamsters had begun to refuse to make deliveries to those department stores and the department stores needed commodities badly.

Not many people had cars right after the war and you took public transportation to work in the morning. You had to go downtown to the center of Oakland and then out in the direction of your workplace. So thousands and thousands of people travelled through the heart of town every morning on the way to work, on public transportation. Very early one morning, here were the policemen of Oakland herding in a string of trucks, operated by a scab trucking firm in Los Angeles, with supplies for these department stores. Some truck driver or some bus driver or street car conductor asked some policeman about the trucks (this is now part of the mythology) and the policeman told him, "This is a scab trucking firm coming in from L.A. to take stuff to Kahn's and Hastings'." Well, that truck driver, that bus driver, or that street car conductor, didn't get back on his vehicle. Truck drivers got off their trucks and that increased till those trucks and those buses and those street cars just piled up and thousands of people were stranded in town.

In a small way it was a holiday. The normal criteria for what was acceptable conduct disappeared. No one knew what to do and there were no leaders. No one called it. Pretty soon the strikers began forming into committees on the street corners. Certain shopkeepers were told to shut down and drug stores to stay open. Bars could stay open if they didn't serve hard liquor, and they had to put their juke boxes out on the sidewalk. People were literally dancing in the streets in anticipation of some kind of new day. Soon the strikers began to direct traffic and only let union people into town and keep out those who it was feared might be against the strike. It lasted fifty-four hours.

I'll never forget an incident in that strike. Some Army recruiting truck came in town through that mass of strikers and the lieutenant on that truck said over a P. A. system, "Why aren't you all out fightin' for your country instead of striking?" Most of the bus drivers still had their Eisenhower jackets with the hash marks on because they could use their Army uniform as part of their bus driver's uniform. And some big ex-top sergeant said, "Where do you think we got these?" With that he sang out, "Fall in!" and about a hundred men lined up and he put them through close order drill. Pretty soon there were several hundred going through this close order drill. They marched on City Hall and demanded to see the mayor. He wasn't in, of course.

It was that vision and the experiences in that strike that I experienced and which my wife saw, the vision in actual life of people determining their own destinies that sustains one and makes one stand fast for a long, long time. You don't have to so often go through all those doubts about, "Are the fundamental ideas of Marxism sound?" if you've been fortunate enough to have had those experiences. It's a matter of being advantaged or disadvantaged through your own life experience that sustains or drives one away from those basic ideas.

In 1951, my wife and I lived again in East Los Angeles, right near the high school where I had gone. I was in the Teamsters Union, freight handling. Some old friends of mine that I'd gone to school with and were from my neighborhood were officials in those unions. I was making a pretty good living. Then I began to realize I was getting a lot of work because the dispatchers were instructed by my friends to give me a lot of work. I went to them and I said, "Look, I want to shake square like anybody else." I immediately started getting only two days work a week. I quit and got a job driving a truck steady.

In that local, which was a local for industrial laundry wagon drivers, there was a terrible situation. The working conditions that had been built up by the membership of the local were slowly being sold each year, bit by bit, for nickel and dime wage increases. Rebellion in that local developed, which I led, and I became chairman of the Negotiating Committee. The secretary of the local, it turned out, colluded with management and I was fired on a flimsy pretext that couldn't hold water. While I was awaiting the arbitration, the men in the local, through collections each week, paid my full wages. What we didn't realize was that even the arbitration had been rigged. Instead of utilizing the American Arbitration Association, they got an arbitrator who was an employers' representative in the culinary industry and I went down the drain.

At first the men were going to strike to protect my job. I was part of the reason why they didn't strike, because I was agreeing to go through the mechanics of the grievance procedure. I really participated in my own undoing, and of the men, because I was simply a symbol by which to break the back of militancy in the union. It was an extremely bitter experience for me. I learned that one does not always use official procedures in circumstances like that if one is going to survive.

This rebellion took place early in 1954, when no spotlight was on the labor movement on this question. I have an honorable withdrawal card from that union, however, because twenty members of that union walked into the secretary-treasurer's office and demanded, right then and there, that an honorable withdrawal card be given me. Their instincts told them that I would need it in the future.

I had at least a dozen jobs within the next year. I'd get a job and two or three days later the management would come to me and say, "We didn't know you were in trouble with the Teamsters Union. We have to let you go." I finally got a job as an apprentice grocery clerk for Safeway Stores. I made about $1800 that year. I had one child and my wife was pregnant. I needed and wanted a steady job.

I saw in the newspaper that they were hiring at the General Motors plant in all departments. They hired me immediately and I was spray-painting again, like I had been for a time at Chevrolet. This time, instead of going into industry in part for political reasons, it was just for a job. The McCarthy period had disintegrated my political movement considerably. The people were not interested in doing anything much but surviving. So there was no movement telling me what to do. I was "just a worker."

I began to discover the subculture in the factory and that I was working in an informal work group with a life of its own, its own informal leadership, discipline, and activity. A whole new world opened up to me. I began to see that to approach any situation like this with a whole set of preconceived slogans was way off the beam. One first had simply to learn what the subculture was so that one's actions were understandable to everyone else, and not to violate what had been created. Because if you couldn't understand the individuals and the groups that they formed, you certainly weren't going to understand anything else.

Then it occurred to me that, by and large, the radicals' conception of the masses was a metaphysical one, an average, which didn't exist except in our minds. Really, the mass was a conglomerate of millions of workers in their subcultures, and rarely were there issues which were real mass issues. One had to try to find common denominators but, even more than that, had to speak to the reality of the people's lives as individuals and in their groups and in the subcultures, in each place of work.

I made friends with the people around me the way you normally do. Most of them were Chicanos from my side of town. We soon had a ride group going. We were on swing shift and one night we'd go to the black community where part of our work group lived and have ribs and the next night we'd go up and have tamales, enchiladas, tacos or burritos, and the next night we'd go and have spaghetti—here and there to each one's house. One guy's mother'd make a big feed and my wife'd make a big feed and so on. We created our own social life, which you have to do on the swing shift, when you work from four in the afternoon until midnight. And the politics that I injected into that group? I didn't even have to try. It came in the natural course of life.

One night when one guy stole something fairly big (from the plant) I told him off. By stealing he was risking his job and he risked us losing a valuable member of our group. And that was irresponsible not only to his family, but to *us* who were his family-at-work. It was the most meaningful kind of politics that one could talk and be involved in. Because we were into that kind of politics we could very easily get into other kinds of politics. Just being *me* was being political. I was helping politicalize those around me without trying to design anything special for a mass.

In 1955, our plant struck against the contract the minute its conditions were announced and before a meeting could be called to ratify that agreement. I'll never forget. I was in the men's locker room on my break. One of my friends up the line came in on his break; he was livid with rage. He had heard the conditions of the contract announced on a news broadcast and he was saying, "Man, he must have really got us something!" I said, "I don't understand. What do you mean?" What he meant was that the settlement must be damn good, for Walter Reuther had sacrificed an opportunity in which the ranks were willing to give their full energies to a fight for working conditions, just to get that improvement in the economic package.

In 1956, I got laid off in a cutback of 1700 men because the boom in auto was over. And by the time they called me back on the basis of seniority I was already back in the Bay Area. But it was in that period, 1955 and 1956, probably the biggest auto years in the postwar period, that some of the insights into the future began to occur to me. I knew from my experience in auto at this point that the next outbreak would be about the nature of the work, the oppressive nature of life in the plants, about the humanization of working conditions.

III

Rank and file revolts today remain isolated and localized. They'll begin to develop to a new plateau once it's discovered how to create an organizational vehicle whereby they can merge and no longer be isolated. But that means a new form of organization, and if that new organization doesn't change existing institutions, particularly of unions and collective bargaining, it will re-bureaucratize rapidly. Rank-and-file movements are already having the experience of sending good rank and filers into the bureaucracy and losing them as fast as they send them in, because the institutions aren't being changed. And, if we don't find a way to avoid rapid bureaucratization, we'll merely create more cynicism.

The only organizational means that I know of that cannot be taken over by a union bureaucracy are the informal work groups in the workplaces. The greatest enemies the groups have are unemployment or any change in the technology that destroys the group's life continuity, internal relationships and group-culture. Industries that don't have these groups, like the teamsters who drive alone on a truck, are at a natural disadvantage. But if informal work groups are the only form of organization that can't be taken over by a bureaucracy, then anti-bureaucratic organizational vehicles have to be based in them. The only way I have been able to think of it is to obtain a ratio of stewards or committeemen representation of about 1-to-15 or 1-to-25. That would mean that every steward would be a working steward, working within the vision of, in direct contact with, these informal work groups—something like the way it used to be in Chrysler before 1955 when Reuther allowed that corporation to adopt GM patterns. In effect, the work day is a full day of meeting within each one of these groups. And if the representative gets out of line, he or she is on the job and can be disciplined by the threat of chill-treatment, ridicule, and worse. If stewards' committees at that representation level were to be pyramided into councils on an area level and finally into congresses on a national level, then the people involved in that pyramiding would still come under some kind of disciplinary hold of people on the job. If the American working class could get an appreciably shorter work week, which is technologically possible, then no matter to how high an office a person went he or she would still be working representatives. The representation time it would take would come out of leisure time as well as work time.

The labor movement in this country has never done a thing with the whole primary work group concept. And that's where the muscle of the workers is and where the union's strength should be. A workplace isn't a collection of individuals so much as a collection of informal groups. Until you recognize that, you're not really into utilizing the power of people in the workplace.

At no time in our society has there ever been a serious discussion of work. The workplace is where most of a human's waking hours are spent. For the first time we have to examine the total oppressiveness of the individual's life. Workers in large numbers can have a fairly good life economically. But the total life experience is a very oppressive one and this goes for all levels of the working class in this country. People seek new solutions to that oppressiveness each day of their lives rather than just in terms of the next union contract or the next strike, and that is not being spoken to, whether it be in terms of heavy industrial, white collar, or professional work. I recently quoted a humorous Big Bill Haywood story to a carpenter with the remark, "Nothing's too good for the workers." He answered, "Yeah, until they get on the job."

The combination of a long period of relative full employment and automation has to a considerable extent destroyed the old values and work ethic at all levels of our labor force. In their desperation to lift morale, eliminate sabotage and increase production, employers are doing dabbling experiments involving piddling amounts of worker control. The official labor leadership fails to grasp the opening this provides to win some real controls. Their piecemeal approach looks to earlier retirements rather than humanizing the work. For the rank and file, life is supposed to begin with pension qualification in the autumn of existence. The view "from below" is quite different and that is the only place where real force generates to bring satisfaction, dignity and creativity to the work process.

GEORGE SULLIVAN

G EORGE SULLIVAN is a member of FASH (Fraternal Association of Steel Haulers), an organization of rank-and-file truckdrivers. He has lived for many years in Gary, Indiana, where FASH originated.

The steelhaulers who belong to FASH are owner-operators. They purchase their own equipment, pay all the cost of operating it plus fines and other incidentals, but are not allowed to haul for hire. They must lease their trucks to trucking companies on terms which are decided by the companies, although subject to bargaining by the International Brotherhood of Teamsters.

In 1967 the steelhaulers had not had a pay increase for eleven years. The Teamsters Union told them there was nothing it could do to increase their rates. After repeated protests, in August 1967 a small group of steelhaulers in Gary began to picket the headquarters of the Teamsters local. They were rebuffed. An even smaller group then set up a picket line at the gates of U. S. Steel Gary Works, one of the largest steel mills in the United States. Drivers began turning back and by nightfall steel shipments in the Gary area had halted.

For three weeks the men in Gary picketed alone. Then a group from Wisconsin came in and asked if they could help. The strike spread to Pennsylvania and other eastern states. In the seventh week of the strike the governor of Pennsylvania called together representatives of seven states, management, and labor. Agreements were reached providing pay increases amounting to eleven per cent over the next three years, and pay for loading and unloading trucks. FASH was born from this successful spontaneous strike.

George Sullivan has told the story of this strike in "Teamsters In Revolt: The Birth of FASH," a pamphlet published by the Writers Workshop in Gary, and reprinted by *Liberation* magazine in May 1971 under the title, "Rank and File Rebellion in the International Brotherhood of Teamsters." He also wrote an unpublished book-length history of FASH from which a few portions of this account were taken.

Here, George Sullivan describes the experiences which formed his ideas. He portrays himself as a small boy, raising and lowering the flag each day day at the schoolhouse, as an ex-serviceman taking part in the beatnik movement, and as a scab during the FASH strike before he joined FASH in 1969.

Since 1970, George Sullivan has been active in the Gary community. He was chairman of the Crime and Corruption Committee of the Calumet Community Congress, founder of the Calumet Action League, and assistant coordinator of the 1972 McGovern campaign in Lake County, Indiana.

Working for Survival

I

MY FATHER was from southern Illinois. His parents were born there and lived on a little farm. My father went into the service, came out and got a service-connected pension, something wrong with his lungs. He acquired a little farm, too. He could do almost anything he was pleased to.

Dad wouldn't take anything from WPA. We had a relief program which people could get. (I remember because I used to sneak off to a neighbor's house and get me half a grapefruit or something like that.) He always talked about anybody who was on that relief program or welfare [as] some kind of a bad individual, to take something for nothing and not working for it. He had a pension and he would get $50 a month and that's what he fed us on.

There were fourteen children in the family. Two died but there were twelve survivors. We were just one year after another until there were about six or seven of us. Unfortunately, I was the first one of the second group. I was at the wrong age to get any clothes handed down to me. I had less than the others because of that.

I had one pair of overalls and I would wear these all week to school. And then on Saturday I'd have to go around the house wrapped up in a sheet while my mother washed them and hung them on the clothesline to dry. That was a very uncomfortable kind of thing. We used to wear tennis shoes all winter because they were the cheapest shoes you could buy. And my feet were always cold.

My father had a lot of attitudes that I haven't seen in other parents. He didn't seem to feel pain very much and for that reason whenever he punished his sons he would overdo it. I think he thought we couldn't feel it, either. I don't remember ever seeing him act as if anything bothered him, and I've seen him in situations where he should have. If he hurt himself it just didn't seem to harm him. We weren't ever allowed to cry around him. He stressed that boys don't cry.

I never knew that other kids sat on their parents' laps. We never did that kind of thing. I don't blame my parents for that. There were just too many of us.

The only one of my grandparents I ever knew was my grandmother. She was always harassing my mother about something. They were always arguing. I never did even know why. She died when I was probably six or seven years old.

My mom and dad didn't go to church but they made us go. Dad kept a Bible in the house and he used to read it a lot and he always justified things by making comments or quotes from the Bible.

Reading was the first thing I can remember that I felt aggrieved about. My sister used to read the funny papers to me every Sunday. She'd get the paper and read it to me and I would watch as she was reading and follow all the action. Buck Rogers was my favorite. I'd spend half the day with the paper just going over what she'd been reading to me and trying to identify the words. If I didn't know I'd go back and ask her. This was before I went to school.

So I reached the point where I felt competent that I could read the newspaper. I got up real early one Sunday morning and went and got the paper before anybody else. I read it over first to make sure that I could understand it. When I took it in I announced to everybody that I was going to read the paper that morning, which I did. They said, "Aw, that's nothing, your sister's already read the paper to you and you memorized it." She said, "No, I haven't read it." Everybody denied that they had read the paper to me. At that time I really expected to get some credit for being able to read the paper without anybody reading it before I did. They just wouldn't believe it or they acted like "so what?" (Now I'm wondering why I didn't get any credit for being able to read it *after* someone else had read it to me!) That's one of the paradoxes that I ran into early.

Reading *Tom Sawyer* is almost like reading about my own child-hood. I didn't have a river but we had creeks. I played in or around water all the time. I spent a lot of time in the woods. We played cowboys and Indians. We carved pistols out of wood that looked almost real. We even used to make our own holsters out of pos-sum hides. We rode horses a lot of the time we were playing cow-boys and Indians. Everybody had horses. We didn't have saddles. (If you didn't have a saddle you had to be one of the Indians.) We made bows and arrows that you could actually kill small game with.

I had a hearing problem but I didn't know that. I thought people didn't talk loud enough. In school I was doing very badly in classes where you had to have a lot of instruction from the teacher. I think my parents really thought I was lazy, but they always just referred to me as being stupid. I was barely passing in some of the grades.

I was in fourth or fifth grade when the school nurse came along and gave us all inspections. She told the teacher and my par-ents that I was hard of hearing. I had a blockage in my tubes. After I got that problem taken care of I never had trouble in school again.

Our school was back in the woods and often the roads were so bad you couldn't get in. The teacher had to drive some distance. If he couldn't get in he might have to walk, he might be late. So he asked for someone to be at the school every day to build a fire in the furnace, sweep the schoolhouse out and put up the flag, and he said he'd pay five dollars a month for that. So I took the job. I was only six or seven years old at the time. I did that for ten years.

I'd always have the flag flying before anybody got there. It was a point of honor with me that I had to have the flag up before any-body got to school. I didn't want them to be at school with the flag not up.

Taking the flag down was the same way. I never did let that flag get down on the ground. It was a pretty big flag too, or it seemed big to me at the time. Sometimes it would get all over the place when I was trying to get it down but I never did let it get on the ground. I would always fold it in a cocked hat like you're supposed to do. We had a little shelf where I put it away. I was really proud of that flag.

I liked to read a lot so I was always reading about American history and the flag plays a great part in the early years. The flag meant all the things I was reading in the books. Everybody is a hero. We were fortunate in never getting a bad guy to be president. We never had a louse in high office. America has always managed to get enemies who were evil. I don't think I ever read in school about us being in conflict with someone who wasn't of a very evil nature. I was just proud of the fact that we as a nation were able to be so selective in our enemies.

When you read about other nations who have been aggressive, the world is full of bad guys. There's always nations that are ripping off other nations and in some cases they're both mean people. In religions, the Moslems and Hindus and so forth . . . I just felt great to live in a nation where we were Christians and we didn't make those kind of mistakes. I can't ever remember feeling that America had attacked someone who didn't really deserve it.

I can remember very well the feeling I had for that flag. I knew what it meant to me. It was not the same as it is now. That's what gives me the feeling that I was cheated as well as lied to. I read the books that talked about indentured servants at the same time they praised the glories of America. I read the books that talked about our great cotton production in the South and the greatness of the nation at the same time that they talked about the slaves. And when I read *Uncle Tom's Cabin* I didn't read any indictment of America into that. I feel stupid. It's like I was sitting there watching someone deal from the bottom of the deck but I didn't even pay attention to it. Why didn't I see it? You feel like an idiot.

Maybe part of it is that I was too young when reading the books to understand what was being said. When I read books about Indian wars, the way the Indians would do in the woods and the things they could do, I related to that because I spent a lot of time in the woods, too. I tried all that stuff, trying to make arrowheads out of flintstones, building a fire with a stick (which I never was able to do). But I could still accept that they were bad because they didn't believe in God. Their god wasn't explained the way ours is. They

were here trying to keep this land away from us and it should right-
fully have been ours because we were smart enough to find it. [The
books] didn't go into the fact that [the Indians] found it a long time
before we did or that they were already here. Naturally when you're
young you don't put those ideas into context.

I read every book in our school library and I was having my sisters
bring home books from high school, but some kinds of books I never
got to see. None of the people in my type of background read a
book like *The Wind in the Willows*. If anyone around had read it
I would have heard of it so that I know that that book is not a part
of our culture. The people who have read it are middle-class or
upper-middle-class. It is not a working-class fairy tale.

In all the fairy tales that we had, one thing came through loud
and clear. There was always the squirrel that wouldn't work, that
wouldn't do anything in the summer but play games. He was stupid.
And he either met eventual death or suffered through the winter on
someone else's charity, was a welfare case you might say. And after
that one miserable experience he then learned his lesson and worked
hard and industriously for the rest of his life. The transgression of
the law may be slight—in an animal story it is always slight, like
an old bear stealing the honey—but the punishment that befalls those
who break the laws is terrible. In my fairy tales I never encountered
an unjust judge or an unfair policeman.

And when I [recently] read *The Wind in the Willows* it was so
opposite. The rat and the mole get together, the rat runs down into
the hole and comes out with a picnic basket packed with a thousand
goodies. It was just there: he probably had a servant. But had I read
that fairy tale [as a child], there would first have been a description
of the work that went into the preparation of that picnic basket and
where all this food came from. There would have been a big difference in the way he acquired it, and the way they acquired food all
through the summer. And never once was there a mention that they
must worry about the winter that was coming. Somehow they were
going to party through the winter or just sleep it off. Like the badger,
when they went into his house after being caught out in the snow,
here he was with this huge larder, well-stocked, and the badger did
nothing but diddle around all summer too. Their greatest fear was

the stoats and the weasels. I immediately related that to us. The stoats and the weasels are those low-class groups out of the woods who might want to take some of the goodies. It made me mad.

There never was any question in my mind that niggers weren't any good. I knew that, but it didn't necessarily mean they were bad people because everyone knew that a nigger's a coward and that he won't cause you any trouble. The one thing I never knew anyone to worry about was problems with the niggers. There weren't any around where I lived.

One did come to the house one time, scared me to death. I saw him at the door, there he was, and I didn't know what to do. Any time we would be doing something wrong, one of the comments my mother would make was, "I'll have some big nigger come and get you if you don't stop that." So I went to the door and there was this big nigger. I just knew that he had come after me. But that's the only association I had. I wasn't taught to hate them. It was like the feeling about animals. It's OK but their place is not in the house or it's not where *you* are. Animals live in the woods. Niggers live somewhere else.

My first association with black people was when I went in the service. They were following the policy of integration. We were in a barracks with three black guys, seventy or seventy-five white guys. The blacks were not hard to get along with. It would have been kind of foolish if they were.

The first real association I had was in England. I transferred to a new base. I got there in the middle of the day. They told me what barracks I was assigned to. I went into the barracks and no one was there. Everybody was out working. I put my gear all in, made my bed and everything and went to the canteen and came back about 3:30 or 4:00. I walked in and I didn't see a white face. It was a barracks full of black people.

I knew, of course, that the sergeant had made an error, put me in the wrong barracks. So I went to the headquarters and told him he'd made a mistake. "No, we've been having some problems about not integrating enough. As new white guys come on the base they're going to be put in there. You just happen to be the first." I said, "But you don't understand. I'm the only guy. You don't put just one white guy in with all those black people." He made me to understand that they did and that's the way it was to be. I wasn't very happy with that.

The first couple of days I didn't talk to any of them. They didn't talk to me. I restricted all their conversation, that was obvious, because they were having a real good time and when I walked in everything just quieted down. It was their first realization that they had a white guy in the barracks. They didn't know how to deal with that any more than I knew how to deal with all of them.

I was a meat-cutter and I got a bit careless. I cut three or four of my fingers. I had them all bandaged up. I had just been promoted to sergeant but I still wore my corporal stripes. I was sitting out in front of the barracks and the sergeant came by and he said, "Sullivan, aren't you a member of the first class?" "Yes." He said, "Well, get your stripes on." "I can't sew with one hand," I said, "and I don't have any money to take them over to the PX." They charged something like fifty cents a set to put them on. He said, "I don't care. You'll have stripes on your uniform by tomorrow or we'll just take the stripes away from you."

I was stitting there by myself just wondering what to do. One of the guys in the barracks who'd heard it, he came out and said, "Have you already got your stripes?" I said, "Yeah, I bought them already." He said, "Well if you go get them I'll sew them on for you." So that was the first thing that really broke the ice. He sat and sewed those stripes on my uniform while we got to know each other.

I was in the service for four years. It was my first experience being in other countries. I was in France, Denmark, Germany and England.

When I got to England I just went wild—I thought I was in the land of my books. Robin Hood had been one of my heroes. And the knights and King Arthur's Round Table and, boy, it was all there. When I first saw Ely Castle I couldn't believe it, still the old castle with the moat around it, the drawbridge. I went to Nottingham, Sherwood Forest . . . I just couldn't stop. From the time I went to England until I came back I was going where my books were.

When I used to read all the time about England and Richard the Lion Hearted, he was mine. So was Robin Hood. It almost felt like these were my people. I felt like that was the mother country. Maybe I felt like it was part of our ancestry or something. But other guys over there didn't have that feeling at all. They treated the English as though they were beneath contempt. It used to anger me, some of the tricks they would pull.

Even before I went to England I had some admiration for the bobbies in England. And after getting there and watching them operate I had even more. I had already been instructed in America by the police to move on or get out of the way a time or two. It's unbelievable, to have a bobby come up and say, "Sir, if you'll excuse me a moment, you are blocking the sidewalk. Please move on." They spoke so polite that for a moment you weren't sure they were serious. They were very serious and when they asked you to move, they intended for you to move. American cops have the attitude of "get the hell out of the way" and start shoving. I never saw London bobbies do that.

When I went to France and other places I would search out someone who was a civilian there, find out what he had to tell me about where he lived. The only time I was in a problem, I was in the Bastille area in France and although I wasn't wearing my uniform I was immediately spotted for an American. It was all Communists there and they started a terrific uproar about "Yankee go home" and all that stuff. But even at that point, when they were doing it, I understood what they were angry about because I had already seen what the GIs were doing to the people over there, the way they treated them, and I knew why they would be yelling "Yankee go home," so it didn't make me angry. I would always go out and look for what was going on and hear the other side of the story. I thought the Communists were a bit silly but I liked to hear what the *people* were saying. I liked to talk to them.

I came home with a different feeling than I had before. I no longer felt as proud to be an American as I had in the past. I just didn't feel that sense of we were unique. I began to have more the idea that we exist and they exist.

I lost a lot of my ideas about what you should and shouldn't do. I began to feel like maybe in America you'd just as well go ahead and do what you felt like doing because nobody really gave a damn about it anyway. Before I went into the service, to do something against the law, to do something you're not supposed to do, was a bad thing. When I came out I didn't have the respect for the law that I had had before because I felt that the law itself was a cheat. I guess I lost my sense of right and wrong.

In the service in the early fifties I had the experience of meeting people from all over the United States. Most of these people were not gung-ho Americans who had enlisted to be heroes for the country. They were guys who had done exactly what I had done. They had joined the Air Force to escape being drafted into the Army and going to Korea. Most of us had older brothers coming out of World War II who had the experience of going to war and they were all giving the same advice: "Man, get into the Air Force. You don't get your ass shot off." So I think that the Air Force was the recipient at that time of what is today the draft dodger.

I came back into civilian life in the mid-fifties. That's when the beatnik thing was beginning, the idea of "let's just get out of it and not be involved." Disillusionment was what was taking place, but the action was to just set down and do nothing, not be a part of what you considered a very phony world.

When I came out of the service I worked for just a little while and then I didn't work any more. I felt that it didn't serve a purpose. It wouldn't lead anywhere. And the idea of being forced to work just for survival—it seemed to me to be degrading that you should have to work simply because you are a human being and you are here. I started wondering, who made those kind of rules and why?

I remember meeting an old guy who said he refused to work because he'd never been able to find a job where someone else didn't make a profit off his efforts, and he was looking for a job where he was the recipient of all he produced. I wasn't looking for that kind of job. I just wasn't looking for a job. But neither were a whole lot of guys at that time.

I think the beatniks were political by being apolitical. They were the ones who were just beginning to set down and say, "I don't want to participate." It wasn't like the strikes in the thirties when people would set down and strike as a demand for something. They just didn't want anything. They wanted to disassociate themselves. And I can see now how it would be really dangerous [to the system] for working-class people to do that.

I met them all over the country when I was going around, and nearly all of them were from working-class families. They had a mom and dad and a small home somewhere and everybody in the family worked but them and they were considered the bum or the outcast of the family. They didn't feel guilty about it. They just felt, "Why the hell should I work if I can do something else?" It wasn't a welfare attitude. I never signed for unemployment or did all that. I somehow scuffled my own living and I did things that were illegal as well at times to get some money or to get survival, but I didn't feel guilty about that because I could have shown a policeman doing something illegal to match what we were doing that was illegal. So, I felt, fair is fair.

I remember jokes that you could very easily relate to at the time. You may remember the attitude of the beatnik when the guy was laying in the street, got run over by a car, and was saying, "Call me an ambulance." And the beatnik says, "OK, man, you're an ambulance," his attitude being, I'm not a part of whatever's taking place and I don't want to be. There were a whole series of them. They called it the beat generation or the cool generation because they were totally unruffled by whatever was surrounding them.

The beat generation made a thing out of saying everything very slowly and very drawn out—no fire, no snap—even in conversation they were saying "I quit." They always stressed the same thing, their disinterest in what was taking place.

Another one of their expressions was "no sweat." That's an expression from the fifties, no sweat. Don't get excited. Don't worry about it. And they didn't sweat about anything.

I had very much the same sense myself, and I'm sure a lot of other guys had it, that everywhere I was at I was a spectator. I remember an incident in Ohio sitting on a hill, looking over the town and just watching what the people were doing and thinking,

"This is ridiculous." I remember hearing a door slam and it's in the evening and a mother calling her kid to come to supper and I was thinking, "She's worried about the kid. He's out playing ball and he doesn't want to be bothered. She's worried about his not coming." I knew other mothers who used to be that way at home and I thought, "Isn't it silly? People all over the country are out now yelling for their kids to come for supper and they're all worried about where the kid is and when he's coming." It's just like a whole big issue over nothing. Everything I saw I was putting into the context of, "Why is everybody getting excited? It's not important." You would see a squad car roaring up and down the street, answering a burglar alarm or what-have-you, and your thought would be, "So what's the hurry?"

Throughout that whole group of guys that I knew there was the feeling that nothing is worth [worrying about]. They weren't bad people and most of them finally got married and I guess most of them are back within the system and working. I don't think they care that much now about what is going on. But somehow or another you get forced into working for your survival.

I knew how to drive and that's one of the things I used to do when I was drifting around. If I got really hard up for money and didn't see any other way to acquire it, I'd go somewhere and drive a truck for a short time. Also I could drive a taxicab. A lot of the guys I knew did cab driving as an odd job, whenever they needed a few dollars.

I got into driving a truck seriously in 1960, drove for a while. . . . Then the guy asked me if I'd go to work in the office. I did and in a short time I was running the terminal. I got bored with that and I quit, went back to doing nothing for a long time. . . .

I went downtown and got involved with some poker games, working for the house joints. I did that until '65. Then I went back to driving a truck again and I drove a truck most of the time up until the FASH strike [in 1967].

Trucking is a job to which a man soon becomes addicted. The young people have been insisting that there is more to life than money and though the average trucker may not know how to express it in words, he feels the essence of this belief deeply. I will not attempt to speak for everyone but, as for myself, I have a weakness for the late hours of the night.

Running late at night through small rural towns I often have the feeling that I am the only one awake in the whole world. Things appear different from high in the cab of a truck. The trees along the road make a tunnel through which your headlights illuminate a semi-circle of green. The limbs across the road are so close that at times I can reach out and touch them. Mailboxes seem to rise up from the ground as my lights pick them up. The dashlights glow softly in the dark and the dials are constantly keeping me informed that all is well with "my horse." The easy snick-snick of the stick as I change gears and the sound of the tires singing in the cool night air, all combine to make my truck seem like a living thing that is keeping me safe and protected in its shell. Oncoming trucks blink their lights in a friendly hello as we pass in the night, or maybe flash them to warn me about the local cop in the next town who may be still awake trying to make another fine before he turns in. Another truck overtaking me comes around and I see the same soft glowing lights in his cab as he lifts his hand from the wheel to wave. I signal him in and he fades off into the darkness leaving me alone with my thoughts again. There is a soft glow in the East and then the rising sun comes up on a new world for I am four hundred miles from last night. These are the hours that compensate for the rest of it and for me they are the best part of trucking. Although the hours are long and hard and the amount of money earned is often less after expenses than in other skilled trades, most truckers will not trade places with anyone.

Truckers who have taken the time to talk to the young have learned to their surprise that they are in agreement on about ninety per cent of the discussion. The two major differences are that the truckers believe that the establishment should not be overthrown as it would only be replaced by another rule that might be harder to handle. They prefer instead to give City Hall the same treatment as the proverbial mule.

The other major difference is in the area of tactics. In spite of all the publicity, the students are far too mild-mannered and don't have enough "clout." A reporter for *Iron Age* has researched the matter and stated that, "The revolt of the truckers has made the student rebellion seem like a Sunday school picnic by comparison."

II

I did not become a FASH member until August of 1969. Along with many other steelhaulers, I had thought that their original protest in 1967 would be a waste of time. They were fighting with the Teamsters Union and I felt that they did not have a chance.

When the protest of 1967 began I was working as a dispatcher for Artim Transportation Company in East Chicago, Indiana. Throughout the protest this company never stopped operating. As trucks began coming in with bullet holes, busted windshields and shattered radiators, I started to wonder what made the drivers keep going out. The clerk typing out the bills thought he had the answer. "They're nuts," he used to say over and over. "They don't know those bullets can hurt you."

Along about the middle of the strike, I started driving again and so began my first experience as a scab. I thought I was missing all the fun but I soon learned that it was the other side that was having the fun. A truck strike is unlike any other because you don't just go through a picket line and have only one danger point. All the time you are on the highway, you are a target and you never know where it is coming from next. The scabs may not like to admit it, but when they reach their destination they all breathe a little bit easier.

I have never met [a scab] who could give a sensible reason for trying to prevent his fellow men from gaining a better way of life. All scabs refuse to discuss the issues at stake or go to strike meetings to hear what's going on. Knowledge is a dangerous thing to a scab's existence for once he learns what it is all about, he ceases to be a scab or else exposes himself to be the kind of no good bastard that some scabs are.

There are many reasons why a scab is such a hated man. There is much more to it than the mere fact that he is working. There is often a long history of injustice behind the man who is aiming the rifle. Just how long that history is and how much effect it has had on him is what determines whether he aims at a tire or the driver.

For myself, there had been very little direct injustice. I had won only one grievance while with the union which should have paid me about a thousand dollars or more. The business agents had told me that I would have to take four hundred dollars or shut up about it. I hadn't thought I was getting a fair deal but the drivers who were old hands told me that it was par for the course and I was lucky to get that.

I joined FASH because I saw that it was a good thing for the owner-operator. When I first met Tom Gwilt, president of the Indiana chapter of FASH, and Paul Dietsch, who is president of the Wisconsin chapter, I was not very impressed. They seemed like a couple of nice enough guys but they were not what I had expected the officers of a growing organization to be. They acted just like truck drivers. We had been complaining for years that no one else understood the steelhaulers' special problems and that what we needed was our own thing. We wanted our own people to run it. Now we had exactly that and here I was thinking to myself, "What are these guys doing in charge? They don't know any more than I do." As I got to know them better, I found out that they knew a hell of a lot more than I did and they had learned it the hard way.

I had never felt any inclination or impulse to change the world around me. I felt in any situation I went into that it was that way before I got there. And if I didn't like it or couldn't make it with that situation, I would just leave it and find another one. For all I cared it could stay that way forever, so long as what was happening didn't infringe on me. I really didn't want any conflicts. I'd done a lot of scuffling earlier and I didn't want to do it any more—unless it involved money or something I was really trying to protect. I had developed the attitude of not bothering anyone who didn't bother me, not trying to take something that wasn't mine, but because of that, I had to make very sure that what was mine was not touched or not bothered. On the street there are certain things that are yours. Your car is a valuable possession, your girl friend is a valuable possession, and your money. Anything else is not really worth so much, if you don't own a house or property. If someone is bothering your girl friend and she doesn't like it, you tell him not to. And if he keeps on, you really make him to understand that he is not to do that. If they're trying to take your money or trying to do something to your car, those are what you have outlined as your rights. I never would have gone out of my way or gotten involved to protect someone else's rights. It had to be mine before I would do anything.

The incident with the Teamsters involved one of the three things that you never surrendered to somebody else. Money, perhaps because it's so necessary to survival, perhaps because the only reason you're going through a lot of things that you are is for that money, is the one thing above all that you never let anyone take away from you. You just don't let that happen. I didn't get into it because I felt that it was up to me to change what was taking place in the union. I was going to fight them because my money was involved.

Really, the only reason I was involved with it was that I was trying to get myself uninvolved, by saying, "Give me what's mine, stop doing what you are doing wrong, and then we'll get along with each other." So [I began] to look around for allies, somebody to help, and the problem kept growing. I knew in the back of my mind all the time the way the whole system was but I just never cared. Somewhere I began to realize this: the only thing to do is to change the whole system or you got to go through this the rest of your life. And I expected that when I was done with this argument I'd be back trucking so while I was at it I might as well get the whole problem cleaned out. So it was for very personal reasons that I was trying to change the Teamster system, because I planned to go back to driving a truck and I didn't want to be harassed later.

At the time that I joined FASH, they had been fighting an unpublicized war with the union leaders for two and a half years. They were preparing to distribute a magazine called *Teammate* which told about the Teamsters officials' nefarious activities with the members' money. As far as the Teamster officials are concerned, it is an unwritten law in the Teamsters Union that what is done with the members' money is not to be discussed.

After reading the first issue of *Teammate*, I was sure that somebody was not going to like it. Just as I expected, about a week after we had started distributing the first issue of *Teammate*, trouble arrived.

I was at the terminal working on my truck when Don Williams, a long-time friend of mine, came speeding up in his car. He jumped out and said, "Hey George, I just heard a radio broadcast that said that Tom Gwilt's house was bombed." "Is anyone hurt?" I asked. "I don't think anyone was home when it happened," he replied. "Come on, let's get over there and see if there might be something we can do."

When we found Tom, he was at a neighbor's home who had been kind enough to give him and his wife Betty a place to stay. Paul Dietsch was there also and he gave us a rundown on what had happened.

Tom and Paul had been in Pittsburgh and Betty and their two children were visiting a relative when their house was bombed. We assumed that our enemy had known this and so the bomb was simply their time-honored method of giving a warning that FASH was getting out of line.

There were several other drivers there and more came in while I was there. Most of them had been with FASH since its beginning. I noticed that Tom was having a disagreement with some of them and I walked over to them to see what was going on.

The men were planning to take action against the union officials in Local 142 and Tom was trying to discourage them. "No! No! you guys," he was saying. "There wasn't anybody hurt so don't do anything foolish. Let the police handle it."

"Police, hell!" exclaimed one of the drivers. "They wouldn't arrest one of those sons-a-bitches if they had watched him set off the bomb."

"Listen to us, Tom," another driver said. "If we let them get away with this there will be more trouble later. I think they are testing us to see what we will do."

Then another driver spoke. "Just one will be enough," he said. "We'll just get one of them and that will be enough to show that we mean business," and he named the man that he thought we should hit.

Tom was adamant, however, and he refused to give in. "This is just their way of harassing us," he said. "As long as they don't kill any of our people, we won't kill any of theirs and if you get

carried away now it might cause a lot of unnecessary bloodshed.''
We had no proof of who had bombed the house, of course, but there
wasn't a man there who thought it was anyone other than the Teamsters Union. Tom managed to cool things down and went inside to
prepare a press release for the newsmen who were on their way over
for an interview.

I went up the street and looked at the remains of Tom's house.
Whenever we hear about gun battles and bombs and other kinds of
violence, we don't usually think too much about it. That sort of
thing always seems to happen to strangers and doesn't make too
much of an impact unless a lot of people are killed or hurt. When
it is someone you know it changes things. No one had been hurt
but that explosion had been a message. Someone was trying to tell
us something and I didn't like it. I had grown up believing that I
was lucky to be born in a country where men had a freedom to
choose their own destiny, and terrorism was something that I had
not experienced. I had been happily helping to build an organization
that would be our own thing and, in my innocence, I had thought
that we had every right to do so. And now, I was looking at a message that drew the line of freedom loud and clear. To me it said,
so far—and no farther.

During the next few days as I watched Tom and Betty trying to
clean up the mess caused by the blast, I did a lot of thinking. Betty
Gwilt had been extremely helpful to Tom in his work with FASH and I
thought that if she were to become afraid to go on, it might cause
Tom to quit also.

The Gwilts had only recently redecorated their home and, like
most wives, Betty had been rather proud of their new furniture and
the new wall-to-wall carpet in their living room. I was thinking about
the carpet because they used the house as sort of a second office
and since steelhaulers usually have their shoe soles impregnated with
oil and grease, Betty always made us take off our shoes before we
walked on the carpet. So now, most of the furniture was destroyed,
the carpet was a mess and Tom didn't have any insurance.

I could see that Betty was having a tough time controlling her
emotions. We didn't have any trouble in removing the damaged furniture because the entire front of the house was gone and we could

just walk from the front yard into the living room at any point we wanted to. Betty was trying to sweep up the rubble that was lying all over the place and once I saw her pick up a broken object from a pile of rubble and she stood there turning it over and over in her hand and looking at it for a long time. The expression in her face was one of deep sadness. I don't know what the object was or what it meant to her, but she didn't seem to want to part with it, even though it was destroyed. She finally laid it back in the pile of rubbish and walked away.

There was only one time when I thought she was going to give up. The carpet she was so proud of was split in several places and had also been scorched where the bomb had exploded. Tom was holding up the edge of the carpet and inspecting the damage when he said, "What do you think, Betty? Maybe if we sewed it up it wouldn't look so bad and we could still use it." She looked at him as if she were about to cry and said, "Oh, Tom," in a very quiet sad voice and then sat down and put her face in her hands.

I suddenly had the feeling that there were too many people in the house so I walked outside. Betty toughened up after that though and never once did I hear her mention the possibility of quitting. I wanted to tell about this incident because afterwards someone was trying to spread the rumor that Tom had blown up his own house for publicity.

After the bombing of Tom's house I began to realize that the FASH leaders had knowingly laid their lives on the line. They had also placed their wives and children in danger. It was not for money because any driver with a steady job earns more than a FASH officer. I am not the hero type and my good sense was telling me that we weren't playing with kids.

There were some other things going through my mind also. I have had the experience of talking to people who talk in glowing terms about the great freedom we have and in the next breath say to me, "You had better not do anything those people don't like or you will get yourself hurt." I think a newspaper reporter summed up the whole situation when he said, "We are not restricted but we know what we should not say."

I don't like to admit it, but I had always belonged to that rather large part of the population that prefers to let other people do the fighting while we set back and wait to see what they win for us this time. After thinking the matter over I decided that I would stay with FASH and if it led me to danger I would face it in the best way that I knew how.

KEN TUCKER

A<small>T THE TIME</small> of the events described in this account, Ken Tucker was the secretary of an independent local union of chemical workers at the Du Pont Chemical Company plant in East Chicago, Indiana.

The situation of workers at Du Pont is like that of many workers in the early 1930s. When Ken Tucker became a union officer the Du Pont union had never been on strike. For all practical purposes it was a company union. Tucker and his fellow-officers bargained militantly and finally led the union on strike, only to find that as a single local union confronting a national corporation their position was very weak.

Before going to work at Du Pont, Ken Tucker had started an underground newspaper for servicemen in Korea. But as he candidly explains, when he first became involved in union affairs it was as a stepping-stone to a job as a foreman. His experience as a local union officer changed his mind.

Ken Tucker is one of a group of younger workers at the Du Pont plant who, like younger workers elsewhere, want not only material benefits but a voice in decision-making. When they went on strike they raised pollution as a strike issue so as to win community support. As an unintended result, Ken Tucker himself became the first president of a multi-issue community organization, the Calumet Community Congress, formed in December 1970.

KEN TUCKER

It Got My Back Up

ᶯᶯ
ᶯᶯᶯᶯᶯᶯᶯᶯᶯᶯᶯᶯᶯᶯᶯᶯᶯᶯᶯᶯᶯᶯᶯᶯᶯᶯᶯᶯᶯᶯᶯᶯᶯᶯᶯᶯᶯᶯ

I STARTED WORKING at Du Pont in 1963, after I got out of the Service. I was single at the time and didn't care especially where I worked. I was just knocking around, looking for a paycheck. My family had a past history of working at Du Pont. My foster father and my uncle had worked there for a total of more than eight years. So it was natural that I had a little pull to get in.

In fact, it wasn't until I was elected secretary of the union and went through the records that I realized my foster father had been secretary years before. I hold him responsible for a lot of the problems at the place!

Du Pont screens very carefully in hiring. One of the first questions you are asked is how you feel about international unions, and how you feel about unions in general. And of course, someone coming off the street and looking for a job is not going to take a militant union stand. At the time, being twenty-three years old and not really caring about people's problems, just caring about myself, I was pretty honest with them when I said that an independent union was fine with me, no union was fine with me, the only thing I wanted was a job.

So I got hired in. After working there for a while, and getting married and having a family, just like anybody else I started to think about ways to move up the ladder. Our plant has a simple way for a working guy to advance. All you had to do was get elected to a union job, work closely with management and show some potential for leadership, and inside of a year or so you'd get a nice job as a foreman. About ninety per cent of the supervisors have come off the union board.

Recognizing that this was the way to get a better-paying job, I decided to run for union office. This was in 1968. I had been there five years and was known only in my own department, where I had been a steward and had raised some hell, done some rather militant things. They were really done for my own self-interest, as a way to get attention and to move up.

I was elected by two votes. For three or four years prior to the election our union had been starting to flex its muscles, trying to become a union and really represent the guys. Those of us running for office attacked the incumbents for failing to communicate with the grassroots and failing to allow decisions to be made at union meetings. Just before the election there was a union meeting at which the president said that a wage offer had been made to the union, and the membership could vote on it if it wanted to, but it didn't make any difference because the offer had already been accepted. Being a politician, I took him on strongly and this probably got me the votes I needed to win. I was twenty-eight years old and the next to oldest man on the new board of the union. John Smrekar, the new president, was twenty-six.

During the years I've been in office my viewpoint has changed, obviously. I've had two offers to go into supervision. The first was a sincere offer, I think, but the last was just to get me out of there.

It's a simple thing that happens. Even though I was still looking out for Number One, I did have the responsibility of protecting other people and they had grievances and complaints. It put me into a head-on battle with the company. It's a tragedy that every wageroll guy doesn't have that experience. Because it didn't take me very long of being involved in a confrontation with the company over a legitimate grievance to begin to see what we were up against. Being on a union board, and doing this an average of once or twice a day, my whole outlook changed. I had worked in one department where I saw maybe one guy get messed over a month, and now I had the exposure to the whole plant, and saw what was happening everywhere.

They were very reasonable demands. A contract is in effect, it's been agreed to by the union and the company, grievance procedure and everything else, and the company refuses to honor it—just completely ignores it—depending on how they feel. When you run up against this enough, you begin to get angry. You start feeling a little bit different about things. You sit down to bargain, you believe that you're supposed to be the bargaining representative of the people who elected you, and the company just puts up a pretense of bargaining so that they won't be liable under federal law. It got my back up.

Du Pont has traditionally been a very paternalistic company. One of the problems that we faced, and other Du Pont unions faced, was that for years Du Pont did take care of their employees. That was at a time when the chemical industry wasn't very competitive and Du Pont was the kingmaker. Every time there was a war, Du Pont expanded and made a lot of dough. That's not the situation today. Today everybody's into chemicals. There's a very competitive market, and in many cases they even try to withdraw the benefits that you already have. I've seen the company slip from a position of being tops in the area in wages to a position of being fifth or sixth. It's gradually falling back in every area of the contract. And Du Pont's whole language changes. When I started in it was, "We will maintain the best pension plan of any industry in the United States." Their policy today is, "We never said that. We said we'll give you one of the better pension plans." In a couple of years it's going to be, "You guys have got a pretty good pension plan."

There's also a split within the union membership. Forty-seven per cent of our employees were hired before 1958. They were there when Du Pont was the best. Many of those guys will tell you that they worked every day of the Depression. For them Du Pont can do no wrong. The rest of the guys, like myself, began hiring in around 1962 or 1963. They don't feel this loyalty, and they don't see this paternalism. Even if it was there they wouldn't want it, because their attitudes are different, they don't want things doled out to them, they want to start making decisions and they want to be involved.

We don't want to bargain on a local comparison basis. If everybody in Lake County got a $10 raise tomorrow, Du Pont would get it, too. That's not what we want. We want to have something to say about our own destiny. Our whole philosophy is that we don't even want to compare. Our position with the company has been, "Look, open up your books. If the East Chicago plant is making a twenty per cent profit this year, we want a twenty per cent wage increase."

As secretary of the union, I had possession of the records. I started studying the history of our union a little. I found out, for example, that in the five years before 1968 there had only been forty grievances filed. With three hundred guys in the union, that breaks down to eight grievances a year. I found it hard to believe that the company made mistakes only eight times a year. The first year we were in office we had to learn what the contract was, what the grievance procedure was, getting our education the hard way. We filed forty grievances the first year. Now we've gotten to the point where I myself last year filed two hundred.

In 1970 we led the first strike in the history of the union. Between 1964 and 1968 there had been three strike votes, but the union had never gone through with it. We felt we had to.

What our strike amounted to was a strike for recognition. We had started to bargain four months before our contract expired, and we had been working without a contract for eight months, so we had been trying to bargain for a year. We were unsuccessful, simply because Du Pont refused to recognize us as a union. They didn't believe that we would really shut them down. They had always managed to evade a strike threat without making a change. So we were very honest with our people. We took the strike vote in January, and we told the members: number one, if you give us the strike vote we will use it; number two, if we strike we won't win. We said there was no way that we could bring a corporate giant like Du Pont to its knees, that they could spend any amount of money to defeat us in a strike, and that from the minute we went out until the minute we came back, we would be looking for an honorable way to come back. But we said we had to strike to let them know we were serious. What we were striking for was the same thing that unions struck for in the '30s, recognition as a union.

We had no experience with strikes. Du Pont, on the other hand, will go to fantastic lengths to win a strike. Du Pont in Niagara was on strike for six months. The company was close to the mayor and the City Council, and within four hours of the strike they had a court injunction guaranteeing them ingress and egress at the plant. The union wasn't even notified of its right to appear in court. They had a second exit which went out through a power company and when the union tried to picket it, they called it a secondary boycott. They organized a dissident group within the union which took the union to court on the ground that it was violating its constitution. Du·Pont will use tactics you wouldn't believe. In our plant, for example, they ran trucks in and out with nothing in them, to give the impression that the plant was doing just fine. They were paying wages and everything else just to run trucks through our picket lines. They fly in scabs from all over the country. There's a law against that, but the way they get around that law is that those people all work for the Du Pont company. They tap your phones: my phone was tapped during our strike. They will hire lip readers, will you believe? They will hire lip readers who stand on top of the plant with binoculars and read what's being said on the picket lines.

We began to look around for support for our strike, before we ever went out. We raised the pollution issue at the bargaining table. We hadn't been able to move the company on anything, so we began to talk about pollution as a health and safety issue, and then we realized that we were talking about a community concern, a social problem. We thought that maybe we could move them off dead center by beginning to bargain about this. And we also thought that, if we were forced to go on a strike, we would be the first union in the country to go on strike over pollution, and possibly would pick up the support of people from the community. That's exactly what happened.

We met with the federal mediator in Chicago and he asked us what the issues were. We said, "Pollution, of the water and the air. That's the only thing we're striking for." He said, "I don't believe it. I've just come back from two weeks at a conference in Florida with people from labor, management, government, and we all agreed that one of the issues that had to come to the bargaining table was pollution. Here I am, my first day back, and that's all you guys are talking about." We went on strike the next day.

We didn't really push for press coverage. But people started to stop by and ask, ''Are you really striking about pollution?'' It was interesting. Our own people, when we started handing out the picket signs about pollution, would say, ''What the hell are you doing?'' To them we would put it that this was a major issue and maybe we could get community support on it. It really was a tactic. But as we got into it, and a citizens' support group was actually organized, it opened up a whole new world.

There was a union board, a leadership, there were union members, that were willing to come forward and testify to the public or any-body else that was interested, about what they knew about pollution. No matter what Du Pont said or did they could say, ''Look man, I work there and I'm telling you what's happening.'' We are the only Du Pont plant that's ever been on strike without being punished, by the company shutting down facilities and moving jobs elsewhere, or something like that. And the reason was that we had community support.

The company called us and asked to meet with the union. They offered us a contract. The contract wasn't much: there was very little change that would seem meaningful to, say, the Steelworkers Union on strike. There were some things in there that I felt were important enough to strike about. For example, we never had the right to arbi-trate a discharge. We won that. We never had the right to say any-thing when the company brought in outside contractors to do mechanical work or electrical work. We won that, too. Monetary gains were very slim, amounting to perhaps $5 a month. But the important thing was that for the first time in its its history Du Pont had changed what they call their ''firm and final offer.''

We went back without settling the pollution issue. But the com-munity group did manage to negotiate a very strong agreement with Du Pont. It created an altogether different situation. Our people became aware of pollution. Our people would call me and say, ''Hey, the company told me to dump something in the river last night, and I didn't do it, and they're going to give me a hard time.'' I'd call the company and they'd send me a written report on the investigation of the pollution incident.

It was very successful. It changed some attitudes. It helped to get our plant manager transferred, which was another reason for our going on strike, and I think that was a first, too. We managed to get a company representative to come to a meeting at Bishop Noll High School and debate the issue. I've never been so scared in my life as to be there confronting my own plant manager, calling him a liar. But I did it. The board members were there with me. I did speak up. That was one of the experiences I went through where our union could never have won anything until we tied in with the community. At the same time the community won a major victory because it had the support of the union, both the leadership and the rank and file.

The next year, when contract time came, we tried to look into Du Pont's taxes. We tried to contrast the taxes of a white employee with those of a black employee, and the taxes of Du Pont with those of a homeowner living across the street. We were going to ask Du Pont to pay its fair share of taxes in the community. I'm sure Du Pont got wind of this because the first day of contract negotiations they said, "We've really got a package for you this year." It was head and shoulders above anything we'd ever gotten before.

Being president of the Calumet Community Congress gave me some new ideas about my union work. For instance, a way to deal with problems that aren't covered by the contract. I used to think, "If it's not covered by the contract I can't file a grievance." Now I began to think of a grievance simply as a statement that you're unhappy with something. I started to say, "If there's anything you don't like, file a grievance on it. We'll interpret it as a working condition." That way, when you go into contract negotiations you can point to all the grievances that have been filed about a particular problem, and you can say, "If the contract doesn't cover them now, let's change the contract so that it does."

However, there was a limit to what we could do at a local level, no matter what we did. We had to find a way to cope with the power of Du Pont as a national corporation.

It's been an educational process that's still going on. Our independent union belongs to a federation of fifteen or twenty independent Du Pont unions. This organization has been in existence for twenty-four years. Its original idea was very good, but very limited. It was brought together on the basis of exchange of information only. Over the years, the independents around the country tried to put some muscle into that and what developed was a very severe split. There were some unions whose only purpose was to come to Atlantic City three times a year, find out what the guys in each place were doing, and then go back. The other unions that wanted to do something more tried to work within that structure, but they were doomed from the outset. Just the name itself, "Federation of *Independent* Unions," excluded some fourteen Du Pont unions that were international.

In our bargaining, the fringe benefits—vacations, pensions, holidays, military service plan, insurance—come down from Wilmington and are put into effect at every Du Pont plant whether there's a union there or not. Locally we bargain over wages and working conditions. We wanted to have some say-so in the pension, the vacation plan, and everything of that kind. After we were elected to local union office in 1968, we tried to make the Federation a more militant organization. But we met with little success.

We decided in East Chicago that the Federation was an obstacle to progress and had to be destroyed. Once there was no vehicle there, people would have to look in another direction. So people from the East Chicago, Cleveland, and Toledo plants got together and decided to go to Wilmington, the corporate headquarters. We wanted to confront the president and chairman of the board of Du Pont, Mr. McCoy. There was to be a union convention in Atlantic City that weekend, and we timed the trip to Wilmington to go there just before. We knew we wouldn't accomplish anything with Mr. McCoy. But we had suggested earlier to the Federation that they send delegates to Wilmington to meet with Mr. McCoy over a strike situation, and they voted that down. They said they could never get in. So we wanted to show that they could get in. We felt that if we could prove this, other unions in the Federation might decide to pull out.

To make a long story short, we went to Wilmington and did very well. The night before we managed to get on radio. So we hit the front page of the morning paper: seven employees in Wilmington,

which is Du Pont land. When we got to Mr. McCoy's office the
TV cameras were waiting for us. We got into his outer office. We
tried to get into his inner office, and were stopped. There were security police all over the place. Vice presidents were running around,
trying to get us to go to another room and talk it over. We said,
"We're not leaving." We sat down. They threatened to put us under
arrest. We said, "Fine, we'll be bailed out. We've looked his house
over. He's got a nice front yard. We'll camp on it."

We got in to see Mr. McCoy. He promised us fifteen minutes,
and we spent three and a half hours. Afterwards we had seven
minutes of prime time on ABC television, and when we hit Atlantic
City that evening every one at the convention was well aware of
what had happened.

The first thing that was placed on the floor the next morning was
a motion to dissolve the Federation. It failed by two votes. So East
Chicago got up and called for a walkout of all those interested in
moving toward a real organization. Ten of the fifteen unions represented walked out. We held our own convention, and invited representatives of the internationals which had organized Du Pont plants
to speak with us.

Initially we in East Chicago felt that we would like to put together
our own international, to do it ourselves. The finances were there.
We felt that even though we might not have the skills which internationals possess, it could be done if people were willing. But unfortunately we got voted down on that. I still feel that would have been
the better way to go. The vote in our coalition of local unions was
to affiliate with the International Chemical Workers Union.

However, when we voted on affiliation with the ICWU at my own
plant in East Chicago, the membership voted to remain independent.
Thinking it over, Smrekar and I concluded that we had let ourselves
become the union, just like the board that we defeated in 1968. We
had let ourselves deteriorate. From now on, board meetings will be
open. Stewards will be mandated to be there. In a way, I'm glad
we lost.

White working-class guys aren't together yet, the way blacks and
Latins are. They say, "Why do I need a union?" I did the same
thing. When they see someone get stepped on, or get stepped on
themselves, they change. But it's a long process.

WAYNE KENNEDY

WAYNE KENNEDY is an organizer for the rank-and-file movement in the American Federation of Government Employees (AFGE). He has been a chief steward for the union of Office of Economic Opportunity (OEO) employees in Chicago, Local 2816, AFGE; a delegate to the Chicago Council of AFGE Locals; and president of the National Council of OEO Locals.

Kennedy believes that public employees should ultimately belong to the same organization as the workers, consumers, and community groups which they serve. In this account he describes the experiences and influences which contributed to the development of that belief.

At the time the interviews on which this account was based were recorded, Kennedy had just been discharged from his OEO job for taking the side of Chicago's urban Indians in their struggle for homes and jobs. The AFGE locals in Chicago issued a joint supporting statement which called on their own agencies to make available to the Indians surplus federal land ''that we not tolerate a new form of broken treaties with the Indians.'' Wayne Kennedy's fellow-workers declared:

WHAT HAS OEO COME TO, WHEN AN OEO EMPLOYEE IS BEING FIRED BECAUSE HE IS ALLEGED, AS AN ELECTED REPRESENTATIVE FOR FEDERAL UNIONS, TO HAVE CALLED ATTENTION TO THE NEEDS OF SOME POOR PEOPLE AND REQUESTED THAT THE VARIOUS

FEDERAL POVERTY AGENCIES TAKE ACTION? HAS IT
BECOME SOME KIND OF CRIME TO THINK THAT MORE
OUGHT TO BE DONE FOR THE POOR AND SAY SO?

On October 24, 1972, a panel of three federal judges reinstated
Kennedy with full pay. The panel ruled that OEO had proceeded
unconstitutionally in failing to grant Kennedy prior hearings before
suspension or removal, thus depriving Kennedy of his rights to due
process under the Fifth Amendment. It also held that Kennedy's
First Amendment free speech rights had been violated because OEO's
rules regarding public speeches by employees are too vague. This
decision may apply to all public workers, not just federal workers.
(For further information see Staughton Lynd, "The Wayne Kennedy
Case," *The Nation*, January 24, 1972. The case is *Wayne Kennedy
et al v. Phillip Sanchez et al*, No. 72 C 771, in the United States
District Court for the Northern District of Illinois, Eastern Division.)

As the account explains, Kennedy gained exposure to the frustration of workers in unresponsive unions through working for five
years in the railroad yards of western Chicago. Here he found that
the memory of the strike of the American Railway Union against
the Pullman Company led by Eugene Debs in 1894 was still vivid
in the minds of railroad workers. The crushing of that strike by
federal troops and a court injunction left railroad workers in a state
of demoralization which persisted more than sixty years later, Kennedy discovered.

WAYNE KENNEDY

An Absolute Majority

I

I GREW UP in a suburb of Chicago—Western Springs. My father taught at Wilson Junior College for about thirty years. He was very active in the teachers union. He was always in opposition to the union leadership because it was in political collusion with the Kelly machine.

My mother was a very, very gentle person. The whole atmosphere was very unrealistic: if you are honest every one else is honest, if you're gentle every one else is gentle; every one should be democratic. Then you go into the real world and you're totally unprepared. I think what I do is largely conditioning from the early years. The older I get the more I want to live it out regardless of the consequences, but when you first get going you have all kinds of problems.

I met my wife in high school. We decided to wait to get married until I graduated [from college]. I was to graduate in '58 and I wasn't even close to it. So we got married anyhow and then she got pregnant so I went to work.

I worked at the railroad yards in Cicero for five years while I was going to school. I was a railroad clerk. I would line up the switchmen for their assignments. If you made a mistake they could put in a claim and collect a day's wages. The management was trying to put them where it wanted and the switchmen were, of course, trying to exercise their seniority. You were kind of in the middle. You could get involved in intrigue right away. The yard master, who is the boss of the yard, he'd tell you, "Oh, skip that guy. I don't want him. Go on to another guy." So you'd have to tell somebody, "Hey, the yard master wants to skip this guy. You'd better get word to him.'' And then somebody would call the yard master and get on him about it. But if he knew you were involved, you'd be in trouble.

The first time I joined a union was at the railroad. I belonged to a very corrupt union, the Railway Clerks Union. I went to some meetings but my interest was more with the switchmen. I got in with the natural leaders there. I was in a strategic place because all of them had to go through me. I got along with them well so I got involved in talking about union problems.

The switchmen also had a very controlled union and the union wouldn't support them in anything. They were always electing a new rank-and-file guy to be the union spokesman for the men in the yard, and then as soon as he was elected he would be going against them. So they would put up another opponent who would say, ''When I get elected, I'm going to do what you guys want. You know this guy (our representative), he's taking orders from the bureaucracy and not from us. When I get elected I'm going to do what the switchmen want and tell the bureaucracy to go to hell.''

They would elect the new guy. But as soon as he got elected he'd turn on them. He'd take orders from the bureaucracy and from the rear door of management. They would take a vote at a membership meeting instructing him to do something. He'd check with the union bureaucracy and go in and make an agreement with management that was just the opposite. So they would never have control.

There was one guy who was always denouncing the union and the union representative, and he was always right. He would say, ''Yeah, we're going to put you in there and you'll do the same damn thing.'' And sure enough that would happen. But he had an in with the management downtown. Even though he was a switchman he could call downtown to this big shot he knew and get things reversed out in the yards. We had a funny situation where the union would go along with the yard management, and here was a rank-and-file switchman who could call a big shot downtown and get something on behalf of the workers. The union was more reactionary than the top management—at least this one guy.

We were captured in this union. But we used to talk about, what were the alternatives? We would talk historically. I read a little bit about Debs. I think he has a fascination for anyone that's connected with the railroad.

A lot of personal hatreds were based on railroad history. The workers had started at different periods. Some workers there had come in as scabs. They could tell you, ''So-and-so, he's a scab who came in in 1920.'' If the guy was a scab back in 1920, he'd be a scab the rest of his life. One group of scabs would have nothing to do with the guys that came in as scabs at another point. Personal relationships to each other were largely defined by the work circumstances that they hired in at. They'd try to work with people that had the same history in the railroad. And this was very important because they were dependent on each other for their lives. You had to be able to trust the other two switchmen or you'd get killed.

You'd think the Pullman strike was yesterday, the way the old-timers would talk about it. Their whole history was the various conflicts and strikes—management tried to pull this and we tried to do that . . . the day we had that last strike you walked out or not—this defined who was buddies with who. They hated the engineers because historically the engineers never supported the other workers. Class conflict just dominated everything—major conflicts.

A lot of these guys had come into the railroad business when it was considered the highest skilled craft. When you were a railroad worker in the 1910s or '20s or early '30s, you were the most skilled workman and you were getting the highest wages. That was when they started out. Now when I was there they were virtually reduced to unskilled laborers who could be replaced with the next guy walking by the yards. There was a tremendous downgrading in terms of wages and in terms of how they were looked at. For most of the white switchmen it was a further humiliation to have blacks, unskilled blacks, coming in as switchmen.

Really to make it they had to work overtime. That's why the seniority system was so important to them. They could get on crews where they would make overtime and work their rest days, and they'd pick their rest days by seniority. A lot of them, to make a living, would try to work ten to twelve hours a day seven days a week. Here they had very responsible, in a way very skilled jobs, and they were reduced to having to work long hours like common laborers.

The productivity of the railroad worker had gone up tremendously. It's measured in ton miles. They'd see these charts showing the tremendous increase in worker productivity and they felt grossly robbed over the years. Had there been any kind of corresponding increase in real wages, the railroad men would have been earning a tremendous salary.

They realized that where you had corrupt authoritarian unions there was more and more pressure to prevent them from striking. It was harder and harder to get their unions to respond. So they felt a destruction of any feeling of importance or having anything to say about their working conditions, even though they recognized how strategic they were.

I think that the failure of the American Railway Union, at least among the oldtimers, was the big tragedy of railroad history. You wonder if it was possible, because of all the tremendous pressure there was to divide the railroad workers, but had that pulled off the railroad workers would have had the upper hand with the industry, I think. Instead, just the opposite happened.

It was obvious to me that the workers knew better how to run the railroad than the management. If the workers had had any say-so about the railroad, it would have been one hell of an efficient operation.

They all drink. They ride on boxcars and go out on ice where you can hardly stand up, and I don't think people can work on that job in that cold weather without drinking. One of the big things for the yard master or the train master was to catch a switchman drinking. Especially the switchmen they didn't like, they were always trying to nail them drinking. They'd have the gumshoes waiting for them or trying to hide on them. (The gumshoes were special agents, plain clothes armed policemen, employed there. They're really labor spies.) It was nothing for the gumshoes to be deliberately spying on switchmen, just waiting for them to make a false move. So there was a constant battle between the gumshoes, and the switchmen and the other workers.

There was also the constant battle of the bosses trying to get each crew to do more work than the crews thought they should be doing, or to do it without enough people around the engine or on the train. They'd want them to move the trains faster and take more chances moving the trains than the crews wanted or thought was safe.

It is a hell of a hazardous job. When I was there some guys got badly hurt and I think a couple got killed. It was just a fact of life that you would get injured. It was a question of how badly, or would you get killed, but it was inevitable that you would get hit. This was the thing that made the guys who worked together feel very, very close. Even away from the yard they socialized a lot together.

Everything they do is an act of defiance. The bosses are trying to get them to do one thing and they don't want to do it. It's a continual struggle between the two. When your physical life depends on your making the right moves and you can be fired on the spot if you're caught breaking the rules, it's an extreme situation.

One thing that used to bug them was that the railroad associations, the management, were always putting on a big campaign about featherbedding—all these unneeded jobs. These guys, here they were risking their lives, they felt they were shorthanded as it was, and they were being accused of featherbedding.* They would react very hostile about it and they wished they could strike back.

---

*Several months after this interview, on October 30, 1972, a crash involving two Illinois Central trains at South 27th Street in Chicago took forty-five lives. A spokesman for the United Transportation Union, AFL-CIO, to which the crewmen involved in the crash belong, made the following statement (*Chicago Tribune*, November 1, 1972):

    . . . The UTU had warned I. C. railroad officials and the Illinois Commerce Commission nearly four years ago of the possibility of a catastrophe because of the dispute over crew sizes and responsibilities.

    A dispute in 1969 which led to a weeklong strike by the UTU erupted over the railroad's attempt to cut crew sizes on its commuter runs.

    At the time the union insisted a flagman be added for "safety reasons." The I. C. cited its safety record and sophisticated signal system as reasons that the addition of a third crew member was simply an example of featherbedding.

    "We won the strike when they agreed to the extra trainmen," Stuckey [the spokesman] said. "But to prove they weren't needed they would not allow the crewman to flag oncoming trains at unscheduled stops and gave them conductors or collectors duties."

The day-to-day reality there was so bad, the job could become so humiliating, that aside from all the intrigue the number one topic of conversation was retirement. Their whole lives, in terms of satisfaction, were postponed until retirement. To me it was unbelievable to have guys in their twenties and thirties talking about, "The first thing I'm going to do when I retire is . . ."

I think if there was any democracy at all in the railroads you'd have one hell of a militant situation. There was certainly a willingness to talk about some kind of direct action. They admired the black movement in the early '60s which was the sit-ins and so on. Even though they were racist, they thought the blacks were doing the right thing and they respected the power that they were developing. Some of the guys now have the Right-to-Vote reform movement going. The big issue is being able to ratify their contracts. There are elements in the railroads like everywhere else that I think will change things.

I think one whole area where there needs to be some very serious thought is, how do you overthrow a corrupt union situation? I am convinced that the reason you have these corrupt unions is that you have a lot of situations that are inherently militant and if management and the government didn't impose a corrupt union apparatus you'd have a very radical development. I'm sure that if there was any kind of democracy in the railroads you'd have left-wing industrial unions. I'm sure that's true of other industrial situations where the militancy is right there so it's just a question of giving it an outlet, some kind of mechanism to express it.

II

After I left school, I went and took a job as a caseworker at the Cook County Public Aid Department.

You had a very depressing situation at the Public Aid Department. The caseworker was taught that a lot of these people were cheating. "They could be working," and "they're getting too much," and it was your job to crack down on them. They would actually count your cancellations per month. The more families you cancelled off aid, the better caseworker you were. They'd want you to look for any pretext to cancel people out. A person might have the promise of a job and so they'd want you to cancel him out right away and it might turn out that the job didn't work out. So he'd have to go through the whole procedure of applying again, maybe not have aid for a while. Any pretext at all, they'd want you to cancel the families out. And yet you could see there really were no jobs for them, that it was a hopeless situation in terms of getting off aid.

They weren't getting the benefits that they were entitled to. They'd be entitled to furniture and some supervisors would just say, "Well, I don't give out furniture!"—just arbitrarily would say that. I had a supervisor that didn't believe in birth control and wouldn't authorize any costs for birth control. The supervisors there were typically matronly middle-class women who were very bitchy and petty, and hated the people they were serving, and it just completely dehumanized people.

The supervisor would give you a rough sketch of every family. It was always negative: this one is just plain lazy, we got to get after her, she ought to be out working, you got to get after her to get a job. This was what you were supposed to do, just follow this negative sketch that the supervisor would give you.

You come there, you're told that casework is a profession, but they didn't want you using your own judgment with the families. It didn't mean anything to hire you; there was no screening at all. We used to say they'd hire Jack the Ripper if he had a college degree. It was very frustrating for people who were trying to be professional caseworkers, to use their own judgment and to act independently with the families they came in contact with. That was not permitted. We were openly told to violate what the people were entitled to.

Also, the caseloads are so heavy that if you don't become callous you have an impossible caseload. The ones who make the adjustment there are the ones who are able to tell them, "I'm not talking to you today." Because if people on your caseload find out you are listening to them, you're trying to do something, you just get swamped. Most people try to fend this off. They stay with the system by becoming very cold and hostile. It is very common there, if a recipient calls up and the caseworker hasn't told him to call, they just hang up on the recipient. It gets to the point where unless the caseworker wants to talk to him he better not bother him. The caseworker has the choice either to become the enemy of the recipient, very hostile, or to leave the system because the workload is just ridiculous. You're continually fighting to get what they're entitled to and being turned down and you inevitably get in trouble with your supervisor and get a bad evaluation.

Before Welfare Rights got going, there was talk and there were some attempts to organize recipients. There was an eccentric guy, I think his name was Jackson, who believed in anarchy and free love. But he would individually take up the cause of recipient families. I worked at the Englewood office, which was the largest Public Aid office at that time, and he would come and picket the front office over some woman not getting her check or something, or he would walk in and raise hell with one of the supervisors or the director of the office. He was something of a threat, not that he had any political power, but it was disruptive and embarrassing to have this guy marching with a picket sign out in front.

Another thing was happening on the West Side. Rev. Mitchell, who was a black minister, was trying to organize the recipients on a right-wing basis: that if they would clean themselves up and think about working and go to Christian ways, that the state, the society would respond, they would have more money and so on. In contrast to Headstart, he had a program called Rightstart. Congressman Crane was very big on that, thought that this guy really had the answers for the ghetto. So those were the two influences. Other groups in Chicago might have been doing things but the only thing that you heard of was this lone anarchist guy and this right-wing minister.

Local 73 of the Building Service Employees was the union for the Public Aid employees and it was corrupt but it didn't have much control over the workers. The young people tried to take it over. Eventually, after my time, the independent Public Aid union was formed by people like Alan Kaplan and Paul Bloyd.

A few years later we all ended up at OEO in the poverty program. The organizing at OEO is basically an outgrowth of people who organized either at separate times or together at the Cook County Public Aid Department.

What I look for in public organizing is two major elements. One is where the professionals cannot, are not allowed, to do their job, where they cannot honestly do what they are supposed to do with some kind of dignity and independence. And the other thing is where you have a large number of clerks and even professionals who are trapped in low grades and low pay. When you have the combination of professionals who are not permitted to be professionals and a mass of clerical workers who are trapped in low grade jobs, to me you've got the two ideal elements for organizing in the public sector. I know it is true throughout the federal government. If you harp on career development for the clerks, and protection of the professional, you've got two basic issues there that people will respond to.

No bureaucracy that I'm familiar with is taking their professionals seriously. Professionals are there to endorse the system. At OEO you are really there, like a commercial, to say that OEO is ninety-nine and nine tenths pure. "We're out there helping the poor. The government is concerned. We're really providing services to the people. We and the government are doing everything we can to take people out of poverty." As long as you have that attitude toward the system—it's wonderful, it's working, we're really concerned about poor people— you have no problem. You can be completely incompetent. You don't even have to do your work. If you give your endorsement you will be OK, you won't have problems. Really, to work there you have to give up your self-respect and go along with the system.

Even the people who do give up their self-respect, if they see a chance of an alternative, they'll come back. I feel that there's no problem with getting people involved, even in the federal government where people are basically conservative and very, very intimidated. I am more and more convinced that there's a lot of inherent militancy everywhere and particularly in the public sector where you have these two elements, where you have a mass of people trapped in low-grade jobs and you have more and more obvious prostitution of the professional people.

In some ways, at OEO, we're the elite of the federal system. We've got people active in the union who are making over twenty grand a year—and they are discontented. I think more and more people are realizing that there's no real satisfaction for anyone. No matter how high the salary you make, people get turned off by the phoniness of the work. They want an alternative.

And no matter how much money you have, no matter how high you go in the system, you're still not reaching what the advertising says you should be doing and, even materially, you're still failing. The advertising standard gets more and more out of reach of even people getting good money. So public employees are being grouped with a large mass of workers that have no job satisfaction, that are trapped in a bureaucratic life, and can never really feel satisfied with their material standard of living. You're going to work, you hate what you're doing, the pay is good compared to other people but you're still not an American success and you see your life passing away. You're treated like a child, you're given no credit for independent judgment, and the more that we bureaucratize the more people hate what they're doing and hate their circumstances and are looking for an alternative.

The American Federation of Government Employees was an old fraternal group until 1961 when [President] Kennedy issued the first executive order giving federal employees some right to have some limited unionism. Federal employees in large numbers took advantage of it and the AFGE was the only available union so there was an enrollment of employees on their own without any real leadership coming from AFGE. We have the right to bargain over personnel policies and working conditions. We can't directly bargain over salaries or fringe benefits. We are restricted to very simple things.

Our belief is that there are so many damn restrictions on federal employees because there is so much potential power here. They want federal employees to be very, very restricted because if they aren't they are going to be a tremendously powerful group. The restrictions have exactly the opposite effect: we have so little to bargain over that we have to be much more aggressive where we can bargain or we wouldn't have any kind of credence among the membership.

Federal employees are at the point where they want a real labor union and the current leadership is a holdover from pre-executive order days where it was a fraternal and an insurance thing. It was traditional that you could get ahead, move into management ranks, by being a local union president. The whole emphasis was on writing your congressman and lobbying with congressmen and showing how loyal and deserving federal employees are in terms of periodic pay raises and some fringe benefits. Our present leadership has developed a pretty fair lobbying operation. There is no belief in direct action or economic sanctions or developing political clout except by knowing congressmen and asking them for things and publicizing their good works and so on.

Our conservative union leadership does not advocate the right to strike for federal employees. But there have been the postal workers and the air controllers and the government printers and others who by actually striking posed the whole question. I think that federal employees are more and more willing to resort to strikes and it is a question of the law catching up with the realities. The postal workers really have won the right to strike; even though they can't legally strike, they have won that right and no one doubts it.

The rank-and-file caucus [in AFGE] is trying to develop in the form of a local officers' organization. We hope to establish an organization controlled by those people who are still in the shops and still on the payroll and trying to service the members at the workplace. This is in contradiction to the professional bureaucracy in our union.

There is a group in Washington called the Washington caucus. They want to develop the political and economic power of federal workers, especially in Washington, D.C., which is just a colony and will never be anything else unless the federal workers make it something. In Washington, the people got involved in social issues like the grape boycott and the anti-war movement. Now they are getting down to the grievance areas and trying to develop a trade union approach.

We started out with a trade union approach and feel that the social issues are just an outgrowth of the working conditions. If you back members on working conditions, they have no problem getting into social issues. If you try to attack social issues without laying your emphasis on working conditions, you're not going to get anywhere. I think that most employees here are for the black movement. They're against the war. But they are very leery of being used in things like this. If you win their confidence on working conditions, they want to participate in the broader social issues because they know that they are not going to be used. You're not working with them primarily to end the war but you are working with them primarily to change their own human situation.

In the Department of Defense agency you have a problem with the war issue because of the job factor. But even there, the DoD employees would like to be out of the war machine. They would like to have better jobs in the social-economic agencies but the way [the union president] is operating, he has presented no alternative to being involved with the war budget. They don't want to be eternally trapped in war jobs. But unless you develop an alternative, they have to be for the war. That represents the only job they have. I agree. It is immoral to make rank-and-file employees the victims of cutting back on the military.

I think that we subscribe to the philosophy of André Gorz and others who are after democracy in the workplace. The government treats federal employees like children in school—they have a lot of petty rules. They treat us so that we will obey orders without question, so we won't resist orders and will carry out whatever the government wants. This is very dehumanizing, especially to the young people. They rule by fear. There is a big fear that if you don't act like a child, there will be very serious reprisals. So our job is to break down that fear and get employees to insist that these petty rules be done away with, that they be treated as equals and have some real influence over their working conditions and the purpose of what they are doing. We have a lot of low-grade employees where the problem is just a decent income. But more and more we get young people in who want some dignity and self-determination.

Government is planning and controlling resources. And OEO is all about comprehensive planning to alleviate the causes of poverty. A lot of people who never thought about it before are getting the rhetoric that we have got to have public planning to control some social problems. The more that people work for government, the more I think they get indoctrinated in public control. Even though it's just rhetoric—it's not serious and it's not intended to work and it's even destructive—at least the rhetoric is there. More and more, it's becoming part of their thinking.

The old bureaucrats who run these agencies are completely unresponsive to their constituencies or to their employees. Special interests tend to control these agencies. The bureaucrats' own mode of conduct is to do the least possible and to make no waves at all, so that they can't be criticized for doing something. This is in direct conflict with the young people who want to see the bureaucracy work, and respond to the people most concerned—not just dish out patronage and contracts.

The bureaucracy is so highly centralized and bureaucratized that it cannot really respond. It is deliberately put as far out of reach of the people as possible. We think that it has to be strongly decentralized and moved out to the regions where the constituent groups can have a much more direct control over these programs.

OEO is the most decentralized of all federal agencies. Its constituency is also the people on the lowest rung of society. This is what I think attracted people to OEO: it is the most decentralized and it is trying to speak to the most oppressed economic class. The structure and the rhetoric of OEO are very conducive to actually trying to respond to people who have traditionally not had any power. In some areas, OEO has enabled poor people to achieve political power.

I started at OEO in 1968. Kaplan and Bloyd started in 1967. Once we got in here, we had to organize for our own self-protection. As professionals we would go out into the community to try to use our influence to see that the program was carried out. We would develop conflict situations in the field and, without the protection of a union, we would immediately be re-assigned or given a desk job. We organized the union to give us some protection in the field as professionals.

At the same time, we were shocked to see what a strong class system there is within the federal government between the clerks and the professionals. We were shocked to see the hostility toward minorities even within the federal government. Our other motivation was to see what we could do to break down this class system and the discrimination toward minorities. If they can be broken down within the federal government, which is the largest employer of all, that would be an example and a base for doing it within the society as a whole.

Our Washington local won in their contract a day care center for their members. In our national negotiations we are trying to do it throughout the agencies. Our theory is that if we can get the federal government to pay for day care and become the leader in day care as an employer, then this will ensure its becoming general throughout the economy. The private sector will follow the federal government. Our salaries have been tied to the so-called comparability of the private sector. There can be a reversal. We can win things like day care and then the private sector will have to duplicate it.

The more we get into it the more we see the implications of the public worker for the whole society. Rather than just [organize] on an occupational basis, if we can do it in terms of the people we serve being in the same organization then I think we'll go a lot further than the other, corrupt unionism ever did. What I think is so interesting—where it's got to be different from anything else in labor history—is that if we do it on a worker/client basis, we're talking about an absolute majority of the country. The constituency consisting of every one on public payment now reaches between 60 and 70 million people, which is a political majority of the country. Just the public workers and those on public payments organized into a collective bargaining unit—the implication is a change in the whole economics and politics of the country. It goes beyond an industrial union. It goes into organizing every one who is dependent on public payments of one kind or another.

I think that organizing just along job lines is not going to carry the society as far and it will corrupt much sooner. Fifteen million public workers getting strong enough where they can demand and have a salary of fifteen to twenty thousand a year could be done sooner and have less impact on society than if you're trying to get the sixty million people to organize. That will definitely change the society and take much longer to corrupt.

The thing that we have to harp on is identifying with the sixty million rather than the fifteen million. When you look at it, like at OEO, our salary is really a form of welfare. We call it middle-class welfare. All you have to do is show up and endorse the system every day. You don't have to do any real work. So you feel like, well, you got this degree so now instead of being on ADC you're on a public payroll. I think people will recognize it's really a payoff. You're not getting rewarded for the job that you're doing. You are basically in the same situation as public recipients. Get away from the idea that we're different than the recipient. You're in the same boat. Your money's coming from the same source. To get your share you've got to get together with these other people. Otherwise, you just get pitted off against each other. In terms of changing the economics and politics of the country, you've got to have the broadest possible base. As the public sector movement you can have a hell of a lot more impact than just federal employees or white-collar federal employees, professional employees, or some such thing.

The attitude now is that these welfare mothers are getting something for nothing. But you turn the question around and say, look, they're getting underpaid for what they're doing. Raising kids is the hardest thing in the world! We've got to get them a decent salary and we've got to recognize them as day care people and we want to pay them enough so that they'll care for other children, too. You'd already have all the natural child or day care centers you'd want if you'd just recognize it and pay the people. When I worked at Public Aid, a number of the recipients I had would tell you, "Look, I'm here to raise my kids. I never got anything out of society and so they're going to pay me to raise my kids." They would tell you that.

I think the basic problem is to get a real shift of money into the public sector, for every one in the public sector, as that's how every one in the public sector will get a decent income. At Public Aid, the money for the salaries for caseworkers is pitted against the benefits for recipients. You're told, we can't raise your salaries because look at how the cost of public aid has gone up, we can't even handle the applications for aid. And, of course, the recipients are told, we have all this administrative cost and the caseworkers want more money. So you're always pitted against each other because of the underfunding of the whole public sector. The only way you can overcome that is to get together and gang up on the sources of taxation, to get the taxes from where the wealth is to finance the public sector.

We are in an ideal position for worker/client organizing because federal employees represent every occupation in the country and they come into direct contact with almost every constituent. There is no movement or reform situation that we are not in contact with because the federal government is involved with everything. I don't think there's any more nobility among the public workers than the private workers, except that the public workers are in contact with the constituency.

The classical situation has been the meat inspectors where they are exposed to a very corrupt industry and they have also had the good influence of the Packinghouse Workers. Single-handedly, through their own union, they upheld the integrity of the federal government in meat inspection. Without their being unionized, very strongly so, there would easily be a corrupt situation. Because of the pressures of a corrupt industry, they have become not only a union, they are really an extended family. They do everything together. They socialize together. They have financial institutions together. They tend to be a very small and very closely-knit group of workers. They are mostly white but they don't have a racial problem (any more than the agency imposes on them). The ones I have had contact with are mostly working-class whites. They are certainly not college-educated professionals. In terms of integrity, they are the ultimate civil servant.

The mine inspectors are more of a potential situation. I don't think that they have developed the unity that the meat inspectors have. They are for strict enforcement but so far they have been controlled by a corrupt industry. Real integrity in the inspection force would interfere with the operation of the whole industry.

One possible way I see public sector organization coming about is for recipient groups to come into a bargaining position, like the federal employees have, by executive order. I think that it is politically very possible to get some kind of executive order that would give the military the beginning of collective bargaining, give the men in the military the right to bargain over marginal issues like their food and their housing. That's all the federal workers have now, other than the postal workers, is the right to bargain over personnel policies and working conditions. But the marginal bargaining is the starting point.

I think that an executive order could be issued that would permit representatives of the government and representatives of people on old-age pensions to sit down and bargain about marginal things.

They've already done it in the area of tenants and public housing. HUD has already issued guidelines that give them some marginal bargaining power.

I think you could issue an executive order giving welfare recipients the right to marginal bargaining, like maybe they could bargain over how their budget would be allocated. Initially, they are not going to let welfare recipients bargain over the size of their welfare budgets. But it could be marginal things like, would more go for rent or more go for furniture? or what about a clothing allowance? What about treatment in the welfare office? I think you could begin to get marginal bargaining going. To me, Welfare Rights is primitive unionism. Where they have been able to force concessions, they have actually engaged in collective bargaining, but it needs to be legitimatized before you can get a real union movement going.

I think the thing that got the CIO off the ground was the indication from President Roosevelt that the government approved of this. The accounts I ever read, workers would say, "FDR wants us to unionize, the government says it's OK." This gives a legitimacy. Maybe we don't like to believe that legitimacy has to come from the establishment, but generally it does have to get a mass of people aroused.

The way I see it developing is, the government consents to very marginal bargaining, so that groups will get organized and begin to sit down collectively with government, and then as that happens there will be more and more pressure for real collective bargaining, till you reach the point where public benefits as well as public salaries will be negotiated.

Our union is the largest in the federal government. I think the most immediate thing is to get the federal unions into a situation where they can merge and have one strong federal union. As this develops, we've got to push harder to get marginal bargaining powers for the military. We have a direct interest in the military since they're employed by the federal government. And then the next thing would be to get marginal bargaining rights for welfare recipients—redefine them as federal employees and bring them into a merged federal union. And then try to do the same for the people on pensions. The National Council of Senior Citizens claim they have two million members. That could be merged into a federal union and you'd have two million people right there.

As I see it, the whole solution to poverty and public services in this country is to get those people who *are* poor and *are* dependent upon public services into the collective bargaining process and develop enough joint power where they can demand that the government pay adequate salaries and benefits. Until it comes from their own power, their own self-developed power, we'll go on not having public services and having welfare and pension budgets that are totally inadequate.

JORDAN SIMS

J ORDAN SIMS is former chairman of the Bargaining Committee
for Local 961 of the United Automobile Workers, and co-chair-
man of the United National Caucus in the UAW. His account presents a view of black struggle different from that of Jesse Reese and
Sylvia Woods (pages 97–105 and 111–129). Like many black
workers who became active in the 1950s and 1960s, Jordan Sims believes that blacks should first get themselves together and only then
build broader alliances.

Toward the end of his account Sims refers to the following incident, which happened in the plant where he worked.

In July 1970 . . . at 4:55 on a Wednesday afternoon shift, a
thirty-six-year-old black employee of the Chrysler Corporation, James
J. Johnson, Jr., walked into the Eldon Avenue axle plant, pulled an
M-1 carbine from his pant leg, loaded it with a thirty-round banana
clip, and went on a wild killing spree. "He's firing at everyone in
white shirts," a worker cried. It is the foremen who wear white shirts.
Within minutes, three men were dead: a foreman who had suspended
Johnson for insubordination an hour before, plus another foreman,
and a job setter. Johnson told the UAW committeeman who captured
him, "They took me off the job I had held for two years and put
a man with less seniority in my place."

The sequel was this:

> Johnson's defense attorneys, members of a radical Detroit law firm,
> contended during a three week trial that the pressures of being a poor
> black from the rural South, combined with the strain of working on
> the assembly line, had made Johnson temporarily insane at the time
> of the shootings. The jury members, two of them factory workers
> and three of them the wives of factory workers, toured the plant,
> which had been cleaned and painted for the occasion. The jurors also
> heard testimony about harsh treatment of workers, violence, and poor
> working conditions at the Eldon Avenue plant. In May 1971, in a
> stunning decision, the jury found Johnson innocent because of tempor-
> ary insanity and committed him to a state hospital. "Did you see
> the cement room in that plant?" one juror cried during deliberations.
> "Working there would drive anyone crazy." (William Serrin, *The
> Company and the Union: The "Civilized Relationship" of the
> General Motors Corporation and the United Automobile Workers*,
> pages 233–236.)

This account is an edited version of a talk to an International
Socialists Educational Conference, at the Chicago Circle Campus
of the University of Illinois, on May 13, 1972.

Going for Broke

B EING BLACK TODAY, forty years ago I was born a Negro, and this makes a big difference in the way I look at things. I happened to be born in a little famous town called Hamtramck. The Negro population was very minute and segmented rather distinctly. If you know anything about Hamtramck you know I got a good, full-fledged, white, all-American education. I didn't necessarily sit at the back of the class because our numbers were so minute that people weren't really concerned about integration at that particular point in time. This doesn't mean that I wasn't affected by my status, even at that time, although definition wasn't really clear. You were always on the outside looking in. The average American Negro, no matter how far back he was born, always has this basic, fundamental attitude. If one ever tells you something different he's lying like hell. There is no way of masking your color, nor your identity, in being an American Negro.

This was my attitude. I played with my little white brothers every day until they b.s.'d with me a little bit, and then I became "black boy," and we fought. I was called "sunshine." We fought. Don't know why, Momma said that was the thing to do. In a white environment you can't get much black history. The only black history I got in Hamtramck was Little Black Sambo, and the tiger chasing him around the tree who turned into butter. That's one of the unfortunate things about being raised in a place like Hamtramck. You never learn your own history or who you really are.

Well, I grew up like that in Hamtramck. And in most endeavors, maybe inadvertently, my family and most others that stayed in Hamtramck earned their own degree of self-respect in their own particular way. We had a basic understanding with the white race in Hamtramck. They knew that if you used derogatory terms like "sunshine," or "Sambo," or "coon," you better have at least twenty pounds on the guy or you caught a bit of hell.

Upon graduation, most of my fellow-students were white and about fifteen of us went down to Dodge Main, the Dodge Main plant in Hamtramck. All got hired but me. This didn't surprise me too much. Disappointed me some, yes, because they made some beautiful speeches at graduation about "the grand, glorious opportunities opening up in America for all you graduating students," and the major contributions that you would make to society today. It took me three months to finally land a job. That's how I wound up at the Eldon plant.

Now we get into the union aspect of it. When I first got hired at Eldon, they didn't teach unionism, not even back in those days. No such thing as an orientation program. No one told you what the union represented. No one told you what the struggles were. One cat came by—I used to call him, in later years, the "white pimp"—and he hustled your dues, because they didn't have the check-off system at that time. He told you that "the union is here and you must pay your dues." That's about all he told you. If you looked around and tried to ask someone else, everyone would give you the same thing: "Oh, you gotta pay your dues, but we do have a union." Never told you what the hell it was.

So we paid our dues like that, until they got dues check-off. In my estimation, looking back, there was the major sell-out. That's what bureaucratized our unions, made them big business, and completely dissociated them from the rank and file, because they no longer had to come down to you and hustle your dollars, and your nickels, and your dimes. From that point on, I think, we got a no-strike clause in our agreement.

At Eldon, in those early days, working with a majority of whites, I noticed there were many gentlemen's agreements, past practices, previous understandings on seniority rights, promotion, upgrading. There were also certain basic understandings. The average black was only qualified to wield a mop, a broom, or a dust cloth. I was one of the luckier ones because the times had just begun to change, a little, and since blacks were graduating from public schools I guess they felt blacks had become a little competent. They could at least run machines. This is the kind of introduction I got to Eldon. Because of my educational background, and I appeared to be an intelligent young man, I was going to get a golden opportunity: they were going to put me on machines.

I got a 5-10 classification. Never forgot it, still can't forget it. Because 5-10 meant drill press. Now it did seem complicated the first time I looked at it, because I didn't know one damn thing from another. That's a hell of a world to walk into, from playgrounds, and football fields, and institutional facilities. I got lost the first three or four days, just walking around looking at all those smoking machines and people milling around. There's not a great hospitality. Maybe there was a great degree of brotherhood between the white workers, because they established the whole thing. There was no welcome mat laid out for me—I never found it. Friends were hard to make. I wasn't too particular about that kind of friend anyhow, because I never liked the factory and still don't.

So I got in there and locked my mind up and put in my eight hours a day and got my money and ran like hell to have a good time. It was the first free breath I'd had off the welfare. My family was on welfare ninety per cent of the time that I was a youngster growing up. You just couldn't get jobs in those days unless you had the money to buy them. If you had fifty dollars, a hundred dollars, you could go to the employment office, didn't have to stand in line, somebody would call down ahead and say you were coming. You were hired. It was quite simple in the early days because they would fire somebody else to make room for you. They changed things around just as they pleased.

I see great, significant changes in unionization. More working people getting together. But it depresses me today, the state the unions have gotten into. To me they're no longer unions. To me they are as much like General Motors, and Du Pont's, and Ford's, as they are themselves. I do not think that they can relate to the problems of the worker any longer, since they've gotten a dues check-off program, and they've tied workers' hands with a no-strike clause in most agreements. There are ways of getting around no-strike clauses if they wanted to. In my estimation, much like the corporations, the UAW has taken a back seat in the corporate houses and they do business with you from that posture, from that position. I have never seen a person who could represent me that had to sneak in somebody's back door and sit down in the damn kitchen.

I've tried like hell to get myself out of this predicament. Put yourself in that position, and when I say "a union"—that's supposed to represent me and be so much more—tell me, "Look up to it, respect it, idolize it." I just can't do it.

I didn't know who the steward was at Eldon. The chief steward wouldn't dirty his hands going around collecting money. He was the central agent. They were bureaucratic even at the plant level back in those days. I never saw a contract until I had been there almost ten years. They said they didn't have contracts for rank-and-file people. I was there eighteen years before I saw a union constitution. My president told me, "You don't want to read something like this. It'll just mix up your mind and get you in trouble." He was right.

We had an administration there where the president had been in office fifteen to twenty years. We were "democratic": we had a vice president, who was half colored, who had been in there twelve or fourteen years. We had a little more colored recording secretary who had been there eight to ten years. So you can see, racial barriers were slowly breaking down, and there was a tolerance that was slowly being developed for the Negro. But only for a certain type of Negro. That's something that used to amuse me.

Our rank-and-file program at Eldon started roughly in 1966. It was a secret thing, like in the old days. Becoming a chief steward took me six years, from 1960 to 1966, running every two years. One thing about whites back in those days, they were honest. They would say, "A colored man can't represent me." And I would say, just as honestly, "One day I will." Well, the day came.

In 1963 we hadn't had a change in our plant for ten years. From 1953 to 1963, that's how bad off Chrysler was and that's how bad off the whole country was: we didn't hire a soul. With ten years' seniority I was the lowest man on the seniority list. But we had a big boom coming up then. Things were on the rise. Jobs became plentiful. Everyone started hiring. The younger whites started quitting, going to better-paying areas. Jobs that were heretofore completely white became mildly integrated. Back in about 1964, we even got a colored inspector at Eldon. In 1968 we got a colored job-setter. About the same time they finally gave us a colored supervisor.

During this period between 1963 and 1966 or 1968, with the white exodus from the hard jobs in the inner-city plants, it opened the door for all of us poor folks. We moved in and took all these good jobs. We became lathe operators, couple of us got into the skilled trades. We completely dominate the inspection department now, books, papers, figures, graphs and all. And one thing you have to say about it, you don't hear about Chrysler calling back as many cars as GM or Ford.

All this black tide moving in there, I started practicing racism—by practicing democracy. I would tell all the whites how beautiful and democratic America was, land of golden opportunity, how great it was to be benevolent and kind and sharing, how blessed it was to give rather than continually to receive. They couldn't deny this American heritage that I was setting right there before them. They had to agree, "Sims, that's the right thing."

I would tell the blacks just the opposite. "You come out of the alley, you've never had a damn thing in your life. Until you get together and support a black program and show The Man that you are here, you will never get any further than you are." You know, that was the most difficult thing I had to do. That's what hangs me up. You've kept the race you've locked me into so well subjugated, so well oriented, that the last thing many Negroes want to be called is racist. And in my estimation, until the black accepts the identity forced upon him by the white American society, accepts his blackness, he will never establish his identity because he'll never have any strength as an individual.

And I preached it. And I got to be chief steward. I beat out an itinerant hillbilly who could neither read nor write by thirteen votes in a plant that was predominantly black and in a servicing department that was about eighty-five or ninety per cent black. And my margin of victory was thirteen damn votes. I was happy to win but I was

sick of the way I had won. Because it was indicative of the attitude
still held at that late date by most American Negroes, that their own
kind aren't competent enough to lead them any damn where.

. . . The average worker is not intricate in his thinking. You're
going to have to drop your fancy speeches. You go too far out some
times. You're going to have to relate to exactly where that worker
is, and educate him. And in many cases you're going to lead him.
Most workers today, white included, would rather be led than lead
themselves. Grumbling all the way, "Yeah, that's the thing to do,
but when you going to do it?"

The same thing applies to political parties, just like it does to
local union leaderships, just like it does to this black jacket I'm wearing: United National Caucus. Some people are going to have to
assume some degree of responsibility, and take a position of leadership. You're going to dictate situations and circumstances sometimes
in this turbulent rank-and-file or workers' force you've got in
America today. You're going to be ruthless in the way you set up
programs to get that worker involved. Even though some may be
hurt. You have never won anything without paying a price for it.
And if you've got the idea today, that there's a smooth easy way
of accomplishing a workers' program, then you are really swept
away with the American dream.

I liked *The Godfather*. Blood everywhere, but the devotion that
was there, goddamn! That really impressed me. If the blacks had
that much in organization, deep family ties, and downright guts, we
wouldn't have to have anybody crusading for us, speaking for us.
There's no way you can kill all of us, not at this late date. Waited
too damn long. If we had just that much of what they had in *The
Godfather*! I liked the composure of the young man. I liked the way
he went from the orthodox all-American, who was averse to the
ways of his family—the old family ways, and the old culture, the
old strength and the old ties—but when push came to shove he got
his hard lesson. He rolled over and did his thing.

Workers are going to have to do the same thing. We no longer
owe our allegiance to our leadership because they don't respond to
us. They haven't in the last ten, fifteen years. It's getting decidedly
worse. In my estimation, workers are up-tight right now. The basic

things we had twenty years ago no longer exist today. Simply to refer to dignity, there is no dignity in the workplace today. You're not as much as an IBM typewriter, or a nondescript lathe operation. And you don't even compare to the importance of a piece of automated equipment. If you damage one single tool in many of their automation projects, that costs you your job. It shows you how significant you are in industry today.

The Man is saying some of the same things he said thirty years ago. "We don't need you. As fast as you go, there's another man waiting in the streets to take your place." We have really digressed back to the origins of when our unions were built. We are having to struggle again for recognition, and just plain downright dignity. And we've sold all these things we used to call precious, like our seniority rights, for things like unemployment compensation, sick and accident benefits, annual improvement factors, cost-of-living increases. They tell you about all these but they never tell you how to keep your damn job, and they won't help you to keep it, even though they're supposed to be obligated to represent you in this capacity.

I wonder where workers are going to be going in the next five or ten years. I'm optimistic, though. We had a few pleasant things occur in our plant. One worker was taken off his job, improperly. He tried to assert himself and ask about his seniority considerations. He was arbitrarily fired. He couldn't believe it. He didn't beg The Man but he asked him rather specifically, "What do you mean, fired? Just for asking about my job?" And The Man said, "That's right. You don't ask. You do what you're told. You're fired!" The brother went out and he got his gun and he did some firing.

Many people thought this was a very deplorable situation. I don't, I think it practical, because we have forewarned that corporation. We warned them years ahead of time that they were deteriorating to just this kind of state. They told us in no uncertain terms, "This is not a sociological department. This is a factory. This is industry, and we're here to make money. We're not here to take any guff from any workers and no goddamn labor rep." That was their whole attitude. This worker knew this.

They have gotten to the point of treating us all the same way, black and white. It's coming down to that dollar-and-cents thing now. That's what it has always come down to in the past, that dollar-and-cents thing. In my estimation, that's the cause of most of the trouble in our country today. That dollar and cents, the way it's always centralized, the way they fight to keep it centralized.

You're going to have to broaden the base of how that money is distributed, how everything else is distributed. You're going to have to learn how to play a major and significant role, not only in industry as a worker. I disagree with GM. I don't believe, "As GM goes, so goes America." I believe, "As working people go, so goes America." I believe that as working people prosper, so does America. I believe that as they grow, so will grow America, to all forms of stature that are relevant to a country that is supposed to be so goddamn great.

In my estimation, workers have been lulled into a sense of security and apathy by good times they've never had before. Not being accustomed to them, they went off the deep end. Many of my white brothers I've seen who twenty-five years ago wouldn't have thought of buying a Buick, or a Chrysler, or a Cadillac. Hell, today I can't tell who the upper class is. I find more industrialists driving small cars than I do workers, nowadays. He has attained a great deal of affluence, monetary affluence, and he's reluctant to give it up.

This is another thing that separates the rank-and-file programs. A man with fifteen or twenty years, who takes advantage of his seniority and takes advantage of his brother being laid off, to make twelve, fourteen hours a day, and says, it's not his responsibility. You're going to have to think about things like that. You're going to have to organize the unemployed. You're going to have to go after a few cats in your own unions, who work the overtime. You're going to tell them, "No overtime."

Human nature is a very peculiar thing. Most people, given a choice, will sit up and think, talk, rationalize, for hours, for days, because they don't have to make a decision. They don't really want to. You've got to make people get off dead center in the working class. You're going to do it by education, by provocation, by force in some cases. I find all these ideas very tolerable, very acceptable, to win an ultimate goal. Because I believe, if your end is justifiable, and you've pursued all reasonable and rational courses, and met with utter defeat, you take any course that's open to you. And you go for broke. Because broke is exactly what you'll be, I believe, when the '70s come down, if you don't get together.

JOHN BARBERO,
ED MANN
AND OTHERS

JOHN BARBERO AND ED MANN are members of the Rank And File Team (RAFT), a national caucus of the Steelworkers Union with headquarters in Youngstown, Ohio. They work in the Brier Hill mill of the Youngstown Sheet and Tube Company there.

John Barbero has worked at Brier Hill since just after World War II. He has used the thirteen-week vacation which steelworkers with long service receive every five years to travel around the world, including visits to the Soviet Union and Japan. John's father is Italian, his mother is Czech, and his wife, Miyo, is Japanese. He once told an anti-war meeting that he is against war because in any imaginable war he would be fighting against a cousin.

As members of Local 1462 at Brier Hill, John Barbero and Ed Mann fought for honest elections and to upgrade the position of blacks in the mill. As members of the international union, they supported the Dues Protest Committee of 1956–1960 and its candidate, Donald Rarick, who ran against David J. McDonald for president of the Steelworkers Union in 1957. And as members of the United Labor Party, a local labor party in the Akron-Youngstown area, they agitated for racial equality in the community, peace, and the redistribution of wealth.

Bill Litch, another member of RAFT, has run against I. W. Abel for president of the international union. RAFT's program includes rank-and-file ratification of contracts, and election, rather than appointment, of staff representatives. It also asks that "each officer return to his home plant and perform one year of uninterrupted work at his old job at least once every four years."

This account combines an interview with RAFT as a group and a second interview with John Barbero. A condensed version appeared as "Conversations With The Steel Mill Rebels," *Ramparts*, December 1972.

A Common Bond

ED MANN: Our union was created from the top down. The Steelworkers Union came from the Mine Workers. It was financed by the Mine Workers, and the hierarchy and staff all came out of the Mine Workers. And they said, "Here's a union. Now you get people to join it." The Auto Workers Union was different: it came from the bottom. I think this is why we've been saddled with a "Big Daddy will take care of you, we'll make the decisions, pie in the sky" sort of thing.

This is shown specifically in the rough time we had with honest elections. Fifteen or twenty years ago the man who was running picked the man counting the votes. We can overcome this now because each side gets its own tellers, which was unheard-of before. We feel an honest election is no longer a battle.

But it sticks in our craw not having the right to ratify contracts. The smallest union created today in the city of Youngstown—for example, firemen, nurses, nurses' aides, garbage men—*everybody* ratifies their contract. If your staff man or your international representative doesn't do a good job you send him back to the goddamned bargaining table and say, "We want something better." Steelworkers don't have this right. We don't have a right to OK anything. This isn't my union: I'm just working for a staff man who tells me, "Sorry boy, you don't have a grievance."

We have to learn how to say "No." The average guy in the mill thinks he can't say "No," he's got to go along with the big shot. The company has a boss over him. The union has a boss over him.

The politician's his boss, and even his wife's probably his boss when he goes home. So where do the people show any fight any more? They've got to learn how to do this all over again. They've got to say, "No, *this* is the way I want it: do something about it."

JOHN BARBERO: I saw the union start. There was a lot of hope in this valley when it started.

My father worked for Republic Steel. He was not political at all, but like many Italians he had a very strong sense of independence. All during the Depression he worked maybe a day, two days a week. He had one superintendent who sold used cars on the side. If you bought a car, he saw to it that you worked for the next six months to pay it off.

Almost every one in Campbell was foreign born. The only people who had American names were the school teachers and the mayor and people of this sort. So everybody felt sort of discriminated against. But they also were people who came here with the American dream.

When the union came to town it was red-baited. Nobody knew what the words meant. I remember one incident where two Communist organizers came to my house and asked them, "Do you want to come to a Party meeting?" My mother said, "Where is the party?"

It was a wonder, the difference the [Little Steel] strike made in our house. My father was one who didn't like to butter up people, but before the strike, there would be a foreman and maybe a girl friend coming to the house. The joke is still around the mill. They would eat, spaghetti and various things. After the strike this never happened again. If somebody came to the house, it was because he wanted them or they were friends. I thought that when it was all over they were actually both better off, both that foreman and my father. There was a new relationship.

I have never seen anything like it in America since. A whole town achieved dignity. It surprised me during World War II that whenever I ran into somebody from Campbell he had this psychology. He was always fair in a question of discrimination, whether to blacks or whites, because the whole little town was this way. Even to this day, when I run into that generation of people out of the city of Campbell I automatically know how they are going to feel.

During that strike, my father was arrested. Then he was blackballed. After four years he went back to work as the result of a Supreme Court decision. He never lost faith. Neither did my mother. Everybody told them that the union was all over with. Everybody said, "Give up. You're never going to get back." But he did get back. After that, even though he was a union man, I sensed that he did not attend meetings regularly or make a big deal of it. There was an objective to be won and they won it.

I had a taste of what unions were like before the war. I worked for nine months in Sharon Steel, the only plant [besides] U. S. Steel that had signed a contract. I started out in general labor and wound up in their blacksmith shop as a helper.

But the big taste I got of what the union was before the war was what I saw at our house. It just changed the whole life of the house. The family was more secure. Our parents got along better. Everything.

Then World War II came and I was affected like everybody else. I actually wanted to go in. I had to go down and sort of sneak in because my mother wouldn't sign the papers; I had to go to the draft board and tell them to draft me. All I can say is that throughout that whole period I believed that what Hitler was doing to the Jews was wrong. We had to get in and had to get in early and stop it. But you wonder. You get into the Service and overnight you sort of sense that you joined the wrong outfit.

Another experience that may have changed my life is that I was sent to Japanese language school. Somehow, when you go to a language school you lose a lot of your hate. If you can talk to the soldier you are supposed to be fighting, you no longer hate him. I remember my experience with the first two prisoners that I had to interrogate on Guam. My Japanese was so poor that they must have laughed at me, except that they were so scared. This guy had a bundle of rags that he had been carrying. He asked me if he could throw the bundle away. He used the word in Japanese which means,

"May I throw it away?" I didn't know. I used the same word back and said, "Yes, you may throw it away." After he threw it away I picked it up and handed it back to him.

I was lucky in World War II. I came through all of it without having to kill anybody. All I had to do was fire my rifle three times in the air and I was sore because I had to do that. One day I accidentally captured eleven Japanese. I was coming around a big boulder and the Japanese were coming around the other side of it. I disarmed them. Before the war was over, I had eleven more. But other soldiers behind us shot and killed people.

We had a Korean that we captured on Guam. Our colonel liked him and never turned him in to the PW camp. So he lived with me in the same tent for the next eighteen months. He was sort of my instructor in Japanese. We used him because the Japanese had a lot of Koreans. When we ran into Koreans we always had a three-way interrogation going.

After the war I worked in Japan for two years. I gravitated to people who had the same sort of experience in unions. I met a Japanese-American—at that time, we had none in this area—who knew all about the organizing on the West Coast. He was a union leader.

After getting married in Japan I came back here. The law was that [my wife] had to be here before the year was out; otherwise, there was the Oriental Exclusion Act.

MIYO BARBERO: Congress had to pass a special law that it was OK for us to get married. I went through a complete physical. They take your picture with numbers—you feel like a criminal.

BARBERO: When I came back in 1948, I started right in to look for a job at the Campbell plant. That's where I lived. They sent me to Brier Hill which is about ten miles away. So that is how we happened to move up to this area.

MIYO BARBERO: He told me that he was a steelworker and was going to work in steel, so that I would know what to expect. When wives came from Europe they had a dream of a wonderful land. Many of them were disappointed so their marriages didn't go well.

BARBERO: When I came back I also went to school. Ed Mann and I took everything that they offered at Youngstown [State University] but never once did I dream of being a businessman, or anything else. I always knew which side I expected to work on. Just the experience of seeing what happened in our own family was always enough to make me say, "This is what we want for everybody." Later I found that people who were active in the union, who participated in that first dream and knew what they wanted, were not against the students at Kent State. Like Bob, whom we hadn't seen for years: automatic good reaction on Kent State and he got into a lot of trouble in the plant over it.

I intended to work for the union when I got out. But the union was already in when we came back from the war, and the union was no longer the union we expected. The president of our local was named Danny Thomas. The man had at one time been a very good unionist, very militant, a very effective organizer. He was for the people he was serving in the beginning. Many people were pushed around on the job, terrorized by informants. Danny Thomas was somehow able to counter, to put foremen up against the wall and say, "You don't push that old man around again." But somehow, somewhere, that wore off. He became a tyrant in his own right. Not only that, it was just the way you read about in the Teamsters. The local paid all his expenses, even bought tires for his car; and everything voted automatic because of his earlier record.

At every meeting you went to you were "out of order." No matter what you brought up, he had such a well-organized machine it was "sit down and shut up"; and he had the goons in the hall to enforce it. An opposition candidate who asked for the right to speak would be thrown out of the hall. Many times I was the only man who stood on the floor. Then Ed finally came. And we'd raise this point: "Give that man a right to talk."

MANN: We had a running battle with that group all through the years.

BARBERO: All through the years. I thought in some ways I was a catalyst. I talked to guys—some of them to this day don't forgive me—broke them away from the machine. I broke up what had been a very tight clique. "A man has a right to speak." I told them how brave they were. "You got a right to stand up and talk in your own union. We've got to have a better system than this." And we put that first caucus together. It took guts on the part of people, because they were part of the machine, they were getting a little bit of a dole.

Talking about it several years later I heard the statement that when the Danny Thomases came in, all they had to worry about was the company. They didn't have to worry about the men. But when people like me and Bill Litch became active, you had to worry because the union could get you fired every bit as fast as the company. You had to watch both sides. You were always accused of being anti-union when you got up and made a motion, like on an honest election.

One of the ideas we came in with was to work with the blacks who were interested for the advancement of black workers on the job. The open hearth department, on the floor end of it, was traditionally all white. But after World War II, many of the returning GIs felt like I did that we fought certain things we didn't like in Hitler and the Japanese, and we didn't like them here either. We were willing to make this fight here. This got to be the beginning of the Cold War on the union floor. Anybody who would do anything of this sort was immediately suspect as a Communist. The labor gang that I was in was almost all college students at that time. It was called the Red Labor Gang. There was not one Communist in there, but this was the automatic reaction.

Jesse Cavaleer with whom I worked at the open hearth belonged to the Socialist Party. He was a theological student, a Phi Beta Kappa from Union Theological Seminary. He wrote on church-labor relations. He came to Brier Hill because he needed a job. He worked there for several years. His primary interest in life was the end of discrimination. In Brier Hill he was one of the first to eye the lily-white departments and to start talking to the blacks about "let's give it a try." He himself was white.

He was the first one to talk to me about patterns of discrimination—how, in every recession, the discrimination somehow reasserts itself. When times are good, blacks can move into jobs very easily. I have seen it many times. But as soon as there is a recession they are squeezed right back out. You can see past discriminatory hiring practices reflected in how men walk up the floor in gangs. The same people who did jobs twenty years ago are doing them again now because there has been a cutback in operations.

Somehow through all this were some permanent gains. Jesse Cavaleer did break a few people into going slagging. One quit because he received such a rough time. Another fellow stayed but finally left for a better job. The third who went was at Youngstown University with us. At the open hearth furnace we tap the heat at something like 2850° F. and the slagger's job is that he goes up to this and throws what looks like road gravel making up all the banks. As he was going up to the furnace one of the whites opened up the furnace door completely and just burned the man. Now you hear, "Where's the discrimination?" Somehow everybody forgets.

In the open hearth we didn't work successfully to end discrimination until the Kennedy years. Somehow, the same people who harassed the blacks in the Truman and Eisenhower years, under Kennedy their sense was to do the decent thing, accept it, and no struggle at all. Our department was desegregated and blacks moved into all the jobs. I didn't hear any complaints at all. This is maybe where the tone of the nation helps. But now, with the recession again, it is an all-white department for all practical purposes except for the few blacks who got in at the early breakthrough. People are getting bumped according to seniority. How do you break in and become a black machinist's apprentice if the youngest machinist has thirty years in the plant? Everybody with twenty-five years or less is either laid off or is doing some other job and has rights to go back to the job of machinist's apprentice first. How does a man get into the skilled trades?

Through Jesse Cavaleer talking to him, Harry Hurtt came to town. I'm not sure any more how they met each other. Harry Hurtt was a rubbber worker. He had been an officer in World War II, and he was from the Akron group of the United Labor Party. It seems to me that the United Labor Party was the sds of its day, very democratic, very free in attitude. They had run Harry Hurtt for Congress, but before that they had sent him to England to study at a school run by the British Labor Party. He married an English girl and brought her back. She thought that we really had a labor party here. At that time the United Labor Party in Akron had five halls.

I think that the United Labor Party came out of the old Independent Labor League which I don't know too much about. All of them looked to Trotsky. The United Labor Party added one other thing that no other left-wing party had: where Marx didn't fit, Freud did. Marie Wagner is an old rubber worker in Akron. And every time a question came up, she would say, "OK, what does Papa Freud have to say about this?"

The people involved in the United Labor Party around Akron were in high school in, say, 1936: they were of the age of the sit-downs. They came out of high school together and went into the rubber shops. Somehow, in Akron, high schools were organized by the Socialist Party and all sorts of independents [see pp. 154–155]. These people all had a history, you know, father, son. They were practically all Anglo-Saxons, or Irish; it was said that Akron was the capital of West Virginia. But they turned out pretty much like the people in Campbell, who were from Europe.

The United Labor Party was the set of decent people we met here. They took Miyo in, they helped Miyo with her English. It was the one group I was in in my life where everybody seemed to trust each other. It was a free group. Ideas weren't discouraged. In fact, they had a slogan in the United Labor Party, "The only left party that treats a member as well as a non-member." But members got to be scarce.

The United Labor Party functioned until the first Eisenhower administration. [Its candidates for Congress and City Council] got a vote of about 10,000 in Akron until 1950 or so. But after that, it just became impossible. We had an anti-war pamphlet on the Korean War that we wanted to distribute at the mill gates but [the atmosphere] was just too hostile. It never got out.

The FBI came around. One of our party chairmen turned out to be an FBI agent. He was the only one who paid dues. Nobody else in the United Labor Party ever paid dues. Every time we would get together, he was taking pictures. He even took Ed Mann's childrens' baby pictures. It wasn't until years later that everybody put it together.

We had something like four basic demands. "Basic industry should be nationalized" is the one that stays in my mind.

I went to the Soviet Union on a thirteen-week vacation. I wondered, how do we get the fifty different can openers that we get in America from private or free enterprise and the job security that you would get in the Soviet Union (except maybe if you are political)? How in America do we introduce job security and still keep democracy?

The United Labor Party considered itself part of the American movement and wanted to get away from Marxist language. We would put the question this way: You have a government in America which is almost like a sideshow. Business really runs its own area and government doesn't interfere. So then, government decisions are nullified on the job. How do we bring the Constitution into the plant? Sure, Eisenhower could say, "Hire more Korean War veterans," or, "Hire more blacks." But he wasn't sitting on the board of directors to say, "OK, let's bring them in." How do we introduce democracy on the job?

We wanted all these things within our union, things that we thought were very natural in America. So all of our literature has always been, "Get for America what everybody is supposed to have." You can talk all your life that the system you want is socialism or job security or on-the-job promotion rights. You say the same thing but you don't use the words that trigger people. Most of the demands, like on-the-job promotion rights, everybody wants. If you get a department that is shut down, a man out of that department coming into a department that is operating has all the problems that the black has always faced. You are not saying, "Give it to the blacks." You say it for everybody. And you could sell it, that this is the American dream.

But then I had a problem wondering about that. Say you are for socialism, but you're selling it as "democracy" or "fairness." The fact that you don't sell it openly means that no education goes on in the process. The problem for rank and filers is that in every election you say, "We can do more for you than the other guy." Somehow there is no education: just appealing to the selfish interests of the individual, primarily economic. I've seen Trotskyists and Communists who when they got to be union officers actually were very good because they could read the contract better. They did a better job servicing their locals. But they never sold Trotskyism, they never sold Communism. The only people who knew that they were Communists were the FBI and not the people. Nobody was ever educated in the process.

But getting back to the early days, one of our earliest fights was to be able to elect our on-the-job stewards. When the machine was built up every steward was appointed by the president. We felt the man on the job has the right to choose his own representative. I won that fight many times. After I had done some groundwork for a few years, I had about as many friends in that local as the president did. I'd get in the meeting and I'd sense the mood of the crowd and I'd get up and make my standard motion that we be allowed to elect our representatives, and carry it. The next meeting, if he was organized better, he rescinded all that. Now it is standard practice. Many times it doesn't mean that we get a better representative, but at least if we make a mistake it is our own.

We knew that we had a corrupt union on our hands. We thought that it was just our plant but it turned out later in the McClellan Hearings that everybody had pretty much the same experience throughout most unions in the country. The corrupt politician also became the patriotic politician. The opposition was always "Communist," even though nobody knew what one was or what they stood for. There may have been one or two Communists hired. But accusations went on forever with us.

We thought that somehow we could force an honest election. With Archie Nelson we put a whole coalition together. Archie Nelson was probably the best speaker we ever had in our local. A black, he was from Alabama and the vice-president. Archie had a knack. Sitting around a table with twenty guys, each with an individual grievance, he could focus them. Instead of everybody fighting each other with different ideas, Archie could refine it and when he got through speaking, people both black and white were saying Amen. He was in a department that was more white than it was black, the scarfing yard. Once Archie Nelson became active and tried to change it, he was forever the grievance man of that department. The white who ran against him once got only two votes.

It was the most effective group I ever organized. We got a man from every department. I never was a spellbinder but I could talk to the man who was on the grievance man level or the steward level.

In the first meeting we must have done something right because the whole red-baiting thing came down on us. Our literature countered that we had the right to choose our own stewards, that the right to have an honest election is the American way.

I remember one of those meetings, the largest I ever saw at our local. We were choosing an election committee. In those days getting nominated was no problem, the whole fight was getting your vote counted. Like Huey Long once said, "If you ain't smart enough to get 'em counted, you ain't smart enough to get elected." This was our reason for getting everybody out. That night they had St. Anthony's Hall, which was an old Italian church right in the Brier Hill area that seated maybe two thousand people.

The whole place filled up. Of the 2,500 people working at Brier Hill, it seemed everybody working there came. Archie, the vice-president, was sitting up front with Danny Thomas. Archie tells the story that the hall kept filling up and Danny looked them over and said, "These people aren't here for me."

The meeting had been going on maybe two minutes. There must have been a space of about ten feet in front of the platform. It was so crowded and there was so much commotion, everybody picked up their chair and they moved up those ten feet. They wanted to hear.

At that point Danny Thomas adjourned the meeting, using the excuse that these people had picked up chairs and were about to attack him. "Don't you lay a finger on me," Danny Thomas said to me. There was no intention of hitting him.

Everybody milled around. Nobody got hurt but the police were called to disperse the two thousand or so people. The regular union office was about a block away and people wouldn't go home for a long time, insisting that we had a right to have our tellers.

Danny appointed all the tellers. We asked for a commission of the international union to hold a hearing on the right to choose tellers. The district was on our side because Danny was a potential candidate for district director. We were told by our staff man, "Come tell your side of the story. You'll get justice here." We figured that if the district director was out to give justice, we had some chance. It turned out that Danny's connections were with David J. McDonald [president of the international union], so the commission was David J. McDonald's people not the district director's people.

A complete set of minutes was written up for a meeting that never happened. Then two hundred people were paid a day's lost time to come down and swear to the fact that the only reason we didn't know about any of this is that we were making too much noise and didn't hear them.

So the commission acted as though nothing had gone wrong. A Steelworker staff man who was sitting on the commission supposedly told this friend of mine, "[some people] can lie more skillfully than the rank and file can tell the truth."

MANN: I think this is where we first got raped and realized it. Two hundred people at the hearing held by the commission perjured themselves for a day's wages.

BARBERO: All the people who came down were his appointed stewards. It's strange. The money was so little. But a lot of these people picked up a day's lost time out of the local's money. They were white; they were black; they were Catholics; they were Protestants; they were Baptists; they were Methodists. It seems that the people who perjured themselves were everything—some were preachers. You just wondered what was this stuff you read about in American history books, that there was a fair system here.

MANN: This is where we woke up. We could no longer believe the international that we would get a fair shake. To get a fair shake we had to take it. If you can't take it, you don't have any right to it. That is the way it is in the Steelworkers Union.

BARBERO: But that didn't stop the fight. They held the election and it was a crooked election. Archie Nelson had put his whole career on the line by testifying at the commission about what really happened at St. Anthony's Hall. Archie should have been a shoo-in but an unknown became vice-president. For years, Archie was out in the cold. In fact, he is now out of the union and has become a foreman. Many times when they needed a black staff man they went and got someone who would toe the international line. These things finally disillusioned Archie Nelson, who had done a great service for our union. Finally, a few years ago they offered him a foreman's job, and he took it. I understand that he is running the department now, except before he ran it as union chairman.

The Dues Protest movement grew out of things like this. Many people suffered the same frustrations in every other Steelworker local. Dishonest elections and absolutely no rights on the job, people being fired: this was general in the Steelworkers. After Rarick ran against McDonald, about twenty people from another local were sitting around a table in a cafeteria. They found out that every man at the table had voted for Rarick. The local had reported more than 2000 votes for McDonald and ten for Rarick, less than were sitting at the table. We were ripe for going into Dues Protest, and we just joined with everybody else from around the country that had similar experiences.

The issue was strange. The dues went from $3 to $5 a month. This happened at the union convention in Los Angeles, and on the train coming back from California—they didn't travel by plane in those days—Rarick started agitating for rescinding the dues increase. He came back to the Pittsburgh area and started there. We picked it up here.

MANN: We had membership cards and petitions in the Dues Protest.

BARBERO: We signed them up like hot cakes. They just came in looking for you to sign this thing.

MANN: It was as if it was payday. You might have been a laborer and black, and I might have been a first helper making $40 a day, and hey, we were buddies. I don't think it was a greedy thing. People resented the international union asking for more money. We don't have the right to strike; so why build up a big strike and defense fund for the international union, when local problems are not being taken care of?

BARBERO: The thing that impressed me was that the dues increase itself was not the issue. The frustration tied everything together. Dishonest elections, no on-the-job representation, no voice: everything that everybody felt.

I recall [a friend] said to me, "What you need is to go back into your plant and have outlaw stuff." It was no longer reds. Our fighters now were outlaws. This was the year of "Gunsmoke." We were the outlaws. "Get your big mouths, your big guns, your outlaws out on the union floor."

BILL LITCH: The international union tried to blackball Rarick as a dual unionist.

BARBERO: Anybody in labor who decides to run against the incumbent immediately becomes a union buster, a dual unionist.

LITCH: The fact that he started another organization . . .

MANN: The membership cards . . .

BARBERO: Even without all that, every time five people got together it was dual unionism. You were creating an organization within an organization.

MANN: Maybe we haven't made it clear enough. I don't think we're cranks, and I don't think we're anti-union. I think we're more pro-union than the people who are representing us.

I believed what I heard about unions before I came to work in steel. We believed the stories they told us, and the literature they put out. Today Joe Hill is a great man but in 1950 you wouldn't dare say you even knew Joe Hill. Now they have a Debs Award in the Steelworkers Union. We're trying to put these things into practice, and there's just no room for it. We believe in justice on the job; and this puts me in a dilemma, because I'm fighting the company on one side, and the union on the other.

We've had some hard times here in Youngstown and the results . . . well, we got a district director elected. This is the group that did it. And he never looked back. We've elected too many people who never looked back. We get a guy in, we have no control over him. This is a fault of ours: we can't keep control, or we're not instilling in these people that there's some kind of an ethic involved. Or, Big Daddy can just do more for them than we can.

BARBERO: I want to emphasize some of the victories won by the Dues Protest. McDonald was taking us down quite a road. The Dues

Protest is the whole reason why the Steelworkers is a little freer organization today. We were part of the same pressure that was building up within the Teamsters, within the Mine Workers, every place else, for democracy.

Through it came the Landrum-Griffin bill. I don't know, maybe the labor bureaucrats are right in saying that it's anti-union like the Taft-Hartley, but as far as on-the-job democracy is concerned this is the first breath of fresh air that came into the trade union movement.

MANN: Right. Especially in elections.

BARBERO: It was a nationwide problem that some locals never held elections. The Landrum-Griffin Act said an election at least once every three years. The union bureaucracy studied the bill to find out exactly how far they could go and stay within the law. So the Steelworkers amended their constitution away from the two-year to the three-year term [for local union officers]. It said that ten per cent of the locals have to nominate, so this is what they did. Actually, they tightened up our union and made it difficult. But the Landrum-Griffin Act [also insured] an honest election.

It didn't mean that rank-and-file groups won—the machine was still better organized—but the rank and file is beginning to feel its oats. We're getting a little more honest guy as a local president, a little more independent. The level is rising. But they are not yet standing when it counts. They are like those shop stewards we had. They are still at the point where they won't stand if there isn't somebody in their ranks who will stand.

MANN: I can give you a good example of rank-and-file action not connected with elections. We had a man killed in the open hearth three years ago. He had seven days to go to retirement. Two or three months before that I'd filed a grievance, requesting that certain safety features be adopted. The grievance was rejected out of hand. He was killed by a truck backing up. One of the items on the grievance was that trucks backing up have a warning system.

The guy gets killed. Everybody liked him. He'd worked there . . . how many years? . . . you know. All right, I led a strike. I had to scream and holler, drag people out by the heels, but I got them out, shut the place down.

We went right to the union hall. We appointed a committee immediately. Every area—pit, cranes, floor—was represented. I said, "I want three men from every area to be on this committee. Now, what is wrong in your area?" Before the company could call us, in two hours, we had a list of thirty demands. When they called, we didn't just say, "Goddamn it, Tony got killed and we're shutting it down." We said, "This is what we want."

The company met with us. They bargained for three days. We got what we wanted. We kept the committee in force. Our local president cut this committee out about three months later but it worked for the time it existed. They still talk about it.

BARBERO: Murray [Philip Murray, first president of the Steelworkers Union] was not for the right to strike. But in the early days, if you talk to any of our people here—and even in our first five years in the plant—we had many shutdowns. If we had an incentive problem, we settled it right there on the job. We had a no-strike clause in the contract. But Pittsburgh would be called by the company, and they were always told that Murray would be out of town for two or three days: just enough time for you to settle your problems. But once McDonald came in this was no longer true. Strikes stopped in Youngstown with the firing of one of our union presidents, at Republic Steel.

LITCH: We had a wildcat when I was fired in 1960, but that was the last until Tony got killed.

BARBERO: Let's go back to the walkout over Tony. We had the men out, we were meeting almost continuously in our union hall. The company had finally agreed to every demand we could think of. We couldn't get the guys back to work! This was strange. You know everybody says, "Labor will strike at the drop of a hat." What I notice is, it's hard as hell to get them out but once they are out . . .

KEN DORAN: You know what happened? After they'd been out for three days they agreed, finally, to go back. Then the company announced that the accident was "human error on the part of the worker."

LITCH: They were going to go back at 3 o'clock that afternoon. Everybody was getting ready to go back. When they heard this, they all came back to the union hall and stayed out another day. Finally the company retracted its statement.

BOB LEWIS: I came to work in 1950. We had a lot of strikes, walkouts in individual departments. Now I think the average steelworker *feels* that he can't strike. It's in his mind.

MANN: That he'll be fired, that the union will see to it that he'll be fired.

RED THOMPSON: My plant walked out about a year and a half ago. There were only two people who got time off: our president got thirty days and the steward got thirty days. The reason they got time off was because the steward and the president have got to stand there [because of the no-strike clause in the contract] until the last man walks out and say, "Come on back to work! You can't go!" They walked right out with the men!

MANN: I think we've got too much contract. You hate to look back, you hate to be the guy who talks about the good old days, but I think the IWW had a darn good idea when they said, "Well, we'll settle these things as they arise." I think we've got to get back to a little workers' rights. Let's say I'm in the research department of the international union. How can I say what's good for that guy shoveling his ass off in the open hearth? First of all, I probably don't know what that open hearth is all about. Secondly, if I ever did work there I've put it out of my mind, because I've got it made now. One of John's points is that anybody who works for the union, on a staff level or any level, must work in that mill at least once every four years, to find out what it's all about again. Because, like I said before, nobody's looking back.

LITCH: Doesn't it go back to the old saying that the union is to rise with you, and not above you?

MANN: I don't know, from being in it all these years, there's a lot of things that I think I might rather do; but I feel that the union is still the best place for a man to express himself. You can talk to people. You can put out leaflets. You can agitate. You can start an organization like RAFT. I can get up on a soapbox in the washroom and say whatever I please. I still have this freedom. Whether it gets much results or not, I don't know. But I still have this freedom, which I don't see white-collar people having. I see that workers still have a hell of a lot of freedom, if they would exercise it.

BARBERO: When Burr McCloskey and I get together we always kid each other, "My fellow failure." Many of our friends have gone on to the U. S. Steel office, or the NAACP, or, of course, the union bureaucracy. What first brought us together is no longer in the picture. You ask the question, have we done anything?

I look over racism. I told you about the city of Campbell. We were the first of the children of the foreign born who went at least through high school. We suffered discrimination, we said we would do better. But racism may be worse in our society today than when I came out of high school. It's more open, deeper. I wonder after all these years. I am sure that we will keep working at it. But other forces, the divisive forces, are much bigger and have done a better job.

Still, Bill Litch, I, Eddie Mann, are lucky. The other Sunday we were down in Akron talking to Marie Wagner because she is sick and we figured that we better see her. She asked me, "Do you have another person in the local that you talk to?"

It turns out that we are lucky in our local. Ed has always been there. He fights things. You wonder where the commitment comes from. Our local had a fighting tradition before we came there. Even though we have had our layoffs, somehow we have forever had a rebel group coming up in our local. She asked me, "Do you have one other person?" I said, "We have twenty."

It goes back to the honest election fights. You could recognize them as they came up to vote. You knew that, despite all the red-baiting, they were working for you and for the local. Somehow this has formed a common bond.

BILL WORTHINGTON, LEE SMITH AND ED RYAN

I N THE 1930s the United Mine Workers under its president, John L. Lewis, spearheaded the formation of the CIO. But the UMW was an undemocratic union and Lewis ran it in an arbitrary and often violent way. Rank-and-file members did not have the right to ratify contracts, nor to elect district (regional) union officials. When Lewis passed on the presidency to a hand-picked successor, Tony Boyle, conditions became worse. America's most dangerous industry had one of its least responsive unions.

In the late 1960s an insurgent movement appeared. Health and safety were part of the reason. Mining disasters like that at Farmington, West Virginia in 1968, which killed seventy-eight men, came to seem intolerable. As Bill Worthington relates, Black Lung was found to be an occupational disease and the demand grew that its victims should at least be adequately compensated.

Union reformers ran on a program of making the union more democratic. In 1969 Jock Yablonski, a member of the international union's executive board, ran against Boyle for president of the UMW. He was defeated, or counted out, and soon after he, his wife, and his daughter were murdered. Miners For Democracy was organized at Yablonski's funeral. Finally in 1972 Arnold Miller, a retired miner who himself suffers from Black Lung, defeated Boyle in an election closely supervised by the United States Department of Labor.

The following accounts were presented by three participants at a public meeting in Gary, Indiana in February 1973. Speaking with enthusiasm of Miller's recent victory, they also stressed the miners' tradition of refusing to work when their safety is endangered. A distinguishing quality of these union reformers is that rather than relying wholly on elected leaders, they expect new leaders to give "backing" to their own rank-and-file action.

BILL WORTHINGTON,

LEE SMITH

AND ED RYAN

Miners For Democracy

I

BILL WORTHINGTON: I was a coal miner for thirty-three years.
I left the mines in 1969 on account of an injury, as well as
Black Lung. I'm going to talk a little bit about the beginning
of the Black Lung Association, of which I'm president, and how we
got our things together.

For years while I was working we were all told that when you
see a miner walking around, wheezing, trying to get his breath, he
had "miner's asthma." We were also told that inhaling coal dust
was really good for us, it was healthy.

About 1953, I believe, a doctor by the name of Dr. Donald Ras-
mussen who did research for the Appalachian Regional Commission
began to study miners. He found out that we didn't have "miner's
asthma," or walking consumption, or any such thing, but we were
suffering from pneumonoconiosis. We cut the term short to say, simply, Black Lung, a respiratory disease.

Finding out from this crusading doctor what was actually going
on, we began to get pretty angry. Our people were dying. They
weren't getting benefits. Coal companies were making millions of
dollars off of us, and then, when we got too sick to work, they
said we had "miner's asthma" for which there's no compensation.
You were just out. You went to the poor house or started begging.

Upon finding this out, we began to get together. We began to do some serious thinking about what we could do. The whole movement started in the state of West Virginia. We found out that the first step was to get state legislation passed that would compensate for this occupational disease. We began to lobby, talk to our legislators, congressmen and so forth. We got state legislation passed, and we got the federal Coal Mines Health and Safety Act of 1969.

We thought that this was the answer, that a lot of people would be paid, that something would actually be done. We did what so many other people have done, what we did earlier, back in the '30s: we thought we'd won a victory so we relaxed.

Then it dawned on us that something was wrong. There were not enough people getting paid. There were too many sick people, walking around, dying slowly, and nothing being done about it. The federal Social Security Administration was not following the law. If they had been, more people would have been getting paid.

So we had to think of something to do to make more people aware of what was going on. We began to study that law closely. We began to do training sessions with disabled miners, widows, as to what the law was all about, and how to make that law work. It's one thing to have a law, something on paper, but it's something else to make it work to our advantage.

We began to inform people of their rights, what steps to take, what bureaucracy could and could not do. Our tendency was to get people to do things for themselves, to say [to the bureaucrats], "Look, man, you *can't* do this. The law says so-and-so." They were able to quote sections of the law.

Such a low percentage of people were being paid, so few of us were off in one little corner doing what we could do, that we decided to combine forces. Instead of one little group over here, fighting the law, being put off, harassed with one harassment after another, we decided that we needed state organization. We managed to get three states working closely together, doing training sessions. And we decided that some of the old law, the '69 law, just wasn't right. We had to do something about that, too.

We got together with congressmen, doctors, lawyers, and what not, and we asked that amendments be made to the 1969 law. These were called the 1972 amendments.* We practically negotiated those amendments with the Social Security Administration. We were also successful in getting them to let us help write the regulations [under which the amended law would be enforced]. This was something that to me was a first-time happening. We had never been able to sit down and work on our own problem. By doing a lot of demonstrating, picketing the Social Security offices and so forth, we got to do that.

As you know, they always try to give you the runaround. When we were in the Social Security offices in Washington we had pickets out at every district office in the coalfields. So the commissioner said, "Look, Bill, get on the phone, tell those people to leave the district offices. We'll let you people help write the regulations." I said, "Put it on paper. Put it on paper and sign your name to it. *Then* I'll pick up the phone." And we accomplished that.

What I'm really getting at is this: it's very possible for people to work together. When we formed a three-state organization we also formed what we called a board of that organization. We kept up communications. Everybody was working toward the same thing. And so there was no more denying of what we wanted, of what we needed. We became a strong, political movement. We have bar-

---

*The best known provision of the Black Lung Law of 1969 (P.L. 91–171) was the benefit program. As of January 1972, there were 350,000 claims filed and 145,000—less than half—had qualified for benefits. The Black Lung Benefits Act of 1972 broadened both the coverage and the definitions contained in Title IV of the 1969 act and made the amendments retroactive to 1969. The amendments broadened the coverage to include surface miners; provided for relatives who had been dependent on the miner; broadened the definition of total disability to an "inability to continue working as a miner"; and broadened the definition of "Black Lung" to include any "respiratory or pulmonary impairment which occurs after 15 years work experience in the mines."

The Social Security Administration estimates that at least 135,000 more claimants will qualify under the new regulations. Approximately two billion dollars will be paid to claimants by mid-1973 and 96 per cent of this money will be given to the residents of Pennsylvania, West Virginia and Kentucky.

However, the program lapses in 1974 and new claims from then on will be paid by the states and mine operators. The state governments are still largely controlled by the coal operators. ("Coal Mine Health and Safety," *Peoples Appalachia*, Winter 1972–73, page 35.)

gaining power. The Black Lung Association board became a bargaining power, a bargaining agent, for the whole Black Lung movement.

Arnold Miller, who is now the president of the United Mine Workers, was the first president of the Black Lung movement. I was proud to stand shoulder-to-shoulder with him. This is why we have him as union president now.

This is how we formed a movement that right now has recognition in Congress, recognition from the Social Security Administration. We thought about all the pros and cons. We planned the thing, I think, fairly well. We asked ourselves, What will we do if we fail with this effort? We looked all around the ball instead of just looking at one side.

Every rank-and-file member of a union ought to know what's going on. This is the purpose of our training in the Black Lung Association: that everybody knows their rights, everybody participates. We feel that everybody ought to have a right to participate in anything that concerns their lives.

II

LEE SMITH: I'm chairman of the health and safety committee at the Federal No. 2 mine near Morgantown, West Virginia. I can tell you some of the things that have happened with the Miners For Democracy. I was with them at the time Jock Yablonski ran, and was murdered.

The company I work for, Eastern Associated Coal, is one of the biggest. And I went in and talked to them about safety. One particular case I mentioned was over a pillar plan.

In the mines they drive headings up on the advance, and when they come back they take all the coal out. There's a plan made for this so that the roof will fall behind the men, so that they'll not be under or near the fall when it comes down. They get in a hurry for coal—more production—and they deviate from this pillar plan.

About 1969 I went in on a pillar plan for Number 9 Section of our mine, Federal No. 2. They had deviated from it, they were completely off of the pillar plan.

I met with the company for approximately two hours before going into the mine. I went into the mine on the afternoon shift, my regular shift. I worked over on the midnight shift. At two o'clock in the morning I was coming back out of the mines and the dispatcher stopped me and said, "Hold it. There's a fall in Number 9 Section." I said, "Anybody hurt?" He said, "I think there's a man under it." So I waited a little bit, and he called back and said, "No, there's four men."

This was the section where the pillar plan had been deviated from. I went up. There was one man who could talk to us, underneath the rock. Finally we got him out and he died the next morning at seven o'clock. There were two more men that were killed instantly. The fourth man had arms and legs broken, but finally got all right.

Tony Boyle was president of the United Mine Workers at the time. I tried to get hold of Tony Boyle but it was just like me trying to call President Nixon. Same thing: I could have gotten just as much. The district headquarters for our local sent out a Tony Boyle-picked man. To start with, the man had only worked a year in the mines, and it was not in a union mine. This was back in the early 1940s. The man didn't know what a continuous miner looks like. Mining today in these big coal mines is modern, it's not pick-and-shovel, it's modern machines.

We got nothing from him. The state and federal mine inspectors said right at the bottom of their report that the company was at fault. But they weren't going to do anything. So we had to take it on: the union had to do it.

We fought for Arnold Miller and we got him in. And since he's been elected we revised the whole pillar plan. Now, the way the procedure goes, I go to the district. It's taken care of, or if it's not, I can pick up a phone and call Arnold Miller direct. I have done it on one occasion. And when I call him, it doesn't bring out mine management, it brings the presidents of these companies down. And they talk with me as if I was their equal, which we should be, we're working in there.

I'm real pleased with our election. We have backing now. We don't have to worry about the company pushing us off to one side.

Before Arnold Miller I was fired four times from our mine, for safety reasons. I shut their mine down. That's the only power whatsoever I have, is to stop their production and withdraw the men. And they fired me four times. But since he took office, it seems they don't have any more of those slips.

When I started in the mines safety was preached in the paper, was preached in any printed material that you got from the mines. There was a big buildup. Everything sounded beautiful. But then when I went to work in the mines, all those pieces of paper were left outside. The more you read, the more people got killed.

I'm a member of the Mines Rescue Team, the ones that go in and try to rescue men after they're trapped, which is a terrible job. And that's the only reason I used to go in. I got in trouble at Blacksville No. 1* over this particular thing. After we couldn't get the men, they were trying to get us to go back in when the mines were about to explode. They were trying to get us to save their coal mine. The president of that division of the Consolidated Coal Company tried to get us to go back in. I said, "There's no way of getting the men. The men are lost." They knew this. Everybody knew this. The men were burned up. I said, "You started the fire. You put it out. Only reason I'm here is to get those men out, alive if possible."

The mine where I work is new. When the company started it they hired all young men. The company took the position, like in the '20s or '30s, "We're going to put these men in there. They're young men, they don't know any better because there hasn't been a union or anything. We're going to train them to do as *we* want them to do." This went on till they got the mine filled with men.

But they made a mistake! These men that they put in there were able to read. Every man that was making a living at this mine had his own opinion. When the company did something that was wrong, each miner knew it. They went to their committeemen.

We have three safety committeemen and three mine committeemen. The safety committeemen take care of safety, the mine committeemen take care of contractual. They are elected in the local.

*On July 22, 1972, Consolidated Coal Company's Blacksville No. 1 mine in northern West Virginia caught fire and resulted in the death of nine miners.

For instance, I am elected in the local. I might add that I'm a mechanic in the mines, and work my eight hours the same as the others. I do my safety work extra, unless I have an imminent danger, when I report off my shift or any shift and go in the mines at union expense.

We have nobody to answer to other than the men we represent. So we take it on our own to make our voice heard, and if management doesn't listen, then we shut them down. That's all there is to it.

III

ED RYAN: I'm from Morgantown, West Virginia. Lee and I work in the same mine. I'd like to tell you about some of the things I've run into, from my standpoint of being a younger miner.

Our national union conventions, a lot of times, were called in places pretty far away from the coalfields. What miner could get the money together to go to some of those places, to go to the national convention? And the ones that could, they couldn't afford to take the time off from work, anyway.

If you were fortunate enough to get the money together, and have the time off to go, a lot of times you went to the door and you didn't get in, because of so-called strongarm men at the doors, with the Roscoes stuck inside their coats which they pull out and flash at you if you want to say anything. Or else if you got into the convention and stood up to propose something, you got beat on the head. "Sit down! If you don't sit down, I'll hit you."

Now we've got us some good leaders. Arnold Miller is calling the next national convention in Charleston, West Virginia, close to the heart of the coalfields. And one of the first things on the agenda is where in the coalfields to move our new national headquarters. It's not going to be in Washington D.C. any longer. Get it down there in the coalfields where it belongs!

There isn't going to be any more of this nonsense when you come to the door. Those doors are going to be open. The only people that are going to be standing there will be saying, "How are you doing, brother? Come in here and have a seat." There isn't going to be any more, "What are you doing here? Oh, you're one of those

rank and filers. Sorry, you can't come in. This is a closed session."
There isn't going to be any more of that.

When I first started in the coal mines in 1967 I did some reading
on my own and found out a lot of things about the leader of our
union at that time, Tony Boyle. So I started talking to people,
informing them of some of these things. "Aw, you're crazy. You're
just one of them long-haired hippies. Don't know what you're talking about." "Well," I said, "you take it for what it's worth." I
told them, "Now, Jock Yablonski is going to get in there, and he's
going to give us some reforms."

I got drafted and had to go to the Army during a good bit of
Jock's campaign. My heart was with it, but unfortunately I couldn't
be.

During Arnold Miller's campaign I did a lot of talking to a lot
of people. A lot of the younger people have the attitude, "It doesn't
matter. I've got me a good job, I'm making big money. I don't
want to be concerned with this union." A lot of the older miners
feel, "Let's see, I have only five or ten years to go. I'd better just
sit back here and be quiet. I don't want no change to come about.
I might get fired and lose my pension."

You can't say that these people are dumb, you can say that they're
ignorant of a lot of facts. After you sit down and talk with these
people a little bit—and that's what it takes—then if they don't pick
it up, and realize it, then you can call them dumb, because they
aren't ignorant any more.

In the union, solidarity starts with your local. A chain is only
as strong as its weakest link. All right, your local is where that chain
starts. From there you can move up to your districts, and then to
your international. This means talking to the people in your locals,
informing them of things which, because you are concerned individuals, you'll research and find out for yourselves—because no one else
is going to tell you. After you find some of this out, tell your buddy
who works next to you. If he's a good enough man that you can
call him "brother," then tell your brother who works next to you.
That's what union is all about. That's your brother working right
there next to you.

I remember one time I was working on a pillar line. I was a miner's helper. So I had to go in and help drill stumps. That's what's left. That's the only thing holding up all this rock that's ready to fall. And I was told by the boss to grab that butterfly drill and hurry up and drill them stumps because she was about ready to come in. I said, "You're crazier than hell. I ain't going in there." Up jumps another man and says, "I'll do it. I'll do it. I'll do it." Off he goes running in there, nothing but a goddamned scab.

You can't have that. I know whenever we take our initiation into the union the pledger says, "I will not take my brother's job." Now that's part of your organizing, that's part of your strength. I'd say the mine I was working in at that time was about 90 per cent scab and 9 per cent who didn't care one way or the other. That's why I was considered a long-haired radical hippie.

IV

SMITH: I want to say something about this being together. On our big strike, there were some mines in Pennsylvania which were sneaking coal in. They were non-union, little "dog holes": pick-and-shovel. But between them they could produce enough coal to hurt the strike.

Morgantown is not a very big place, but there were enough pickets to shut down Morgantown, a complete town, just going through it. We went out there and they came down in their trucks, hauling this coal. So we told them to dump it out. They dumped it out and called the Pennsylvania State Police.

The police came out and looked the crowd over, called back in, and told the State Department of Highways to clean the coal off the road. A trucker came along in a big truck which could haul maybe thirty tons of coal. This guy knew he was in the wrong, that the pickets were going to get him. He looked down the road and saw all these guys. He laid the brake on that truck, set the emergency brake, jumped out, and took off back down the road. Left the truck and all.

We didn't have to go out there any more.

RYAN: Let me tell you one thing, about coal mines. Maybe it's because it's awful dark down there, maybe it's a psychological factor. I don't know. But when you're underground, by God you'd better be a brother. Coal miners are close. They are brothers. That's what a union's all about.

SMITH: You're either company or union, there's no halfway between them. Here recently they offered me a safety division manager's job for Eastern Associated Coal, which is a *fabulous* job. I mean, $50,000 home, maybe not a Cadillac but pretty good. And I asked the man, "Is it a company job?" He said, "Yes." I said, "I don't want it." He said, "Well, think it over." I said, "I did. I don't want it."

I would think that people in all unions ought to be brothers, also. I would think that if you're working for a living the same as I am, and your goal is to make a paycheck at the end of the week, then we all ought to be brothers. The coal companies, the steel companies, they're not only brothers: it's all one thing.

RYAN: You don't usually see a picket line in a mine strike. If one man stands in front of the mine and says, "No work today," and gives a good reason, no one goes in. It's just not done.

A lot of unions have to have picket lines when they strike because you do have people who work when their brothers are out there not working. You just can't have that. Rank and file, that's where your strength is.

List of Abbreviations

AFGE	American Federation of Government Employees
AFL (AF of L)	American Federation of Labor
CIO	Committee for Industrial Organization; later, Congress of Industrial Organizations
CP	Communist Party
FASH	Fraternal Association of Steel Haulers
GM	General Motors
ICWU	International Chemical Workers Union
ILD	International Labor Defense
IWO	International Workers Order
IWW	Industrial Workers of the World
KKK	Ku Klux Klan
NLRB	National Labor Relations Board
NMU	National Maritime Union
RAFT	Rank And File Team
SIU	Seafarers International Union
SP	Socialist Party
SUP	Sailors Union of the Pacific
SWOC	Steel Workers Organizing Committee
UAW	United Automobile Workers
ULP	United Labor Party
UMW	United Mine Workers
UPWA	United Packinghouse Workers of America
USA (USWA)	United Steelworkers of America
YCL	Young Communist League
YPSL	Young Peoples' Socialist League